Chocolate

Chocolate

© Copyright 2005
Anthony Hamilton

Dedication

I wish to dedicate this book to my grandmother,
Miss Ida B. Bolton,
who just happens to be ninety-four years young.
Though our times together have been few,
it is my hope that our love for each other
can remain forever new.
This novel was written to say Granny,
I love you.

Acknowledgments

Those who know me on a first name basis know why writing my first novel was so important. Though I have always strived to do the unexpected, I couldn't have achieved any of this without skeptics, and those who dared to believe in me. Because God knew, in order to succeed, I needed them both desperately.

To my editor, Bridget DuRuz, thanks for agreeing to become that necessary someone in a writer's life who helps lead them to literary promise.

To my wife, D. J., thanks again for giving me the time to express myself to the world and for blessing me with the most beautiful daughter in the world.

To my daughter, Elyscia, I am an advocate of yours who staunchly believes that greatness is your birthright. To my sons, Anthony Paul, Anthony Darnell, Emmanuel, and Toddrick, it is my hope that you all will grow to become better than you've ever hoped, brighter than you ever dreamed, and more humble than God has ever deemed.

To my sisters, Alice and Doretha, without our ups and downs, we would not know how far we've come. And just in case you've ever wondered… if I had it to do all over again, I would choose the two of you again. To my brother, Terry, you have paid an enormous price to find an emotion you lost. It is my wish that soon you'll be dancing to and endless waltz with her. To Phillip Askew, your support was evident and your love for this brother has been dully noted. To my brother-in-law, Christopher Spencer, thanks for caring enough to proofread for me through the night and for always saying, "Bro-law, it's gonna be all right." To my other in-laws, Sonjia, Lisa, and last, but certainly not least, Ms. Spencer, thanks to you all for making me earn your respect. I hope by now I have.

To my best friend, Leonard Anderson, my hope is that some day I might be able to place reassurance in the minds of those I come in contact with, just as you have in your life. To Carlos Watson, it was you who taught me about the window of opportunity. I hope that I've proven to you just how skinny I could get.

To my father Chester Hamilton, though we have a long way to go, it is still my prayer that somehow we will get there. To my stepfather, Wallace: Now how could I write anything without saying thanks to my guy? Thanks for all of the support.

To my mother: Here we go again… I told you this would happen. God went and gave your son some words, and now he's hoping the world will read his stories. Thank you for having me and for being the mother you are.

Author's Note

I knew writing this book was going to be a grueling task for me… seeing that I started on the project when the tides of elation were at their lowest. It was a difficult process at best because a part of me had to die before I could give my readers this gumbo-like rendition of what I've come to know about life.

In my attempt to remove many of the myths that have plagued so many of my people, I was forced to stroke vigorously through the mighty waves of ignorance and against the strong currents of self-denial. Taking on this endeavor was my way of challenging my own beliefs, and a way to not be afraid to admit when I was wrong.

We must all call out for a cease-fire and bring a halt to the verbal assaults blasted by bullets of degradation. As we battle our way over hills of promise, we will undoubtedly have to deal with our lies. Together we can travel through the in's and out's of trust, and well past blame. We may venture up and down the streets of worry, or take a peak at Point Deception now and then, yet we must be sure to stop along the way to soak up passion.

I wrote "Chocolate" so that people could simultaneously learn why it is important to bridge the gaps of deceit. Writing this book made me reevaluate my own place in life. It made me check my chauvinistic hat in at the door of reasoning, and it forced me to unclothe my fears and set down naked at the table of truth. Enjoy.

CHOCOLATE

The Basics

The inability to identify our own self-worth is clearly one of the most immortalizing acts ever inflicted upon us as human beings. Whether subjectively or socially established, the fact remains... ain't nobody better than the creator... and the last time I checked, He hadn't made any mistakes.

Society's physical mandates have become the unwarranted compass by which so many of us are judged. And it comes from listening to badly informed individuals, who were no doubt the descendants of overly opinionated fools.

My mother used to say, "Child, we all have our ugly moments, some of us just lose track of time... that's all." She'd also temper that with, "There is something beautiful about us all, but beauty alone does not invoke self-assurance."

It was my father who taught me that opinions are only as good as the minds that own them. When he spoke, the world stood still and an undivided spirit of awareness would humble my soul.

With each honorable act of concern from either one of my parents, my will to honor them grew stronger. But from day one, I was Daddy's little girl, and when he left my side, I felt exposed.

As far back as I can remember I have had complete trust in my father, especially as a child. I loved the way he thrust me into mid-air when he came home from work. I ran as fast as I could towards the front door, and as soon as it opened, I leaped into his out-stretched arms. Each time my smile was as wide as if I had just gotten my first tooth. As I stretched out my hands and feet, my father would turn me around and around, then he would throw me up high in the air as my mother stood across the room in a state of panic, just hoping my father wouldn't experience his first case of the dropsies.

I believed in his love, and that alone gave me more than enough confidence to take that leap of faith into his strong arms. I would do it again today if…

My parents were both practical jokers. Sometimes my mother would tell my father to hide in the house just so they could see if I would be able to find him. After she made sure he was hidden well enough, she put me down and followed me as I crawled with determination in his direction.

The love I had for my father heightened all my senses. When he wasn't there I knew it, not just because his voice had vacated my surroundings. No, it was his scent I missed. I could literally smell him from as far as fifty feet away they told me. He had a peculiar scent that set off something inside of me. When I sensed it lingering, but could not see him, I began to cry.

Even though I had a right to love my father the way I did, sometimes his undying affection made me feel selfish as I grew older. I felt selfish because he was always and forever there for me, when so many of my peers lived fatherless lives. To this day his strength feels like the comfort of fresh warm fabric.

His eyes had a way of gauging the course of my life. Long before my birth they had seen a violent side of society, much too dreadful for my mind to comprehend. He floated on a raft through a sea of violence and hatred growing up. He saw his ancestors and many friends beaten down by the hands of the mindless, spineless few, and often tried in vain to rescue them from drowning in the torment of inequality. To save himself, his ears became deaf, and he was able to turn down the sound of racial injustice and march to his own beat. Over the years he developed the patience necessary to outlast ignorance.

My father was a self-made philosopher of human reasoning. He was the reason why I always felt compelled to be more than society suggested I could be. He taught me that a shallow mind would think small-minded thoughts, but a mind that inhaled knowledge shall exhale wisdom. I saw my father as being a lighthouse of undying hope and a navigator of logic, especially when the ways of the world attempted to steer me away from its truths.

He continually compiled information for a book he was writing entitled, *Ignorant-ology 101*. Though it was never published, he continued to quote himself and other citations whenever he saw fit. He meant for his book to show one hundred and one ways to identify a distorted mind by detailing what he called, "Baseless out-bursts of actions displayed by ignorant people."

None of his observations were ever racially motivated though, because he wanted to see the good in everything. But he learned early on in life, as he so carefully put it, "Just as wrong ain't never been right… there ain't nothing clean about being nasty." He often said that, "A man will never be greater than his heartbeat, nor will he ever be taller than the distance that he's willing to stoop in order to help lift up his brother."

Although my mother never ceased in her efforts to point me in the right direction, it was my father's overshadowing wisdom, which ultimately influenced the major choices I made. When adversity would stick its evil head out from underneath the rubble of torment, the embedded words of my father, the self-proclaimed scholar, would almost always prompt my next move.

He was my private teacher as well as my own personal preacher. At times his sermons could be a bit long and grueling, but he had a way with words that made even deaf ears crave the sound of his voice. It was piercing, and his timely delivery was often heart-warming. He spoke with a passion that separated him from normality. So I gauged my highs and lows through my father's eyes, not because I loved my mother less, but because it was more helpful that way.

My parents taught me that I was beautiful, not in spite of the color of my skin, but because of its darkness. They never flinched in their efforts to equip me with a bag of forgiveness. They knew sooner or later I would need to reach inside and use its contents throughout the course of my life.

When it came to my own skin color, I would be swinging vigorously against the perceptions of my adversaries for the better part of my life, they warned. And like so many others who have come and gone before me, I realized that I would possibly have to fight battles I might never win.

Though I knew my mother loved me whole-heartedly, I never felt that she could possibly understand my plight. She was nowhere near as dark-skinned as my father and me. But they knew I would see that so many of us desperately need to take a walk back into our own past before emotionally denying someone else's future. None of us were as pure in color or in truth as we might have wanted to think.

Both my mother and I internalized my father's advice about fighting back. "Attempting to swing against the ignorance of hatred is equivalent to a hopeless-romantic that chooses to fight against passion," he said. "His efforts will fail, more often than not, because no one thing is ever stronger than its originator."

We observed my father closely as he exposed his theories one after the other. He said that society had led him to study the 'small-minded' syndrome. He was teased most of his life as well, seeing that he was also darker than nearly everyone he encountered. But his wisdom enabled him to remain unmindful of the cruelty inflicted by others.

My pops saw to it that I never suffered from low self-esteem because of that. Long before my parents ever tied on my first pair of training-shoes, I was showered daily with any reassuring phrase one could think of: from 'You are the most beautiful child in the world' to 'Baby, you are the greatest.' So by the time I came face to face with the likes of ignorance, I had been armed with just about every positive mental device I could possibly need.

School Days

All through school I had been called almost every derogatory name imaginable. Kids could be so cruel. My peers would often tease me about the color of my skin, as if I had been given the choice of choosing the shade of black I was to become.

In grade school, sometimes I ran to the restroom at lunch just to take another glance at what all of the commotion was about. I would stand in front of the mirror and wish I was even a few shades darker… just for good measure.

Later on in junior high, it did not usually bother me that my peers couldn't see the love that went into producing the wonderful human being I was. They seemed to be reaching towards the arms of stupidity while I was able to ignore their every word. Instead of allowing them to affect my emotions I was able to place their cruel words under my feet as I continued inching my way upward to success.

It was more than okay for me to be called out of my name, Claudia, for most of the individuals who mocked me could not even spell half of the mean words they used. And I had seen my pops tolerate worse. Unbeknownst to most of my peers, I was an only child and I figured some attention was better than none.

Despite my efforts to go with ease from one class to another and try my hardest to remain focused through the day, there was always a wanna be comedian in the crowd – someone just waiting to get famous at my expense.

Stanley Jackson was a thorn in my side from day one, but in just about every young girl's eyes he was the prettiest boy they had ever seen. During a period in our lives when the rest of the boys' faces were either marked or bumped up, Pretty Boy's was neither.

He was a high-yellow brother with curly hair and smooth skin. And all the little prissy-tail girls just adored him. For some strange reason in a quiet little way, somewhere hidden in the back of my mind, I guess I did too. Stanley wore little bitty shirts that made his arms look pleasing to the eye, if you know what I mean. It was hard to make fun of Stanley, because he wasn't slim enough to be called skinny, and to the naked eye he was as close to flawless as they came. But like all good things, I knew that even he had to fall from his pedestal one day.

It was Stanley's relentless comedy routine that finally got on my last nerve. I had to do something. It would have been better if at least every now and then he gave those 'hey-darkie' jokes a break. He could have taken turns and teased somebody else, but I got the full brunt of his insensitive attacks. The 'stupid little black girl' he always referred to was eventually going to get tired of his verbal antics and fight back. Whatever I did, I knew it would have to be well planned. I knew when I fought back, my verbal swings would have to count.

Though I really could have cared less about a boy, I would have felt better if Pretty Boy had just sent me a note.

CHOCOLATE

You know, the ones with the boxes you check to answer 'yes' or 'no.' I was that sucked in at the beginning of the year.

My mother told me that when little boys like you, "They play silly games. That's just what they do." I loved my mother for sharing her wisdom, but I wasn't trying to swallow that tender morsel.

Trina, a girl in my fourth period class, liked Robert McFarland. He wasn't easy on the eyes but he knew how to treat a young lady, and that was always very attractive to me.

At least once a week, he'd bring something to school and give it to her at lunch just to let her know he cared. He gave her those small things that matter, but which most people take for granted; a photograph cut out of a magazine, or a pretty little rose he had stolen from his neighbor's backyard on the way to school.

Rhonda Patterson and I had been friends since we were about five years old. She was my girl, next to Sweets that is. Even though I did have a few friends at school, nothing could ever have meant more than my sweet friendship with my cousin, Sweets.

Rhonda was always getting candy thrown at her by Bernard Anderson. He was a nappy-headed little boy who used to wear high-waters to school. He wore his pants at least an inch over his shoe tops.

He was a peculiar young brother and easy to tease, but he had the thickest skin I had ever seen a kid display. No matter what the others kids said, it never seemed to get to him, and he actually enjoyed the attention. If I didn't know better, it seemed the more he was talked about the higher his pants got. There were times it looked like Bernard was wearing Capri's!

Bernard 'High-Waters' Anderson and I were cool, mainly because when he was around he took the attention off of me.

Rhonda was silly-crazy about him in an unconditional way for girls our age. She especially liked him because his rear end set up real high. From what I could tell, that was probably the reason his pants were always too short.

Sometimes between classes, Rhonda and I would walk down the hall past Bernard. She would look over at him and point. "Ooh, look girl... do you see that?" she asked.

I knew the drill, but I always played stupid. "What? Did I see what?" I responded.

She was a little too curious about boys, so there was only so much time I could spend with her. I knew what she was getting at, but playing dumb gave me a way out. So there I was, just acting like half-blame... looking dumfounded, as she continued to go on and on about 'High-Waters.'

"Girl, you can't stand here and tell me that you can't see all that. Shoot! That's a big old buuutttt."

We were too young, I felt, to have those conversations, so I always shied away from the subject, if for no other reason than for us to continue being friends. I didn't mind talking with her about Bernard, but I was not really into boys like she was.

What I didn't like, however, was the way Bernard threw candy at her. I was quite cautious and his passes seemed a little too hard and potentially very dangerous. One day he threw a piece of candy like a crazed baseball pitcher. She merely laughed when it hit her.

I asked with great concern, "Rhonda, why are you smiling like you've just won an award or something? Don't you know that if he had thrown that piece of candy up a little higher, he might have put your eye out?"

CHOCOLATE

"It's my favorite candy girl, a Butterfinger, and besides, Bernard is the starting quarterback on the Little League football team now..."

Rhonda was a little on the hefty side and she played rough like that. To me that was a bit much.

"Fool, I watch football with my father sometimes and I've seen quarterbacks throw bad passes. You're way too klutzy to be anybody's wide receiver. You better watch yourself 'cause Bernard ain't no quarterback like Doug Williams or Warren Moon... and you ain't no Drew Pearson, who happens to be such a fine wide receiver, in case you didn't know." My knowledge of football was sure coming in handy, and I was feeling so good.

"That boy's gonna mess around and put out your eye and then you're not gonna be able to see no Butterfingers anymore; no high-waters, and no high-butts for that matter! Now I suggest you pull his funny looking tail to the side and tell him you have switched positions. Tell him you are now a running back... uh, like Tony Dorsett, and from now on you would like a simple hand-off."

"Claudia, girl, you sure know a lot about football! But, you're right. He does kinda throw the candy hard sometimes."

"Sometimes! A couple weeks ago he almost broke one of the windows in the lunchroom! Have you ever seen him play ball himself? Rhonda, as you can tell, I know a bit about football, and from what I have seen, High-Waters is not very accurate at throwing anything."

She didn't know that every once in a while I had seen her take one to the head. She was so silly-crazy for Bernard she said, "It's all good." I guess that's what they meant when they said that all is fair in love and war.

There was another wanna be friend named Moesha Wilson. She was tall and lanky and on the real skinny side.

She was several shades brighter than anyone at school, and every chance she got she made sure I knew it. Her parents were well-to-do, but I learned through watching her that money ain't no friend. Moesha could have been a very sweet person, but the lust for attention made her bitter. She made a grand entrance getting dropped off at school every single day. She made sure everyone noticed that she rode in her family's long, freshly detailed, black Mercedes.

The boys all called her 'Big Bird' because of her skin color and elongated frame. But I called her 'Old Nasty-Mouth' because of the snobbish way she pranced around school saying one foul thing after another. I could never call her my friend, knowing how she felt about me. At first sight she seemed like a good person, but the second her mouth flew open she put an end to any assumptions simply by speaking. There were times I knew she was laughing at me and I felt her spiteful eyes cutting into me. That behavior removed all doubt of ever becoming friends.

Moesha wore braces with rubber bands on both sides of her mouth. They always appeared to need changing because they had food and saliva dangling from them. For the life of me, I could not believe that she couldn't feel what was going on inside her mouth. Because of her attitude... no one ever told her that her mouth was nasty; not a teacher, not a janitor, not a student, and certainly not me.

But she was silly-crazy too, about a boy named Tyrone, who could be quite violent. Sometimes at lunch he and Moesha would walk around outside holding hands. Without warning he would swing her around and throw her to the ground. She would get up real fast and brush herself off, and look around to make sure no one saw her being tossed about like a rag doll. One day Tyrone got even rougher and placed her in a headlock. Every time you saw her though, she was smiling like she was dating a wrestling superstar from the WWF.

As I mentioned, I wasn't into boys yet and Tyrone, Bernard and Stanley served as the perfect deterrents. Neither Tyrone nor Bernard would have worked for me, but I would have gladly taken them over Pretty Stan, or Stanley the Jokester Jackson. It was only a matter of time before I had that figured out.

If there was ever such a thing as a human sex repellent, Stanley Jackson was it. Before opening his mouth he was as appealing as another victory to a winning team. But as soon as he spoke, he became as sour as the taste in a loser's mouth. Though I couldn't find it in me to ever hate 'The Jokester,' I longed for the day I could get even.

Stanley had a way with words, and boy did he know it. When he spoke he commanded attention, and sometimes it seemed like I was the only one who wasn't giving it to him. Just when I felt there was nothing else bad he could say about me, he proved me wrong.

The dismissal bell rang one day and it was time to go home from school. I was wearing simple blue jeans and a nice pink blouse my mother had bought for me a week earlier. I was also wearing my first training bra and was feeling uncomfortable. I was a bit unsure of myself, but walking down the hall with a few classmates helped me feel better about the new bra experience.

As we approached our lockers, out of nowhere, Pretty Boy appeared and had to notice us. Like always, 'the pointers' accompanied him on his stroll. The closer they got, the more nervous I became.

My feet wanted to move but for some reason they felt shackled. I grew numb with anticipation of what was about to be said. With every step Stanley took towards me I grew weaker. I felt like the walls were closing in on me.

As if on cue, 'the pointers' lived up to their collective name; they started tapping Pretty Boy's shoulder pointing in our direction. One of them singled me out and Stanley's reaction would always be one of my most embarrassing moments. There he was, The Jokester, just leering at me with a cocky smile. He stood and stared at me like a hungry vagrant stares at a piece of freshly cooked meat.

Just as I began to place my books inside my locker The Jokester started in on me. What he did next was a young girl's nightmare.

Without any hesitation he yelled out, "Hey, Claudia! Are you in training?"

Everyone in the hallway started laughing along with Pretty Boy and his pointers.

"I heard that tryouts for the Junior Olympics are this week. Is it true that you're competing for the 'little-bitty-titty-comity' award this year?"

I was confused and embarrassed. "No, boy, I'm not trying out for the Junior Olympics," I shot back trying to sound confident. Not quite sure he would continue with his line of questioning, my voice became defensive as I said with naïveté, "I'm not in training for anything either. What made you ask me that?"

"Maybe it's got something to do with the little bitty training bra you have on. What are you doing with that thing on anyway, training your chest to stand still?"

The volume of laughter increased to a deafening range. I couldn't let him get away with that. I had to say something. I was quick on my feet too, and I needed to show him he wasn't the only one who could get a laugh at someone else's expense.

I mustered all my courage and pushed my way over to stand amid him and his pointers. Now I did the pointing and said in a loud voice, "You know, Stanley," and I pulled on my bra strap, "I hear they have this same size in jock-straps. In fact, there is a set of two put aside down at the corner store with your name on it."

That made everyone start laughing again. Stanley just stood there shaking his head back and forth. He shrugged his shoulders and lifted both of his hands palms up.

"Okay, Claudia. You got me... That was a good one," he admitted. "I had that one coming. Okay, okay, the little jock-strap down at the corner store routine, that was good... that was real good."

I knew it wouldn't be the last time he would take a shot at me, or the last time I would take revenge. I recalled my father saying that 'a hit dog will always holler' and Stanley had just been run over by a Mac-Truck.

About three weeks later, we all went skating and my father allowed me to go to Denny's afterwards with a few of my friends. We were minding our own business when out of nowhere it seemed, someone found it acceptable to try out some darkie jokes. We had just been seated when the idiot started in on me.

It was Pretty Boy and 'the pointers' sitting a couple of booths down from us. Stanley stood up with a fork in one hand and a glass in the other. He started banging them together in hopes of bringing more attention to himself.

His clothes could have done that on their own, however. Stanley was wearing a blue and white sweat suit with matching running shoes that day. He was always coordinated from head to toe, or like my friends used to say, he was 'doing the dang-thang.' What he was wearing at the time wasn't really what mattered, though; what mattered was what he was saying.

"Hey, Claudia! I heard you are so dark that your hairdresser couldn't tell where your hairline started."

When he felt like he was getting the desired reaction, his voice became louder and like any good comedian, he moved in for the kill.

"What kind of lotion did you put on this morning? Whatever it was, you look... uh, burnt. Yeah, burnt." He hollered for the waitress and pointed to me, "Hey! Miss! She'll have the 'Sambo-Slam' and a glass of 'Brighten-Me-Up' on ice."

When Stanley saw the waitress come over to our table with a pot of coffee in her hand, he couldn't resist another opportunity to challenge me.

He stood up and shouted, "Oh, Miss... just give her a glass of water. Can't you see she's already had more than enough coffee? Pouring her a cup of coffee would be like trying to serve the night a bowl of darkness. It just ain't right." He was on a roll and 'the pointers' were in fits of hysteria.

He insisted on continuing the attack. "Get this. When they're camping, her parents use her eyes as reflectors to guide them through the night. If you don't believe me, turn the lights off in here and tell me the first thing you see. If it ain't her eyes, I'll gladly pay for everyone's food in here. Now where is your light-switch?"

He was in rare form and loving it, and I just sat there as he gave me his best. While he was rambling on and on, I was able to zone out to avoid several of the worst brainless comments.

There I was, as predicted, once again having to defend myself from the ignorance of a brainless, narrow-minded, insecure pretty-faced nobody. This must have been the thirteenth confrontation in a year. Not that I was counting.

CHOCOLATE

I was tired of being the 'Black Girl' this and the 'Black Girl' that. I didn't want to believe my mother was lying about my beauty, but after a while I couldn't help but doubt her. In fact, it was down right humiliating to think that in order to be accepted I would have to deal with the same insulting crap my father had warned me about.

While my father and I were at the grocery store a few months prior to the Denny's incident, I had the opportunity to see Stanley's parents for the first time. They were standing in the checkout line but I didn't know who they were until they called out his name. Stanley appeared from around the other side of a store display as I moved behind my father to disappear. Pretty Boy grinned at his lily-white pretty mother, and I noticed his father was as dark, or darker than I was. I had never mentioned my observations.

All kids' minds are filled with thousands of unanswered questions. Often, instead of a genuine search for the truth, their discomfort of not knowing or understanding makes them mean. Their own insecurities drive a need to hurt others. Perhaps they have something to hide. For the most part, answers elude them because they lack the patience necessary to prove whether their theories of life are true. I had given Stanley the benefit of the doubt for too long.

"Hey… Claudia," Stanley's voice continued and brought me out of my private thoughts. He was simply making sure he had my attention and then his voice droned on.

Privately I could handle the abuse, but it was the way Pretty Boy always wanted to place me on 'front-street' that really bothered me. I didn't enjoy playing the dozens, but it was time for all of this to come to an end. I wanted the teasing to stop.

'Why must I continue warring against the miffs of my predecessors when they have no ability to determine my future?' I asked myself.

I had been taught that only by yielding to my sense of emotional self-worth could I allow another human being to diminish who I was. "No one can inflect mental anguish against us as a people, unless first given permission," I recalled my father telling me.

I had given Stanley permission to disrupt my emotional state of mind. Now, only I could denounce that right.

The time had come for 'the pointers,' and anyone else for that matter who dared laugh at The Jokester's stupid skin color commentary, to get some insight into Pretty Boy's home life. Not a single soul gave a damn about the repercussions from the mental abuse I had endured. I was tired of being the center of negative attention. It was time for The Jokester's truck to roll to a stop, and I was getting ready to make it pump its brakes.

I felt a surge of that selfishness and I didn't care who I hurt. I had become bold enough to make the jokes stop by revealing Stanley's secret. I had always been told that the best way to keep a man down was to get down there with him. I finally reconnected to the mindless chatter and interrupted The Jokester with my own insulting barrage. I tentatively stood up ready to give him my best ten minutes.

"Hey, Pretty Boy, while you're at it, let's bring your father in here so no one gets lost, seeing that he is my twin. I find it hard to believe that none of your 'pointer brothers' have seen your father yet." I had his attention.

"Hey... Jokester, do they know?" I was ready to drive home my point. "Do they?" I repeated. "Your devoted 'pointer brothers' there," I indicated his posse with a dramatic full arm point. "Do they know your own father is darker than I am? Haven't you ever mentioned his extra shade or two of darkness? Maybe they don't know that if he stood next to a rack of Michelin tires, he'd blend right in. Maybe you should invite them over and introduce them to your 'real-dark' father. In fact, isn't it true that *Webster's Dictionary* is making up a new name for him as we speak? I hear they are going to call him 'Redark,' that will be defined as 'real-dark' in the big book."

Oh, Stanley didn't like that, but I was feeling too clever to quit.

"And speaking of coffee," I said addressing the Denny's waitresses, "all you really need around here is water. Stanley's father is black enough to place his finger in a cup and make his own coffee."

The crowd sat stunned in silence, but I continued, "So yes, Jokester, turn those lights off so that the whole world, not just the folks here at Denny's, can see me and my twin brother… your father." I was exhausted when I finished. I sat back down trying to get my breath.

I could tell Stanley was devastated, and for the first time in years he was at a loss for words. I didn't feel good about what I had just done to him. I knew it was wrong, but how else was I going to get him off of my back?

Stanley stood after hearing what I had to say, and slowly walked over to my table. He stretched out his hand towards me in a gesture of peace. It was his way of saying he gave in. The irony of it all was a sad thing. It dawned on Pretty Boy that his own father had the same color of skin he had teased me about for years. He was finally forced to answer some of his own uncomfortable questions. Stanley never again took a shot at me about the color of my skin, or anything else.

Chocolate

My mother loved my father's dark skin, which made me jealous at times. He was even darker than I was. But if it was good enough for her to love, it was good enough for me to be proud of. I was, after all, the proud daughter of two of this world's most influential human beings. I liked to think of myself as being a seed of truth. For I was born happy and happy I shall die. Though my skin had always been the rich mahogany color of fine graded coffee, it was an evenly toned color of earthly perfection. I was darker than almost anyone I knew, yet my soul dawned the brightest demeanor this world had ever seen. The skin of truth is what I liked to call it, and 'Chocolate' is what they called me.

My mother and father were true soul mates. They were inseparable; emotionally joined at the hip, and mentally in tune with each other's needs. I was the result of passion, the unmodified distinction between lust and love. Everything I did was recorded; my every move was cherished because my parents treasured me as they did each other. I was a happy child for obvious reasons.

They named me Claudia Renee Williams but it was my father who first christened me 'Chocolate.' My guess is that sooner or later I would have been given a name similar to Chocolate anyway, considering my dark complexion. It didn't hurt any that my skin was pure and smoother than a baby's butt.

I acquired my nickname just before my fourth birthday, as I sat in the middle of the kitchen floor devouring leftovers from an unattended mixing bowl. My mother had left it on the edge of the kitchen counter while she delivered my father the three things he seemed to crave most after a long hard day of work: a glass of red wine, his slippers, and his daily dose of the *Wall Street Journal*.

The story goes that I stood up on my tiptoes and pulled a plastic mixing bowl down off the counter while Mama was out of the room for a moment. When she came back into the kitchen she saw her only child straddling a massive bowl, wearing a smile larger than life. I smiled up at her as my cheeks blushed through the chocolate goop, just like a kid who had tasted candy for the first time. She couldn't help but smile back despite the mess I had made.

Mama had returned to find my entire face covered with chocolate, and when she saw me, she turned and screamed as loud as her soft southern voice would possibly allow.

"Maarrrvviiin! Come here! Come here baby! Hurry up! You've got to see this!"

She never took her eyes off of me, as she laughed until her stomach started to ache. Not knowing what all the commotion was about, my father immediately dropped everything and ran to the kitchen.

There I was, enjoying myself to the fullest, unaware that, that day would be of tremendous symbolic meaning in my life. I was still dipping my hands into the mixing bowl, grinning out of control, happy I had gathered an audience. I have been told that I was a character growing up and that momentous occasion was proof positive. When I finally acknowledged my parents, I raised up my hands into mid-air, obviously quite proud of the mess that I had just made.

"Look at her, Marvin," my mama said. "She's smiling like she has just found a pot of gold."

My father responded matter-of-factly, "She has, baby, and for her, it's chocolate." Within a matter of seconds I had a name that would stick with me forever.

As I sat there in the middle of the floor, I covered myself from head to toe in the sweetest tasting chocolate I would ever come to know.

My father yelled out to my mother, "That's my baby! That's Daddy's little 'Chocolate' baby."

When I heard my daddy call me his little 'Chocolate Baby,' I got up and started dancing wildly as he rushed to get the camcorder.

"Hurry up, Marvin," my mother urged. "You can't miss this! We've got to get this on tape."

"Hell, I'm running as fast as I can, Janelle." He was looking everywhere for the camera.

"Where is it?" he yelled running from room to room. He finally found it on the top shelf of the bedroom closet, where they always kept it.

"I've got it! I found the camera! What is she doing now?" he asked as he ran back to the kitchen.

"Oh, she's still at it," my mother reassured him. "This girl is crazy. Just look at her… she's such a happy child."

By that time, I was running around the kitchen touching everything I could get my hands on. I was even chasing my mother attempting to turn her dress to chocolate.

"Oh, Janelle, this is priceless," my father said while filming. "Look at our pretty little baby. Doesn't she look just like her daddy?"

That made my mother stop short.

"Nope," she replied with a straight face and her hands on her hips. "She doesn't resemble you at all. Come on now, Marvin… just because she's got a little bit of chocolate on her hands and cheeks doesn't make you two twins. She definitely has her mother's features. Marvin, when I look at her all I see is myself as a child. Just look at those dimples."

"Ah, come on, Janelle. Are you serious? Not even the chin?" he asked hopefully.

"Nope, not even," she said with a smile.

My father continued taping as my mother scooped me up and danced around the kitchen with me. There I was in her arms, as I must have been so many times before, but none of them was more memorable than that moment. I must have seen that tape over a thousand times, but each viewing was like the first.

My mother spoke with a southern drawl and walked with the noble poise of a European queen. She was always being teased about how flat she spoke some of her words, but Daddy loved that about her. When other people talked about the way she pronounced her words, my father would embrace each horizontal expression she uttered.

My mother once told me that her fair skin was passed down through generations by the very souls that claimed to hate her. She spoke to me about the depths to which a man would stoop to put an end to the craving of his flesh. It wasn't until later that I fully understood her claim.

Mama said, "Child, please believe me when I tell you that the fleshly desires of a man don't have a thang to do with love. He ain't trying to leave you his affections, he's trying to release his troubles - and his troubles ain't never something you want. My skin may be beautiful to the eye, but it was given to me in an ugly way. You see, baby, you can't just relieve yourself of affections.

"Not unlike the chains that were once worn by our oppressed ancestors, harsh words still possess the power to emotionally shackle so many of our people today. No, it's true, Chocolate, the plantation owners never meant for our skin to be as pale as theirs but their lustful act was symbolic in nature."

Here she let biblical implications come into play.

"Though God's uncompromising conclusions have become self-evident, my skin color gives proof that no deed, whether right or wrong, will go unscathed. For it has been written that, 'whatever is done in the dark, shall one day come to the light, and our skin color is a perfect illustration of that."

She explained to me that the color of her skin represented the mitigating reflections of our ancestors' past. She said our skin was our coat of protection given to us at birth to shield us from the rays of the world's indiscriminant madness and the chills of its ignorance. The only choice we would have when it came to how we were seen by others ultimately depended on how we viewed ourselves.

My mother was one of the lightest individuals I had ever seen; yet vanity was not part of her vocabulary. She understood the myths that came with being a shade or two brighter than the rest, but she was too well read to fall prey to the stereotypical findings of the few anal-retentive knuckleheads of this world.

"Child," my mother once said, "I was never given a chance to choose the color of my skin, but if I had my choice, I would much rather be colorblind."

My mother called my skin warmed over butter slightly burnt by nature, yet to a gorgeous shade of perfection. My father would often tell me that the color of my skin was like newly polished brass, soothing and refreshing to the eyes; like freedom within reach.

His skin was as dark as they got, but intellectually he was as bright as they came. Though he was nearly one shade away from being blue, Mama loved him for being refreshingly new.

He never showed any ill affects due to his being darker than most. He was a genius, so why should he? Obviously he had reasoned that out as well.

The color of a person's skin never invaded my mother's thought process. She was intrigued by a man's soul instead of the temple that stored it. She came to love my father initially for the intense level of his emotional awareness.

Even though I was too young to state my findings, I knew that my parents loved each other and that there was nothing they wouldn't have done to cultivate their love. What they had was hypnotic in nature and absolutely overwhelming in size. As a child I was often captivated and even mesmerized by their emotional connection. It was a degree of perfection that would always remain immeasurable. Their love for one another had a way of downplaying their inadequacies, while at the same time it lifted their convictions, destroying any possible hunger for external affairs.

When it came to reasoning with the essence of life, my mother simply closed her eyes and allowed her soul to lead her. Love was the cadence their hearts danced to as their faith in each other catapulted them to the apex of its premise. Together they co-mingled and made the most precious shade of chocolate this world had ever seen.

When Mama walked beside my father, her shoulders were always adjusted firmly in a proud position. When she spoke of my father, an amazing glimmer of joy rolled off the tip of her tongue and the essence of the few words she uttered forced one to smile. Why? Because she had fallen in love, not with the shade of his skin, but rather the color of his soul. By doing so, true love had no choice but to unfold.

I watched my parents profess their love for each other sometimes without ever uttering a word. I watched them embrace one another with a smile, and knew even as a child that their love for one another had to be uncommon. They had a moral appreciation for their vows. They had promised to keep them by never allowing the stimulating fires of their desire for each other to cease. My parents had a non-materialistic appetite and they loved each other seductively. By doing so it prolonged their relationship.

Pay Attention, Child

Mama was what the southern brothers called a high-yellow woman. Janelle Williams was her name. She stood about five-feet six and had a caring personality, at times a bit impatient, yet with a quiet soothing voice. Her face was blessed with a set of dimples that most people would die to have, and her dark brown eyes enhanced the structure of her face. When she smiled, she indirectly affected others' anger and caused it to dissipate, but it was her uncanny ability to reason with sadness that invoked a feeling of promise to those who came in contact with her.

I craved many things in life over the years but no craving was as strong as my love for my mother. I respected her for the way in which she denounced her outer blessings and redirected attention with her exquisite substance.

Mama and I would often converse about many miscellaneous things in life. When we talked she let me know that I had her undivided attention.

Over the years she had acquired a wide range of wisdom and at the drop of a hat she could summon it. Mama hated talking to the deaf ear of ignorance, as she so gracefully put it. She didn't mind repeating herself; she just refused to waste good air on those who didn't care whether they lived.

When she called me Claudia, I knew to pay special attention to her every word. Something meaningful was about to be said and I knew that it was time to concentrate.

Once, when I was nine years old, Mama was in the middle of an important statement, and she thought I wasn't paying close enough attention. She just shut down and didn't talk to me for almost two weeks; she was just that way.

It was just after the two week silent period when we went to a local mall. We went window shopping and quietly enjoyed each other's company, but it was obviously one of those let-me-see-where-my-daughter's-head-is kind of outings. I could see the nourishment inside my mother begin to seep out as it had done once or twice before. I was about to get her best, whether I wanted it or not.

We were standing in front of a large department store when I finally decided to break the ice.

I turned towards her and asked, "Mama, it's been a while since you've said anything to me. Did I do something wrong? I mean, what's going on? Will you please say something?"

She was reaching into her purse but stopped to reply, "Claudia, I never stopped speaking to you child, I was just giving you time to think about everything that had happened. Now, are you ready to answer my question?"

"Sure," I replied. The next thing I said seemed to anger her dearly. "Mama, do you even remember what you got so mad at me about?"

"Child, although I've forgotten more than you're ever going to learn, I remember exactly what we were talking about. I was telling you how important it was to be able to listen, and you didn't seem to be paying attention."

"But, I was paying attention, Mama," I said, but obviously she wasn't convinced.

"Child, do you know what a lie is?" she asked.

"Yes, I know what a lie is, but I'm not lying," I insisted.

"If you're not lying, then the truth ain't in you."

"But I was, Mama, I was."

"You were what?" she asked.

I was too consumed with my own concerns to remember what had just been said. Just that quickly I had already forgotten half of what was being talked about. She wasn't there to hurt me, she was there to guide me, but I was too blind to see. All I needed to do was just shut up and listen. I was too caught up in myself to allow someone else's opinions to override my thought process. My pride was getting in the way and I was out of control.

I just needed to get one last shot in for good measure, though. So I stood in front of my mother, looking at her like the world owed me something.

I tried to outsmart my moralistic teacher by wearing the most dejected look on my face when she asked, "Well, do you, or do you not recall what you were doing when I was talking to you?"

"Yes, I mean, I think I do."

"Which is it?" my mother emphatically demanded. "Do you, or don't you remember why I stopped talking that day?"

I stood there too nervous to respond. I knew I wasn't paying enough attention and something told me that whatever I was about to say was only going to prolong things. When it came to interrogating her child, my mother was a scholar and a manipulative detective; a real life Elliot Ness. I was no match for her and she knew it.

I only had a few words available in my all but depleted vocabulary, so I did what any solider would have done in my position: I held up the white flag and surrendered as she moved in for the kill.

"Speak to me, child, and please make it plain." Though her voice was soft, the few words she did speak were rigid and to the point.

I was frustrated and just wanted to throw up my hands. I said, "Okay, Mama, I get it."

"Oh, do you really?"

For the most part it was fun to be around my mother but she had a thing about paying attention. She was the kind of woman with a lot of patience for most things, but disrespect wasn't one of them. She insisted that she and I become the very best of friends. She would often tell me how proud she was of me, but just as she kept her bag of 'positives' handy, her bag of 'constructive criticism' was readily available.

My mother had a low tolerance for any mental lapse and didn't mind displaying her displeasure towards it. I can count on one hand the times she hit me, but there were occasions when I would rather have taken a whuppin' than listen to one of her famous southern tongue lashings. She was notorious for what my family jokingly called her 'verbal-ability,' and her attacks should have been outlawed in every state. But when she got started she couldn't stop.

She was as sweet as could be, but you didn't want to rub her the wrong way. If you did you'd better brace yourself for one of her lethal outbreaks. She was a painfully honest woman with punishing truths. I called her 'the queen of open-ended questions.' She demanded the same respect she held for herself and she remained uncompromising in her stand. When she was ready to make a point, she would always wear a smooth, confident smile… right before she slapped you across the face with some realism.

My next lesson began right where we were standing; near the food court on the lower level in the mall.

CHOCOLATE

"Chocolate, the very next time I part my lips to express myself, I pray that you find a way to undress your attitude long enough to listen to the naked truth."

I had listened to her truth enough times to write a book on it. I knew enough to straighten my face, undress my negativity and pay closer attention to what she was saying. Those days if my mother decided not to speak to me, it taught me a great lesson. I didn't want the silence to reappear, not when all I had to do was listen, for God's sake. Over the years she had taught me so much. I needed her wisdom in my life.

I knew that my attitude could eventually destroy our relationship and I wouldn't let that happen. Deep down inside I didn't want to lose what we had. She was always so real, so easy to touch, so available to feel. Her love was so timely, so sure, so forever.

When my mother finally finished talking, the words she spoke had given 'the ability to listen' a whole new meaning. I loved her for reaching into her bag of love's correction and I still can remember the intense words of emotional alteration.

In the Twinkling
of an Eye

At twelve, I was barely old enough to reason with life when God came and did the most irrational thing He could have done. He took my mother away. Without any notice, or any request of emotional eviction, He simply removed her from this earth.

She was a woman of extraordinary conviction, a real vision of promise when society was too afraid to commit. She possessed a hopeful kiss when the lips of compassion and ultimate affection had all but lost their ability to reconnect.

My mother was an optimist when it came to giving… she displayed it by the way she lived, rather than the words she spoke.

But in the twinkling of an eye, the maker of all of the mountains and the flowers came and quietly took her away. Without any reservation He confiscated the reason why I became the woman I did.

There was so much to remember; countless pages of memories to turn: the smell of her freshly washed skin as she straightened up the house throughout the day; the things she said without ever saying a word; the way she stared at me proudly from a distance with her head tilted ever so slightly to the right, while smiling serenely at her only daughter.

My mother spoke clear messages with few words, and those she did speak made up for her silence. She was a doer when the world was full of walkers; a giver when life wasn't giving up a thing. She pledged nothing she couldn't fulfill and when she ordered something from life, she was always ready to pay the bill. She had the tenacity to continue to love those who, from afar, seemed too trifling to ever care about. Her courage was unyielding.

She loved both my father and me equally and she made sure we knew it. When we were ill, she tended to us. When life became discouraging, she pulled us near and held our heads close to her bosom, stroking our brows until a spirit of relaxation consumed our minds and the power of slumber took over. Though her arms were frail, they possessed enough compassion to slay an angry giant.

When the cold night air crept through the cracks along side my window, she would come into my room and tuck the blankets ever so gently around me. Her love for me was the soothing pillow of my life. She was my problem-solving guide long before I ever had the displeasure of meeting trouble.

I loved my mother for instilling in me how vital it was to know when to speak as well as when not to. I would come to miss seeing her point her anointed hands towards the skies of immorality, causing them to calm. But not even she could have possibly prepared me to deal with the ramifications of death.

CHOCOLATE

Death is the most common denominator of them all; it holds the one truth that we all share: we shall all come face to face with it one day.

Life is so precious. The moment we feel we have a grip on it, something happens to cause us to perspire, and just like that, the worst happens. The grip I had just wasn't strong enough, and like the last slow dance with that special someone, it just wasn't long enough.

When she left for work on the morning of October 3, 1989, Daddy and I had no idea that it would be her last time to see the two people she loved most in life; that it would be our last time to see her.

There was an unusual sense of calmness in the air the day God sent death to meet Mama. She got up from her chair and came around to my side of the table as I complained about my burnt toast. She picked up my toast and began to scrape it over the trashcan. I saw her glance at my father as he smiled at her seductively.

"Can you guys save that for later?" I asked.

"Save what, baby," my mother asked with a guilty look on her face.

I interpreted their smiles and asked, "Daddy, is that why my toast is burnt?"

"Child, I don't know what you're talking about, and besides ain't nothing wrong with a few little burnt areas on your toast. I mean, look at me, Chocolate. I'm burnt and your Mama lu-u-uves me," he said.

"You've got that right, Big Daddy," she said to him.

Then she looked over at me. "Baby, when the boss speaks, you better listen. Because don't nobody know burnt like I know burnt," Mama said.

"Look, it's too early in the morning for all of that," I winced. "You two are so mushy."

"No, baby, we're in love, and that ain't just grits and bacon you smell, that's affection in the air. And don't you forget it."

There she went again swelling up my father's head. When she started talking like that, he'd stick his chest out like a proud strutting peacock. Mama knew what she was doing, and when she poured it on, she poured it on thick.

My father ate it up word for word, never missing a bite. I loved the way he stared at Mama. He looked at her like she was his prize lamb and together they had won first place at the summer fair.

And there I was that morning thinking about how I had made it through a tiny earthquake while they were pleasing each other in the other room and my toast was burning in the kitchen.

As Mama handed me back my two pieces of toast she said slyly, "Baby, can you ever forgive your Mama? I had to help the boss with something and it took a little longer than I thought it would."

My father's smile stretched his face out of proportion.

"Mama, if you don't stop stroking his ego, he's gonna have to call in sick and tell his boss that he's got the big-head again."

They both started laughing their heads off at that.

"That's your child, Marvin. Get her…"

"Oh, so let me see… when she does something crazy, then she's my child, and when she does something creative, she's yours. Do I have that right, Janelle?"

My mother looked over at me and said, "Now, Chocolate, baby, do you see why Mama married your daddy? He's the smartest man I know."

After a long look at us both she sighed, "Well, I'd like to stay and chat with you two beautiful people but I have a job to go to, and I'm going to be late if I don't hurry out of here."

She walked over to kiss my father on the forehead as he hurried to finish his breakfast.

"Bye, Mom," I said, as she leaned over to kiss my right cheek and with her palm, she gently stroked the other one.

"Bye, my little angel. Listen to your teachers and concentrate on your schoolwork. Do you hear me?"

"Yes, Ma'am, I hear you, Mama, and I will," I promised.

As she got ready to leave the house, she stopped and said, "Hey, Chocolate, about that toast... it'll never happen again, I promise. Bye-bye, baby. I love you guys."

"We love you too," we called simultaneously. And she was out the door with a twinkle in her eye.

She had been gone for over three minutes and still my father was smiling. They had that effect on each other. It was a bond that few relationships rarely get a chance to experience. They had made not only a promise, but also an emotional connection that surpassed the normal realm of thought. It is only acquired through the love that stems from one heart to another and can never be bought.

That day Mama was wearing low pumps and a beautiful sundress, loosely fitted. She walked out with a smile that could cure the common cold. Not knowing it would be her last chance, she waved good-bye. I can remember a connection between the three of us that would never be duplicated. We never dreamed that the kiss we received that morning would be our last. But the bombshell that was yet to be delivered would more than wake us up.

After work that day, my father had come home and was winding down. We were just waiting for Mama when there was an unexpected knock on the door.

"Chocolate, get the door!" my father yelled from his study.

By the time I made it to the door, the two gentlemen who had come knocking were already walking back towards their car.

"Hey, mister!" I yelled.

They heard me say hello, and came back to the house.

"Hello, young lady, is your father at home?" one of them asked solemnly.

"Yes, he's here, wait just a minute. I'll get him." I opened the door to the study just wide enough to peek inside.

"Dad, there's someone at the door for you, and they sound mad."

"Who is it, baby?" he asked.

I ran back to the door to find out. "Excuse me, what's your name?"

"My name is John Wilson," said the taller man. "What's yours?" he asked politely.

I wasn't supposed to talk to strangers, and besides they weren't there to see me, so I didn't respond. Daddy came out to speak to them.

When they left the house, he closed the door without saying a word. He walked silently into his bedroom but slammed the door. I heard him yell out at the top of his lungs, "NNNNOOOOOO! NNNOOOOO!" he wailed.

I ran down the hallway and knocked on the door as hard as I could.

"What's wrong, Daddy, what's wrong?" I asked fearfully, and barged into his room.

"It's your mom, Chocolate. Something bad has happened," he managed to say.

"What? What is it, Daddy? What has happened to Mama?" I asked as I stood helplessly in front of him.

"She's been in an accident, Chocolate," he replied with no emotion.

"Well, she's going to be all right, isn't she?"

The look in his eyes told me all I needed to know. Before I could blink, I was in my father's arms. There we were, holding each other and I was weeping uncontrollably.

"No, baby, not this time. She's not going to be all right."

"Well, when is she coming home? Are you sure it's Mama? What if they were wrong and it is not my mama? They're lying... we just saw her earlier this morning. She'll be here in a few minutes, just wait... you'll see."

The questions were pouring out of me and I remember saying things like, "I don't believe it, it can't be her! They're wrong, Daddy. Mama's coming home."

Then my selfish side asked, "Daddy, what are we going to do without her? Who's going to cook for us? Who will scrape my toast?" I sobbed.

Standing in the middle of my father's bedroom I was unable to move. The shock of hearing of my mother's passing was devastating to say the least. A numb feeling invaded my body; a feeling as if the world had come to an end. I couldn't think of living without my mother. She was always there, and just like that... she was gone.

As my father spoke, I gazed across the room and stared at the picture of my mother he kept near his side of the bed. Just looking at it made me feel weak and instantly lonely. I wasn't ready to let go. Our hearts were too connected. But I had to be strong; strong in the face of adversity because that is what I was taught.

"I want this all to be a lie, Chocolate, but it's not looking good. Please, baby, I need you to be strong for me. We'll get through this together," my father tried to reassure me, but his voice was dejected.

Disbelief was slowly fading, but I couldn't handle the thought that I wouldn't be seeing my mother anymore. I walked into my own room and fell to the floor, too weak to stand and too hurt to move.

As soon as my eyes adjusted to the darkness, I picked up the phone and called my cousin and closest friend, Pamela. Both Pamela and I had always been there for each other no matter what we went through. She was the best friend ever, with the best name ever. Pamela was my Sweets.

When she was born, her mother, Aunt Jackie, developed complications while delivering the twins. Paul, her brother, never made it. Sweets had trouble dealing with his death for quite a while. She and my mother had been close and this news would be a great setback. I still had to call hoping we might be able to cope with another death together.

With my hands trembling out of control, I reached for the telephone in my time of need. The numbers just wouldn't stop whirling before me, and a phone number I had dialed so many times had suddenly become hard to remember. But after several attempts, the phone rang and within seconds Sweets answered.

"Hello…" she answered sweetly.

When I heard her voice, I lost my own. But Sweets knew my cry, as our spirits were forever connected.

"Choc, what's wrong? Girl what are you crying about now?"

"Sweets, something happened to Mama today, something real bad," I managed to sputter out.

"What? What's wrong with Aunty Janelle?" she asked with great concern.

"She's gone, Sweets. She's gone and she ain't never coming back," I sobbed.

"What? Chocolate… come on, stop playing."

"No, Sweets, it's true… she's gone."

The phone grew quiet as Pamela began to absorb the implication of my tragic news. She was contemplating how to deal with death's instant transformation, while at the same time how to comfort me.

As I waited for her to respond, the thought of never again being able to hear my mother utter my name consumed me. The reality of tragedy was creeping in and I almost hung up the phone.

Sweets broke the silence. "She's gone, Chocolate? Not Aunty Janelle... She ain't never harmed a soul. How could God let her die? Choc, I'm sorry... I'm so sorry. Let me get off the phone and try to find my mother; you know she's never home. Like always she's got her trifling tail out in the streets. Let me get off this phone. Don't worry, Choc, even if I have to walk, I'll be over there as soon as I can."

Aunt Jackie arrived home from hanging out in the streets all day not too long after Pamela and I had talked. After hearing the news, they both rushed over to be with my father and me, but it was still almost two hours before I heard Sweets yelling out my name as they walked through the front door.

"Choc... where are you? Hey, Chocolate! Where are you, girl?"

After it was clear I wasn't imagining things, I pulled my tired soul up from my bed and ran towards the sound of her voice. By the time I reached them my father had come out of his room as well and together we greeted them.

Aunt Jackie, my mother's younger sister, was crying heavily as she walked over and gave us hugs. Even though Aunt Jackie led a questionable life, we still loved her and could tell she had genuine concern. After all, she and my mother both gave birth during the same year. And there we stood,

Chocolate and Sweets, the products of two sisters; cousins and best friends in their saddest hour.

"Marvin… is it true? What has happened? What happened to my big sister? Why did she have to die? Please tell me that this is all a lie," she begged.

"Jackie, you don't know how bad I want to tell you it's all a mistake, but it's true and our Janelle has gone to heaven. I still have to go down and view the body, but from everything I've been told, it's her."

"So what happened, Marvin? When did this happen? How did she die?" asked Aunt Jackie.

I could hear in my father's voice that the words were hard to form but, being the man he is, he braced himself as he swallowed to speak.

"On her way home from work, she stopped at the grocery store to pick up something for dinner," he started in a monotone voice. "There was a man in a hurry to get home just to tell his wife that he had won a measly eighty-five dollars on a lottery ticket… On her way back to the car, he struck Janelle in the middle of the parking lot! She must have stepped into his blind spot," he tried to reason.

"She got hit by a car? By what man? Who is he? Where is he? Did he get arrested? How could he not see my sister?" She blurted out a flurry of questions.

"I don't know, Jackie," he sighed as his voice trailed off. "This is all I was told. The information came so suddenly, and I was so shocked I never thought to ask for more details. I do know that he claimed he never saw her."

"Don't ask him anymore questions, Mom," Pamela urged her mother. "Can't you see Uncle Marvin is hurting? Let's just think about how she lived, and let's stop talking about why or how she died," said Sweets.

Aunt Jackie stopped questioning my father and we all hugged in agreement to try to let the healing begin.

CHOCOLATE

A week later we had the funeral. As everyone gathered to pay their respects, I could see the impact my mother had had on the lives of so many others. Everything was beautiful and she lay there looking like an angel. My father just sat beside her coffin, numb from it all. He was motionless as he listened to all the emotional accolades spoken on her behalf.

When the funeral was over, everyone was invited to our house for dinner. As the house filled with mourners I knew my heart was too empty to cater to their presence. I couldn't bear to be around the crowd so I walked into my mother's room and hid inside her closet. My soul was robbed, as was my father's, but I was too selfish to feel for any one else. I was hurting dreadfully as I sat there in the middle of the closet. I held her favorite blue sweater in my arms, crying and rocking back and forth feeling so detached from the world.

The woman who had for years shined a beacon of light upon the distant path of my womanhood was gone. I felt my womanly sense of direction become dormant. I sat there pleading with the Spirit. Why? Why, oh why?

I could feel my mother reaching down from heaven to wipe my tears. I could hear her whisper, "Be strong child. Be strong for your father. Stand tall, and for God's sake child, get up off that floor before you mess up your knees."

After feeling my mother's presence, a wave of guilt came over me and lifted me to my feet. I leapt up and opened the door with the urge to find my father. Though he was as strong as the Rock of Gibraltar, the fact still remained, he was human. He had lost the love of his life, his best friend, his emotional sounding board, his beloved wife.

It was time for *I*, to be replaced by *us*. So, I reached deep down inside myself and placed a firm grip on the knob of self-pity to turn it off. By the time I became myself again, most of the people who had come to pay their respects had gone. There were a few close family members still lingering but for the most part, the mourners were gone.

I had never heard the words, 'I'm sorry,' used so many times. I knew they must be sincere, but a part of me wondered why they were smiling at me. Was their conscience bothering them or were their sentiments really genuine? I was starting to feel like a priest in a confessional.

I was on a mission in search of my father and really too tired to care one way or the other about their concerns. I decided not to talk to another soul until I found him.

One older lady did stand out, though. She appeared to be in her early sixties, yet her skin dawned a radiant complexion of light brown magic, which simply tugged at my eyes and demanded my attention. She wore her hair fashionably short and had a captivating smile. She was wearing a yellow and white sundress with all of the matching accessories. The hat, the gloves, the shoes, the purse, the whole nine yards. But it wasn't only her attire or appearance that caught my eye, it was the magnetic way she approached me. I had never seen her before, and was in a hurry to go to my father's side, yet I allowed her to reach me.

"Hi, darling, how are you doing? Are you all right?" she asked gently.

"Yes, Ma'am…" I said.

"Well, baby, I just came by to pay my respects and to make sure that you and the boss were okay."

Instantly my body grew cold and my feet became too heavy to take one step. Who was this stranger standing in front of me? Only one other person had ever called my father 'boss' and God had already taken her away.

My eyes widened to saucers. "What did you say your name was?" I asked tentatively.

"Now, Chocolate, child, I never told you my name. You don't know me, I just stopped by to pay my respects."

Her voice was wrapping around my soul, and this was getting eerier by the second. I was almost about to pee on myself, but I took a step towards her and reached up to touch her face.

"Mama, is that you?" I asked incredulously.

With that, the woman took my hand and placed it against her chest, just as my mother had done a thousand times before. When she released my hand she turned and walked softly towards the front door.

A few months ago my father had intended to fix the front door latch. When it was closed only the three of us knew how to unlock it. When I mentioned that detail, she smiled back at me as she gently put both of her hands together like my father taught us and pulled up on the knob to open the door.

"Mama, is that you?" I asked again. "Please tell me," I begged.

Before leaving she said, "Go on, Chocolate, go on now and straighten up your face. Then go find your father."

I couldn't move. I tried to, but I just couldn't. God had allowed my mother to come and visit me one last time. I knew it was her. It had to be, but I never mentioned it to anyone.

With the door closed, I ran to the window in an attempt to see which way she was going. But there was no sight of her. She was gone. There was no car, no cab, no one outside to pick her up; she had simply vanished.

I ran back to her room thinking, 'Chocolate, are you going crazy? Dark Child, have you gone insane?' My thoughts came to a halt as I noticed something on her bed. The placement of the item almost made me choke. The same blue sweater I was holding just minutes ago was now folded up neatly and set in an all too familiar place.

My mother and I had always gathered up our things and folded them together, but she left them for me to put away. They were always placed right where the sweater now lay at the foot of the bed. I ran over to the sweater, and picked it up.

As I hugged the sweater tightly to my chest, I looked up to heaven and said, "Thank you, Mama. Thank you for letting me know that you were really here. I know it had to be you."

When I finally located my father he was standing in his study holding a picture of Mama. I noticed the tears of emotional displacement streaming down the side of his face. He was just standing there, no doubt still in shock. All that had taken place had weakened the strongest man I knew. Too weak to muster up enough pride necessary to hide his pain, he was now finally ready to submit to the power of sorrow. I slowly walked over to him and reached up to wipe away the tears. I gave him the biggest hug I could.

"Daddy, are you okay?" I asked quietly.

My father had done so well in front of so many, but the show was over. There was no more strength left inside his heart for suppressed sorrow. The time had come for the weight of it all to be lifted. As he began to cry, our souls bonded like never before. He needed me then as I had always needed him. I was there to be given a chance to truly feel love at its highest point.

He fell to his knees, but I wasn't strong enough to lift him back up. God knew that I was more than willing to try. Too weak to speak and too broken to keep himself together, he wept until his tears were dry. Somehow my presence gave him the necessary strength to endure this dreadful moment. I know he could feel the strength of my mother inside of me.

CHOCOLATE

There I was, old beyond my years at twelve, and feeling like I had lived forever. I was comforting a man who had never forsaken me and who had loved me since my own conception. I was feeling his pain as he felt mine; wondering where we would go from there; wishing like he did, that tomorrow we could wake up and be told that this was all just one big misunderstanding.

Before too long, my father began to gather his strength. He looked up at me and said, "Oh, child. Mama's gone and there's only you and me."

"But, you know what, Daddy? We're going to make it and ain't nothing going to stop us," I said with confidence.

"Yes, it's true, God has called Mama home, but she stayed here long enough to show us both how to love, and right now that's all that matters. Right?"

"That's right, Chocolate." His face began to light up as he spoke. I could tell most of his worry was focused on me. I took his left arm and placed it around my neck in an attempt to help him to his feet. God knew what was in my heart and I thanked Him for placing enough strength inside my father to get up off that floor.

Long before I was able to gain my balance and discern the difference between distances near and far, it was my mother and father who carried my concerns in their arms. It was my turn now.

"Oh, baby, I love you so much," he said.

"I know you do, Daddy. We'll be all right. Mama's gonna be proud of us because we are stronger than steel, and ain't no other love in this world ever been more real."

"That's right, Chocolate. You and I are inseparable. We're going to make it."

He hugged me tighter than ever before, and I could feel his hurt melt.

"I love you, Chocolate," he repeated.

"I know you do, Daddy. I know you do," I whispered.

In the midst of sorrow, he was reaching out for me, not with his hand but rather with his heart. I had felt so guilty and wrong for not coming to him sooner that day; but by the looks of things I was right on time.

I loved my parents for showing me how love is supposed to be between two people. I loved them because their minds had divorced ignorance as they inducted themselves into a higher plane of understanding. Instead of succumbing to man's baseless predictable views, together they stumbled upon their own as they ran their minds across the pages of literary promise. As a child, they literally washed my brain with the edifying waters of educational acceptance.

My mother lived her life as though she were a queen. She never found it necessary to undress my father's manhood; instead she enhanced his life by teaching him the difference between quality and quantity.

She was everything he desired in a woman and made him know he possessed all the traits of a wonderful man. She bathed her body in alluring oils. She fed him as though he was a king and she bedded him down like the southern belle she was. She used her smooth brown skin to entice the beast that was caged up inside of him.

She was our nurse when we became ill, our keeper and sorter of thoughts when the world caused us to become confused. She was my emotional mentor, my window of reassurance and the picture of splendor.

I missed believing that Mama was always going to be there. She was always so right, and the thought of having to go on without her was so wrong. How could my shoulder of reassurance be forever removed? What was ever going to take its place? Who would show me how to become what she was to me? She was an aunt, a sister, a granddaughter, a niece, a loving mother and a devoted wife; just a beautiful, lovely, elegant lady. But more than all of the above, she was the epitome of love!

I would always be Daddy's little girl, no matter how grown. When life felt gloomy and all forms of logic and reasoning escaped my storeroom, it was his voice that I reached for to redirect me. My father was my guiding light. But, there wasn't a single day that went by, that thoughts of my mother didn't run through my head.

The driver's remorse rewarded him with a mere involuntary manslaughter conviction. No jail time, as if killing my mother wasn't a crime. We fought the decision to no avail and decided to remember the time she spent here on earth rather than re-open wounds unnecessarily.

Though my mother was given the opportunity to see thirty-eight summers, in the twinkling of an eye she wouldn't live to see her thirty-ninth. Her premature death made the situation all the more tragic. May her intelligent soul rest in peace and memories of her never cease.

A Life Lesson

My father, a man who loved me more than life itself, Mr. Marvin L. Williams, bestowed most of life's lessons upon me. He was a businessman who retired in suburbia of the South Bay Area of California a year after Mama's death, staying close to where I grew up. In his early fifties, he was still a very attractive man; built tall and slender but with a little belly bulging out ever so slightly over his belt. Even so, he wore it well.

He had always enjoyed reading and stock trading. When he was not absorbed in a book on Economics, or collecting material for his own publication, he was teaching me ethics and values. If he was not learning, it was only because he was asleep.

Mama said that while she was carrying me, Pops read out loud to me; quotes from famous authors and historians. He read beautiful poetry and prose. He read historical passages. He read about scientific discoveries. He read about the lives of significant men. It was important to him that learning became important to me. I was intellectually sure of my predetermined educational future.

My father was a great speaker, and would often use words to pacify and motivate those who were battling with low self-esteem. Because of my upbringing I developed a love and appreciation for words, not unlike him. When I wanted to, I could communicate with the best of them, my pops saw to that. By the time I was ten, other people noticed I had an exceptionally well-developed vocabulary. There were so many words at my disposal, but one seemingly useful word was not allowed. I was never supposed to use the word 'typical' when it came to describing myself. Indeed, I knew I was special.

My pops believed in the power of logic and reasoning. He was determined to teach me about life, whether I was ready to hear it or not. He dismissed the notion of entertaining anything that influenced or enhanced the growth of ignorance. For the better part of my life he had been the editor of truth and the brook from which my values flowed.

He reminded me to not allow the unfounded views of my peers to taint my journey towards success, for failure is as unproven as the words that they speak. He would often caution, "Child, if you dance in dirt, no matter who you are, you're bound to get dirty."

Like so many of my peers in junior high, though, there were times I wanted to be noticed for all of the wrong reasons. I wondered what my face would look like made up, and if boys would like me better if I bared just a tad bit more flesh.

I knew Pops had become worried about my reactions to typical teenage draws. My eyes lit up when I saw celebrities flash across the television screen, often times wearing clothes that he felt were distasteful. A part of me wondered what I might look like dressed like that. I was filling out in all the right places and a spirit of self-centeredness had begun to hover. I had no plans to invite immoral behavior into my life, but there were moments when my thought process had become tainted with visions of, 'what if...'

CHOCOLATE

Although Pops had stated his displeasure many times about the way many of my peers were dressing, he never thought that the immoral-attire-virus would enter our home. He knew I could only be one-half a second away from losing my self-worth if that were to occur. My father knew he had to somehow deter me from succumbing to the ways of typical adolescent life. He was afraid of where that could lead. So many others before me had already fallen prey to the mental perceptions often inherited by those suffering from low self-esteem.

I loved my father for being the great spectator of truth that he was. His impeccable timing in the unveiling of its reality was second only to my Father in heaven. I always admired him for the way he unselfishly rerouted my emotional derailment and then carefully placed my inadequacies back on the tracks of self-empowerment. Whatever I became was because of his unrelenting tutelage.

He taught me the basics from how to change tires and give cars a tune-up, to how to hang pictures on the wall. At the same time he instructed me not to ever hang my head down. He taught me the unforgettable life lesson of never allowing life to catch me with my pants down.

When my father wasn't around, though, I would sometimes close my bedroom door and stand in front of the mirror pretending to be sexy in clothes I wouldn't dare wear out of the house. I knew he would not allow me to go anywhere wearing skimpy clothes.

But nevertheless, I remained curious. I had borrowed an outfit from an 8th grade girlfriend, Tam, and one day I stood in front of the mirror wearing a pair of her pants which had taken me over five minutes to pull on. My circulation was nearly cut off from the jeans that, at best, I should have worn ten or fifteen pounds earlier. As soon as I put them on I began hoping the fabric would relax before my thighs collapsed. Sure

I was able to get them on, but I reminded myself that just because I was able to wear them didn't mean they were my size.

Regardless of the impracticality, I was looking good. The jeans were a little tight and the blouse was a bit on the small side, but I was sexy. Or so I thought.

Without anyone there to witness, I did one of the latest dances, and this particular one called for a dip. I figured out in a hurry that wasn't about to happen. And I had gotten so into myself that I had forgotten to close the door to my bedroom

After walking past my bedroom and catching a glimpse of me in jeans that were two sizes too small, Pops knew that it was time. He had seen me carrying on for a minute or two, and I'm sure it was the precise moment I had been prancing around in front of the mirror. If I had known he was watching me, I would have stopped and searched for a place to hide. By the time I turned around and saw him it was too late.

There we were, just the two of us, ready to endure another emotional battle. I was standing in the corner of stupidity, waiting on the bell of enlightenment. My father stood in the center of the ring ready to sound the bell, yet wondering why this fight had to continue. Without saying a word he turned and walked back into the neutral corner of his study.

Pops called me into his study to 'check my water.' I knew he was about to gauge my level of obedience. Suddenly I got a wake-up call. It was only a year after Mama had died and I was only thirteen.

He had waited for the most opportune time to unleash his wisdom as he had done so many times before.

"Claudia, come here," he called from his study.

I walked down the hall into the small smoke-filled room. He had taken up smoking a pipe after Mama had died, and I had to place my hand over my mouth and nose in an attempt to keep the smoke from penetrating my lungs.

I bravely walked over and stood directly in front of my father and said, "Yes, Dad?"

With that strong, stern voice of his he said, "Pull your pants down, Claudia."

I was horrified by the command. I looked at him, and tried to verify that I'd heard correctly.

"What did you say, Daddy?"

"I said pull your pants down," he repeated plainly.

"You heard me." He was reading the newspaper and not once did he bring his eyes up to meet mine.

Up until that moment, my father and I had had a great relationship. I will never forget the emptiness I felt at that very moment, nor the betrayal I felt was creeping in.

"Do as I say, child," he ordered.

Instantly I felt cold chills as I reached down to unfasten my jeans. I reluctantly unzipped and had to wriggle to drop the jeans. I noticed my father lift the newspaper up a bit higher. The top of his head disappeared behind the paper as he shielded his face. He was decent enough and considerate enough, and probably uncomfortable enough to avoid viewing my half-naked body.

I stood there frozen in the midst of my own stupidity. My jeans were wrapped around my ankles. My panties were exposed and both of my hands were covering my crotch. I was trying to pull myself together.

"Daddy, why did you make me to do this?"

He ignored my question for minutes, by simply turning the pages of the newspaper as pipe smoke swirled over his head. My father continued to sit there holding the newspaper, staring in silence at page after page of now meaningless words.

My soul felt bare as he indirectly exposed my deepest fears. This wasn't funny and only he knew when it was going to end.

"Daddy, can I pull my pants up now?" I pleaded in a soft and desperate voice.

My father was a very theatrical man, who defied those things he felt it necessary to defy. He called himself a moralistic teacher, a cultivator of promise. He prided himself on being able to reach the unreachable.

The silence finally broke and his point was about to be made. Without setting down the newspaper he asked, "Chocolate, how exactly does it feel to be undressed in front of me?"

Before I could answer he continued, "And what reason could you possibly give to make me understand, why you, my only child has to bare her flesh to be noticed? Haven't I taught you that it's better to be thought of as a fool than to speak and remove all doubt?"

"Yessir, you have. But I wasn't even speaking, Daddy."

"Sure you were, Claudia.

"Body language. Haven't you ever heard of body language? I don't think that you young ladies, and now you are one of them, give these young boys enough credit. Why do you think they have to be telepathic to see your motives?" he asked.

"Telepathic... what does that mean?"

"It's a mind-reader. When you are uttering these suggestive words with your flesh, you not only invite the possibility to be disrespected; by doing so, you create the opportunity."

"Invite the possibility and the opportunity to do what?" I asked innocently.

"Baby, when we allow ourselves to believe that the essence of who we are is a direct result of what we wear, we allow our values to be confiscated. And in exchange for giving up our own identity, we are then no longer identifiable."

"So, Daddy, do you feel that wearing tight clothes is going to change who I am?"

Without flinching, he asked yet another question.

"Why are you wearing those tight clothes, Chocolate? Is it because you have forgotten how developed you are? Or could it be that you now wish for others to notice that for themselves?"

"But, Daddy... that's not it at all. I just wanted..."

"Stop while you're ahead, Claudia. You'll never be able to justify why you now, after only thirteen years, feel you have to wear clothes that cut off your circulation," he pointed out.

"As a man, I look for a certain amount of purity in a woman. When it is not visible, I am then presented with two choices: to move on, or settle. Don't ever settle, Chocolate, not as long as you're able to savor your standards. Don't choose appearance over substance, and stop trying to be like others just to get attention."

I stood there cold from the shame that each of his words unveiled. I felt the wrong in my behavior as he swung his truth in my direction with a vengeance.

"Chocolate, baby... association with wrong has never led to right. It is the mixture of bad decisions along with less than desirable associations that shall ultimately imprison us. If not mentally or physically... then both. Chocolate, don't allow this world to play you like a cheap deck of cards."

His lecture was making its point.

The room was quiet as my soul was humbled and reached for regret. The only sound left was the soft crackle of newspaper pages as they turned.

While still holding the newspaper up as high as he could he uttered these words.

"How do you feel at this very moment, Chocolate?" he asked, breaking another unendurable silence.

"Embarrassed and humiliated," I replied honestly.

"Seeing you this way embarrasses me, Chocolate. I flinch at the thought of my only child not having the common decency to clothe herself in a respectful manner. Pull your pants up, child, and never forget how it felt to endure such a moment. When you're out there in the world baring your flesh to society, remember me as you carry on."

I held up my head as high as I could and responded meekly, "I'm sorry, Daddy."

I knew he wanted me to be an individual; to lead instead of follow. I felt I had grown beyond my years again, as I stood there unable to move.

My father was much better versed in this area and with each word, I was humbled and my tongue was made short. He rejected vague, open-ended answers, as if they were doors of missed opportunity; left open deliberately to excuse the actions of any man's deeds.

"What exactly are you sorry for?" he inquired. My father always said anyone can apologize, but a person who wishes to make it right, should display it through his actions.

"Are you sorry that you were caught? Or are you sorry that you allowed the world to fool you into believing that you have to show your ass to be noticed?"

His directness left me speechless. I couldn't say a word, and it was senseless of me to try. The fight was over. I was guilty and the verdict had come in. My sentence was fair and just and the humility that accompanied it was well deserved.

He was right. I was sorry that I had gotten caught, but I was more grateful for the lesson I had just learned. My apology wasn't necessary.

"You know you should be covered at all times and some things should always remain private, right, Chocolate?"

I forced my chin to remain high.

"Yes, Sir!" I exclaimed in total agreement.

"Then stop running around here with your stomach exposed and your ass hanging out! Respect yourself enough to wait for the appropriate time to share your body. Chocolate, trust me, you'll have more than enough opportunity to show off. For right now, you need to keep developing your mind and start showing that off. Let the world see how intelligent you are, and let others merely wonder what color panties you have on. Anyone can get naked, but not everyone can be bright enough to see past the shallow views of life. Clothe your mind with the knowledge necessary to make the correct decisions. Become an individual and the rest will be easy. Never be led by fashions and don't allow the standards of a season to alter your morals for a lifetime. You are a star, Claudia. Now get out of here and start shining so the world can see your light."

I picked up my jeans and walked back into the hallway. After taking a few steps I stopped and leaned back against the wall. I thought for a second about what my father had just done and said. He always had a creative way to express his views and although this one was the most creative, I got the gist of what he was saying.

His message was simple: "Claudia never give of yourself anything less than is necessary to accomplish your goals, and never accept anything less than your best. Or anyone else's best for that matter."

I loved Pops enough to rise to the occasion and make him proud. He taught me that life is a process of accomplishments and struggles. No one had ever become successful without both. He told me to plant the things I wanted to grow and water them with patience.

He wasn't against my inability to understand the consequences of my actions. He knew I was gaining ground with each of life's lessons. He never stopped testing me, and I knew that as long as he lived, the challenges would continue.

Sweets

Sweets was my cousin, Pamela. Her full name at birth was Pamela Renee Montgomery. We were born only two months and two days apart, and practically grew up together. Sweets and I were inseparable, like darkness is to night, or honor is to right.

We both had a thing for hair too. As far back as I could remember, we played with each other's heads. Everyone always hoped that when we grew up, we'd open our own hair salon one day. Sweets and I would just laugh at the crazy notion.

"We're just doing this because we don't like the way our mothers comb our hair," was our answer.

By the time we entered high school, everyone knew about our artistic gifts. Just looking at each other was proof we could do some hair, but we were too selfish to take it to the streets. We didn't want anyone else to look as cute as we did. We passed on the potential hook-ups and just kept wooing the on-lookers.

Sweets' father, Uncle Jimmy, left my Aunt Jackie for a white woman. Aunt Jackie claimed that he left because he couldn't handle her goods, but I knew better. He left her because he wasn't the *only* one handling her goods. Uncle Jimmy was a handsome man, with the same fault that Aunt Jackie found in every other man; he only had one dick.

He was a successful international real-estate broker and had done well for himself over the years, but he was frequently out of the country making deals and acquiring additional assets. Now he was gone for good.

My Aunt Jackie was a high-yellow woman, but she wasn't white, and after being burned over and over again by black women, Uncle Jimmy developed an allergy to their attitudes. He refused to be involved with a black woman again as long as he lived. I realized that it wasn't Sweets' fault, but every time Uncle Jimmy sent for her to visit, Aunt Jackie always had an excuse as to why she couldn't go.

I could tell that Sweets missed having her dad around because she always talked about him. I was the lucky one because my daddy, Marvin Williams, wasn't going anywhere.

Aunt Jackie was what we called a 'mover and shaker.' To be blunt, she was a whore. She was always dropping Sweets off at our house and jumping into a car with some horny old man she had just met. She had a nice body for her age, or any age for that matter, but she was nasty as hell and could never get enough sex no matter how long she stayed on her back.

Before Mama died, I often heard her and my father carrying on about Aunt Jackie. She was a sight they said, always running around half-naked. She was just nasty for no reason at all. They said she was born like that; that she came out of my grandmother with her legs wide open at birth. She lived each day hard and fast as if someone had told her it would be her last.

CHOCOLATE

One weekend a few years back, Sweets was over at our house while Uncle Jimmy was abroad on a business trip. He arrived home early and caught Aunt Jackie naked in bed with both a man and a woman. We were all shocked.

So I don't feel that my father was really surprised to hear what I told him that sad day…in the summer before 9th grade. I just think it was the last straw.

That was the day Sweets broke down. We were just hanging out in my room one Saturday night and she became distant.

"What's wrong, Sweets?" I asked as she started crying.

"Oh, nothing, Choc. I've just got too many things on my mind, that's all."

"What kinds of things? You can tell me."

"Chocolate, you don't want to know," came her flat reply.

"Sure I do. If it's bothering you, it's bothering me. You're my girl."

I reached out to pull her close to me as we lay across the end of my bed. I began to cry with her without even knowing the details.

"Don't cry, Sweets, don't cry," I cooed, trying to soothe her sorrows.

I could tell that whatever was wrong, it had done a job on her. Sweets was my best friend, and as tears began to touch her face, I could feel them penetrate my heart.

"Tell me what's wrong, Sweets. Let me help you."

By that time, my father was making his last rounds before going to bed. He couldn't help but overhear the tearful commotion in my room. The door was cracked and he gently pushed it open and entered the room.

"What's going on in here girls? What's with all the tears? Was dinner really that bad tonight?"

Right away we both started smiling, but I couldn't explain why we were crying. I honestly had no idea.

I just shrugged my shoulders and said, "We are just dealing with something sad we heard, that's all, Daddy."

I was never good at lying and my father knew it. He could see right through me and he knew I wasn't telling the truth. He also knew that whatever was wrong couldn't be revealed at that time. So he simply walked over to us and gave us both big bear hugs and gentle kisses.

"Ain't nothing like a good lie before going to bed," he said with a wink as he closed the door.

We both looked at each other in surprise, as if we had expected him to swallow our feeble explanation. But we were relieved that he left us alone.

"So," I stared back at Sweets, "are you going to tell me why we're crying?"

She was good at avoiding people, but I knew all of her moves. There was a desk near my closet on the opposite side of the room, and as she got up to walk towards it the chase was on. Before she could reach the desk, I was in front of her, attempting to console her pains, but also trying to get her to reveal them to me.

"No one's going to sleep in this room tonight until the truth comes out," I declared.

Sweets knew how persistent I could be, and I knew I had to stay on her to get to the bottom of things. I could see she was squirming but I was ready to apply more pressure if need be. Sweets looked at me with dread in her eyes.

My best friend in the whole wide world was hurting and I wanted to know why.

Sweets turned to me, her eyes brimming with tears. She gulped to swallow the last bit of denial.

"Chocolate, I feel dirty," she blurted out.

CHOCOLATE

I didn't have enough information yet, but was willing to give her some time. She walked away from me as if to leave, but instead she slowly turned back and fell gradually to the floor with her head buried in the palms of her hands. She was finally ready to speak, and I could see she was too tired to fight, and too weak to run any farther. I was about to have my heart broken, through the breaking of hers.

She pulled her hands away from her head and told me a story that pierced my soul.

"Chocolate, one night right after I had gotten off the phone with you, I opened my bedroom to investigate a noise. It was quite dark so I waited a few seconds to let my eyes adjust. I listened to the night a bit longer but the sound had stopped. After several seconds I headed towards the kitchen to get myself something to drink. I walked softly like we did back when we used to try and steal your mama's cookies out of that jar she kept on top of the refrigerator. Do you remember that?"

"Yeah, Sweets, I remember. But what happened next?" I asked, anxiously awaiting her next words.

"I poured myself a glass of milk and got a couple of cookies to snack on. I walked back down the hallway to crawl back in bed, but before I reached the door I felt an enormously strong hand being placed over my mouth."

"What?" I said in disbelief.

My eyes were wide with fear as I clutched my pillow. She carried on, and I was just hoping that she was not about to go where it seemed she was headed.

"I was petrified. Whoever he was, I didn't know. He had to have been tall, because when he gabbed me, my feet were dangling as he carried me into my room. He had one hand covering my mouth, and a knife, which was pressed against my throat, in the other. The knife was sharp, Chocolate, and cold. I was so scared, and even though my mother was there, I still felt so alone. I d-d-didn't even know where my m-m-milk and cookies were," she stuttered.

Sweets dropped her head back into the palms of her hands and began to sob deeply. I was emotionally drained, searching for the right words to help. For the most part, anything I might say was too late in coming. So I sat there wondering if I could stomach hearing the rest. The room had grown extremely quiet and all of my questions had disappeared. I was ready to forget that anything like this had ever happened, but Sweets had only just begun.

I knew she had to go on with her story, so I encouraged her by nodding and closing my eyes. I tried to comfort her the best way I knew how; by just listening. This time when she started in, it was real intense. The way she described each pathetic moment was heartbreaking.

"When it first started, I thought it was just one big bad dream. I wanted to believe that I was going to wake up from this awful nightmare. But it wasn't a dream, it was real, Chocolate.

"He told me that he wouldn't hurt me, and that it would all be over soon. But it will never be over. I have never been able to forget that night.

"I felt him stretch something around my face in an attempt to cover my eyes and I shook my head back and forth trying to loosen his grip. He kept pressing the knife against my throat, telling me over and over again to be still.

"I was going crazy, but I didn't want to die, so I gave in and stopped fighting back. He told me that he'd be gentle and that he wasn't going to hurt me, as if he knew what forced penetration felt like. He reeked of cheap liquor as he rubbed his hairy face against mine. I could hear rage and lust in his voice as he brushed his stubble-filled face against my breasts. Licking them over and over again, he was like an animal in heat. He reached down between my legs and pawed at me with his filthy hands. Before I knew it, he tore my panties off with one stroke of his strong hand.

"I was so afraid, and even more confused, as I lay there underneath the stench of his evil lust. I tried once more to call for help but he shoved something inside my mouth when I tried to scream.

"Seconds later my t-shirt was torn off and one at a time my arms were tied to the headboard. Chocolate, I was wearing that t-shirt you gave me for Christmas two years ago. You know, the one you're always asking me about?"

"Yes, I remember the t-shirt I gave you," I said with barely a whisper.

"Well, that's the one I had on when he attacked me," she repeated as if she felt guilty it was ruined. She continued as if she was on a mission.

"He turned on the light to see as he tied my feet to the bedposts. Strangely, I felt somewhat grateful as the light slightly brightened the darkness burning against my eyelids." She looked at me for understanding and I nodded.

"I attempted to brace myself for what was still ahead but there was nothing I could have possibly done to prepare myself for the kind of violation I had yet to endure. I was losing my virginity to a man I'd never met. My soul was barricaded beneath the pit of his self-inflicted hell," she sobbed.

"With his left hand he pressed all of his weight against my right shoulder as he positioned himself to penetrate me. I could hear him breathing out of control as he tried to force himself inside of me.

"His evil soul mustered a most pathetic voice. 'It'll all be over soon. You'll see.'

"He never asked me how old I was, or if I had a disease, or if there was anyone else in the house other than my mother… He sounded like an addict who had come face to face with his fix. I was so scared, Chocolate… scared out of my mind! I needed my father to rescue me, but like always he was nowhere to be found," she mourned.

"His nasty sweat was dripping from his forehead, and it stung my face with every disgusting drop. It made me feel dirty all over. While he moved in and out of my fragile frame, I asked God to lessen the pain. When the pressure grew too much for him to stand, he released himself inside of me like the heathen he was.

"I lay there feeling like a research animal, as blood from my wound ran down between my inner-thighs. I could not move. I was helpless and emotionally numbed by each unwelcome thrust. I was robbed of what I had been assured all of my life was my jewel. It was not my choice, Chocolate! I did not invite him into our home!" she implored.

"For twenty or thirty minutes I endured this creature, while my own mother laid motionless in a stupor next to a stranger in her bed, a mere thirty feet away!" The disgust in her voice indicated to me that was the worst part of it.

"I can still feel the stubble of his unshaven face scraping against my skin. I can still smell his putrid flesh as it rubbed against mine. I still feel him as if he violated all of my beliefs. He relieved himself inside of me as if I were a public toilet on the side of the road!"

I let her cry for a moment as I held her hands.

"When he was satisfied he loosened up the t-shirt he used to tie me down with and whispered in my ear, 'Sleep tight, don't let the bedbugs bite,' and if you can believe it, he had the nerve to give me a good-bye kiss on my forehead! Chocolate, I was so disgusted and humiliated."

I tried to reassure her that I understood the emotions she endured. We held hands in silence just looking into each other's eyes. I knew she could feel my love and concern.

"I didn't want to see him, Chocolate, I was too ashamed to open my eyes the whole time, even when he turned the light on. So I just laid there lifeless until I fell off to sleep, wishing I could somehow sleep long enough for it all to have been a lie. But there wasn't enough sleep left in the world to undo what was and make it go away. I wanted so badly to believe that none of this had happened."

"Sweets, have you told anyone else? Did you tell your mother what happened?"

"Yes, I told her the next day," she said dejectedly.

"She ran to me and asked if I was okay. She kept saying over and over again that she was sorry. She admitted that the man who raped me was the brother of the bum she slept with that night. She never even asked their names. She never really cares who she's with anyway."

"So, let me get this straight. The man who raped you was her john's brother?"

"Yes, from what my mother said. He was waiting on his brother in the living room… that was until I came out of my room to get a drink."

"What did he look like?" I asked.

"I told you, Chocolate, I never saw his face. Our eyes never met because I couldn't bear to open mine throughout the whole ordeal. I can only tell you what he smelled like, what he felt like, and about the pain I never want to feel again. He made me feel dirty and useless, like an old candy wrapper discarded in the gutter, or like a broom that has lost its bristles. He will never have a name, but he will always be inside of me and that is what haunts me.

"I hate my mother for inviting wrong into our home. I hate her for not ever placing my needs before any of her wants. She says that she needs to get herself together, but it means nothing to me any more. She merely utters words that have been spoken so often before, time and time again."

As she spoke, I could feel the void that led to her emptiness. As she wept, I could feel the heavy fall of her tears dripping against my compassion.

I nervously brushed my hair while I listened to Sweets finish her horrifying story. I had listened so hard, her sad words darn near busted a hole in my heart. After Sweets stopped talking, I knelt down beside her. I took the brush and began to stroke her hair as we wept. I could tell she was relieved that she had finally revealed her deep dark secret.

I crawled a few feet over to reach the nightlight on the right side of my bed. I had used it many times for reassurance while the world was asleep, and we both needed a little extra light. I went back over to Sweets to offer continual comfort. I continued to brush her hair and it made her sleepy like it did when we were little kids. Her eyes began to close as I stroked her long black hair. She was obviously emotionally spent after saying good-bye to a secret she had held inside for over a year.

The next morning I woke up with the early morning sun touching my face. With Sweets' back to me, my right arm was draped over her, and our legs were intertwined. Our legs were knotted together just like our love for one another.

It took a moment, but I was successful in my efforts not to awaken Sweets as I got up. Something had to be done. I had to tell someone about her ordeal. I was always looking out for Sweets and this time would be no different. I crept down the hall in search of my father. I peeked inside his study but he wasn't there. Before I could turn around I felt his hand upon my shoulder.

"Chocolate, are you lost?"

"No, Daddy." I wanted to tell him he had just scared the wits out of me but I respectfully said, "I was just coming to say good-morning is all."

I wanted to take the opportunity to tell him about Sweets, but I was too nervous.

He knew I had something on my mind, and I felt like I was lying. As I turned and walked away he took me by the arm and pulled me into his room. With the door closed he confronted me.

"Chocolate, now you know how I feel about lying, don't you?"

"Yessir," I nodded and dropped my chin.

"Well then, don't you feel it's about time you came clean? What's going on with you girls?"

"It's Sweets, Daddy," I said.

"You have to promise not to do anything crazy when I tell you…"

"Now girl, you better tell me right now. What the hell is going on?" he demanded before I could reveal anything. "I won't make any promises I can't keep. But I will do all I can to help. Now, you must tell me, what is wrong with my Sweets?"

I sat down on the end of his bed and told him everything, almost word for word just as Sweets had told me. He didn't say much while I spoke but he moaned every now and then like a father in pain.

After hearing me through, he looked over at me and asked, "Chocolate, are you okay?"

"Yes, Daddy, I'm fine," I nervously replied.

He lit up his pipe and nodded his head back and forth in a sober motion.

"I will handle it, Chocolate. I promise I will make it right for our Sweets."

Smoke swirled around his head as he assured me, "Baby, it will be all right."

Within minutes he was ready to leave the house. He walked by my room and announced, "Chocolate, I'll be back in an hour. I'll bring you two something to eat, okay girls?"

He was actually gone for several hours, and we were getting worried. But when he returned he brought closure with him. He also had a few bags of McDonalds. We knew there were a number of other things he had yet to disclose.

"There's some food here for you girls," he offered. "You better eat it while it's hot. Come on out so it doesn't get cold."

We were famished and while we were eating we noticed he unloaded some bags from the car. For some reason he took them directly into the guest room. It wasn't long before some of the things began to look familiar.

Sweets noticed first and yelled out, "Hey, Uncle Marvin, I've got a TV at home just like that!"

He looked back over his shoulder and smiled. "Sweets, this *is* your TV. And from now on, *this* is your home."

I would never forget what I felt inside for my father, and the joy I felt for Sweets. Pops had become our instant hero. We both started jumping up and down in realization of what he had just done for us.

"Daddy, Daddy, I love you!" I screamed.

"Don't love me any extra for the things I have to do, love me through my mistakes and praise me through my failures," was the wisdom he offered for the moment.

Sweets didn't seem to care that her Uncle Marvin knew about her personal horror. She was finally safe and that was the bottom line. She wanted to know if her mom was okay with the new arrangements, though.

"So, Uncle Marvin, what did my mother have to say about all of this?"

He knew Aunt Jackie really didn't care one way or the other about Sweets' well being, but he had a way of putting things delicately when necessary.

"Your mother loves you dearly, Sweets, but sometimes people have a tendency to misunderstand love and responsibility. It's hard for people to be responsible when other things, such as drugs and alcohol, influence them. Jackie loves you, but she has a problem taking care of herself, let alone you. We love you, Sweets, and you have always been welcome here. You're here so much already, you might as well call it home."

The part about us loving Sweets was the truth, but the rest was what my father delicately called propaganda, a play on words, the half-truth and whatever else he called his brand of lies. Oh well, it sounded good and it worked for Sweets.

I loved Sweets as far back as I can remember. We went back as far as cooking on Easy-Bake-Ovens, play-acting with Barbie and Ken, and learning how to jump rope. We went back farther than all that.

For years she was my confidante. Our love and sisterly bond had been able to dismantle the lies of our peers and the wrongs that stemmed from our fears. I believed God wanted me to protect her, and that He placed her in my world so that I wouldn't ever be lonely. I believe that God helped us name her Sweets, so that having her smile around could help remove any bitterness in the world.

Sweets had a bubbly personality that drew people to her and she was a joy to have around. Though we each had our own room, we were rarely apart. She knew the house rules almost better than I did, and she never made a mess, and she always picked up after herself. And, she always had my back. I was glad to have her there, but I hated knowing the deciding factor that brought us together as sisters.

It was the latter part of the summer when Sweets moved in and we were ecstatic to be under the same roof and in the same school after all these years. We were good for each other, and we were good together.

Sweets had her own money, Uncle Jimmy saw to that. He had opened a bank account for her when he left Aunt Jackie when Sweets was about ten. He had been depositing money into her account on a regular basis ever since. He also left them with a home that was paid for and even sent a yardman by the house to make sure the yard was kept up every month.

My father called Uncle Jimmy and told him what had happened to Sweets. He agreed it might be best that she stay with us. My father loved Sweets like she was his own, and she knew it. In fact, he would always joke around and say that Sweets looked so much like my mother that she gave birth to her and just handed her to Aunt Jackie at the hospital.

Aunt Jackie was always too busy running the streets to help Sweets out before she lived with us. I was told that Uncle Jimmy threatened to cut off Aunt Jackie's finances if she didn't step aside and agree to the move for Sweets. Jackie didn't want to lose her money, so she agreed to let her only child go, rather than put up any sort of fight.

Of course Sweets has never been privy to that information. It would have destroyed her if she ever found out. Uncle Jimmy was too far removed from her life for his parental instincts to kick in, so he did what he always did when Sweets was in pain: he put more money into her account and wished her well. My father became all she needed and I saw to it that she never hurt again.

I hated Aunt Jackie for years after that. When I saw her I cringed. There was no explanation good enough to justify the neglect that Sweets had to endure. At least not one I was ready to hear. My father saw the hate in my eyes and it ate at his soul to know that he couldn't remove it.

She was my mother's sister, yet I had lost all connection to her. After knowing that a man had raped my only child, I would have searched for his nasty ass as long as it took, to the ends of the earth.

I couldn't understand how anyone could not love Sweets. She was always such a good child. She earned good grades in school and she never disrespected her elders. She made people laugh when the world was full of anger. But that was all right. She was finally home, and wasn't nobody ever gonna hurt Sweets Montgomery again.

Love Was Not Enough

Almost two years went by with Sweets as my sister. We did what we could to bridge the gap of deception and deceit both her parents had created, but it wasn't enough. Towards the end of 10th grade, my father and I could tell that she was still dealing with something bigger than herself. Something bigger than us. Something that perhaps our love alone couldn't soothe.

Every day that passed by became more difficult for her. Sure, we laughed and went on, as the emptiness she felt inside was easier to conceal than it was for her to reveal. But she was suffering from a broken heart and a neglected soul.

There were times when Daddy would kiss me good-bye on my forehead and without intending any harm; he simply waved good-bye to Sweets. It affected her deeply, I knew, because she developed the same blank expression on her face each time. She wasn't being selfish; she was just being human.

There were times when I could feel her leave this world for hours on end. She had an escape hatch inside her head and tried to minister to her own sorrows. It was frustrating to watch my best friend leave my side, while I was still able to stroke her skin.

I worried endlessly, like a big sister does, when something or someone poses a threat to one of her siblings. Because my love for Sweets was so strong, the weight of her anguish began to show on my face too.

That spring, just before school was out, there was the time when Sweets and I went skating at Percy's Skating Rink over on Jefferson and Ninth. It was where all the kids hung out on Friday nights. My father would let us go every once in a while just to see if we had learned the things he had taught us over the years.

That night Sweets and I had played on each other's head for over three hours. Every curl and flip was in place. We wore pretty little outfits that helped emphasize how beautiful we were. Of course, we had to get the nod of approval from the tasteful eyes of my loving father. We knew that we weren't to wear anything too short or too tight. If we were caught dressing inappropriately, we could kiss the skating rink, or any other privileged outing for that matter, good-bye.

After passing my father's strict dress code, he dropped us off at Percy's. The skating party was usually over around midnight, but Sweets and I rarely saw the other side of eleven o'clock.

"Chocolate and Sweets, I'm going to be right over there underneath that light at…"

"I know, Daddy, ten forty-five, and don't be late." When I interrupted him, he gave me his million-dollar smile and waved good-bye.

Sweets and I felt like two high school Cinderellas with just a little less than four hours of freedom standing in front of us.

CHOCOLATE

Before entering the rink, we stood together and did the hand shake we had done a thousand times. We each took our right index fingers and together pointed firmly, high in the air. We simultaneously lowered them and extended our arms out towards each other, until both of our fingertips met. This was our way of confirming that we were inseparable.

We smiled at each other as we made our grand entrance. All eyes were on us and we knew it. We had what my father called class, and it was time for us to take it to the streets. It was like having an American Express... we never left home without it.

There was a crazy DJ there who we all loved. He called himself 'Wild Man!' and, man, was he ever wild. When he played his dance music for the skaters, he stood up on a chair and did a crazy dance himself, holding a record in each hand. He never missed a beat and believe me... it was all right with us.

Sweets and I loved to dance out on the rink, but we mostly preferred to dance with each other. That night we jumped at the chance to be on the floor when Aretha Franklin's *Respect* came on.

Every once in a while we'd dance with a brother we knew who had his hormones in check. But finding one was like trying to spell Hatred without a capital H.

The brothers seemed to think that, 'Yeah, sure I'll dance,' meant that for the next three or four minutes they had the right to pull, grab and squeeze anything they could get their hands on.

While Sweets and I were dancing that night, a couple of brothers came on to the rink and tried to move in. They sure were braver than everyone else there.

"So, what's up with the two of you skating all alone?" they asked.

"We do it all the time. It's fun. Why don't you try it?" but they didn't get the hint and stayed with us.

So we paired off and gave them a few minutes of our best moves as we started back dancing to a real good song. We had fun just laughing and grooving to the music. I was so into it that I closed my eyes for a second, but a second was all it took. The brother dancing with Sweets reached down and grabbed her ass. The next thing I knew she was kicking his.

Sweets had temporarily lost her mind. My guess is that she flashed back to the night she had been taken advantage of and gave this brother the ass-whuppin' that the other bum had coming to him. Sweets had lost all of her dignity and half of her right foot in that brother's behind.

I had never heard nor seen her go off like that. She was letting all of her frustration out on him, as she wailed away on the brother.

He was losing out on getting his cheap thrill and yelled, "Man, get this bitch up off of me!"

I was doing fine until I heard that. I wish he could have just taken his ass-whuppin' like a man, instead of crying out like the jerk he undoubtedly was. I wasn't about to let Sweets be disrespected by another man again as long as I could help it. She had been through the ringer and had taken all she could from the perverted ass-holes of this world. I was glad she decided to fight back, so I joined in.

This unsuspecting brother didn't know that there were two sides of crazy, and that Sweets and I were both of them. I reared back and tried to kick a field goal with the brother's tail, and managed to kick him square in the ass with my skate. I knew that it had to hurt him because my foot was aching for days after.

"Sweets, are you all right?"

"Sure, Choc. I'm fine, how about you?" she replied in an eerie monotone.

I had never seen Sweets handle herself that way. She had reached a level of insanity unknown to man. Her cup of patience had run over and she was fighting back for all she was worth. Her once soft and gentle soul had become hard, and the world was being shown a glimpse of her reality. She never even cried.

Security came and escorted us into a private room where we could supposedly cool off. A few minutes later a police officer stepped through the door.

"What seems to be the problem, young ladies?" he asked.

I was waiting for Sweets to explain what had happened, but she wasn't willing to say anything at all. She just put her head down and began moaning and rocking from side to side.

"Is someone going to tell me what's going on?" asked the officer.

I walked over and stood between the officer and Sweets. I was able to stare him straight in the eye and say, "Did you ask the boy out there what happened? Did he tell you what he did to make her so angry?"

"No, but my partner is taking a report from him as we speak," he admitted.

Something was happening to Sweets. She had never avoided a conversation like she was attempting to avoid this one. As the officer and I stood there going back and forth, Sweets retreated back into that special place inside her head. There was a savage look in her eyes and a peculiar smile on her face. I had never seen that before and her animalistic state frightened me.

I turned to the officer. "Get her some help," I pleaded. "She's sick and needs help right away."

"Wait just a minute... I'll do the ordering around here," he replied.

"My sister is sick, can't you see?"

He agreed and didn't wait long to call an ambulance. All of the questions ceased when the paramedics came flying through the doors. Bystanders were jostling for a better look. Flashing lights made the atmosphere even more chaotic. I felt so bad for Sweets. She had already gone through so much… and now this. She had been mentally and physically robbed of her virtue, her dignity, and the delicate nature of life.

She had become a victim of unfortunate and devastating circumstances. Betrayed by those who were sworn to love and protect her, and ridiculed by the voice of shame speaking endlessly inside her head. She had become a walking time bomb and only God was aware of the length of its fuse.

I attempted to cover her face as they wheeled her past the onlookers and towards the ambulance. She never lost that maniacal smile. I was hurting for her, but I couldn't for the life of me reach deep enough to summon a smile equivalent to hers. She was high on a sad reality most of us would never fathom.

Inside the ambulance I continued to hold her hand, whimpering with fear like a lost baby at an amusement park. As soon as they had her hooked up to an IV, I closed my eyes and I cried out for God to help my Sweets.

'God, please don't let Sweets hurt anymore. Give her pain to me and free her from agony. I will do anything you ask of me, just make Sweets whole again. Please heal her mind and bring back her smile,' I prayed.

The ride to the hospital seemed to take forever, but it was not even ten o'clock yet. We were far from Percy's and my father didn't know where I was.

Out of nowhere Sweets said, "Chocolate, I kicked his ass didn't I?"

I smiled at her and answered, "Yes, you did Sweets. Yes, you certainly did."

CHOCOLATE

When we arrived at the hospital, they took her in for observation. I wanted to call Aunt Jackie but something told me not to. Sweets was already in enough pain, so I decided to let sleeping dogs lie. I called my father first, and he rushed to the hospital as soon as he could. He handled all of the paperwork and checked on Sweets.

I told him what happened at the skating rink and he shook his head in disgust. He loved making points, and it was even better when things he previously mentioned came to pass through my behavior.

"Now, do you believe me when I tell you that we all have our boiling point? Chocolate, Sweets is no different. She just got fed up and let go of the pain she was holding inside."

"I know, Daddy. To tell you the truth, it was kind of good to see Sweets lose it for a moment. She showed the world that she wasn't taking it no more."

We waited without further conversation for hours. The last thing I remember was placing my head on Pops' lap. He folded his coat underneath my head and jiggled his leg until I went to sleep. The doctor came out and gave us an update. I woke up when my father got up to shake his hand

"Hello, I'm Dr. Skipper the on-call psychologist. And you must be Pamela's uncle?"

"Yes, I am. I'm Mr. Williams. Pleased to meet you Doctor."

"Well, to put it plainly, Mr. Williams, what we have here is an acute case of anxiety. Pamela is feeling somewhat better now, but something has triggered a painful memory releasing tremendous fear and anxiety. This could be caused by a traumatic event in her life that she's afraid to talk about. We would like to keep her for observation for at least twenty-four hours."

"We know she's been dealing with something and we're trying to help her get through it the best we can," my father offered.

"Has she sought any professional counseling in the past?"

"No, I can't say that she has," he admitted. "We just thought we could love her through it."

"Love has tremendous healing powers, and we all need love, but Pamela needs to seek professional help as soon as possible," said the doctor. He said that she may have blacked-out at the rink, and there was a chance she might not remember anything that had happened that night.

I couldn't take it anymore. It was burning me up inside just listening to this stranger basically tell us that my Sweets had gone crazy. He was quite annoying I thought.

"So, how is she doing now?" I butted in. My voice conveyed my frustration and concern.

"You must be Chocolate?" he asked. "Pamela has been asking for you. Why don't you follow me?"

"You mean I can see her?" I asked eagerly. My irritation with him was waning already.

"Yes, just follow me. I gave her a little something to calm her down, and she's still somewhat sedated, but I'm sure she'll want to see you."

When I entered her room, Sweets was just lying there staring at the ceiling. She was higher than a Boeing 747, smiling like she was Oprah Winfrey's daughter on Christmas day.

I was afraid she wouldn't notice me, but it wasn't a moment before she said, "Chocolate, come here, girl. You should have put more gel in my hair, all that dancing made my curls fall out."

She started going in and out on me and I could tell she needed to rest.

Right away I knew something was still wrong. She never mentioned anything about beating that brother down. The whole thing seemed so strange. How could someone forget all of that? I wouldn't be able to forget one second of the night's events. I didn't want to leave her, but my father assured me she was too sedated to know she was alone.

I gave her a big hug and adjusted the covers just as Mama had always done for me. Daddy and I both kissed her on her cheek and promised that we'd come back the next day.

Early the next day my father took me back to the hospital and dropped me off, so that I could visit Sweets. He gave me some money to get her a card and some balloons. The lady in the shop was taking her precious time and I became very impatient. I needed to see Sweets I needed to know that she was okay. I had a feeling something else was wrong, as if I had some kind of telepathic gift. As I reached her floor I convinced myself I really did possess some kind of sixth-sense when it came to Sweets.

I heard familiar voices the closer I got to Sweets' room. Sure enough, there stood trouble. Aunt Jackie had somehow found out about what happened to Sweets. Apparently she managed to close her legs long enough to visit her daughter.

The first clear words I heard were, "Why, Mama? Just why did you come here?"

I didn't want to interrupt anything so I sat quietly in a chair outside the room. Sweets had a million questions for her mama, and Aunt Jackie seemed to have very few answers.

"When was the last time you told me you loved me?" Sweets asked her.

"Do you even know what my favorite color is, Mama?" Aunt Jackie had no reply.

I could feel Sweets appraising her mother before she asked, "Mama, how long ago did you lose it?"

My aunt, being unaware, fell quickly into one of Sweets' famous verbal traps and finally broke her silence.

"Lose what?" she asked naively.

"Respect for yourself, Mama. Self-respect." Sweets' voice was short-tempered.

"I haven't been a good mother I know, Sweets, but that doesn't give you the right to talk to me this way," Aunt Jackie said defensively.

"Mama, please, why don't you tell me what gave you the right to bring those men into our home that night?"

Sweets was quickly pinpointing her pain.

"Can you tell me who you were thinking about when you were laying on your back as I listened to you give yourself to stranger after stranger? Who gave you the right to constantly embarrass and disappoint me?"

The room grew quiet as my aunt, once again, searched for a response. Sweets, wasn't finished, though. It was her time to speak and she took advantage of it.

"For years, I watched you screw around on my father. I watched you do one selfish thing after another. I hated you for not being woman enough to love the only man who ever truly loved you. I listened to my father sometimes at night as he cried out openly about your adulterous life. I saw you break his spirit, strip away his compassion, and tear apart our family.

"Your promiscuous ways allowed a complete stranger to rob me of my virginity in the most humiliating and degrading way. As I lay there on my back with my hands and feet tied tightly to the bedpost, I thought of you. Let me tell you how I felt when that man placed hisself inside of me," Sweets threatened.

"No, no, Sweets. Please don't!" my aunt begged.

"No, Mama. You need to know how he took your only child and turned her into a frightened young woman. You need to know how violated I felt. You need to know, and I have a right to tell you."

"Please stop, Sweets, I can't take it anymore."

I heard her coming towards the door, running from the truth like she had done all of Sweets' life. I quickly stepped inside to block the doorway. I confronted my aunt to save my cousin.

"All of her life, I've listened to Sweets cry out for your love, Aunt Jackie. I've heard all, and I mean all of her stories, and believe me none of them were cute. Now, excuse me for disrespecting you, but it's time for you to turn your nasty ass around and listen to your daughter. Sweets hasn't finished talking."

My aunt knew I wasn't playing and that it was going to be hard as hell for her to leave, so she walked back over to Sweets. She sat back down in the chair next to her bed.

"Now Sweets, where were you?" I urged her to continue.

"Mama... I need you to know how humiliating it was for me to have that dirty thief take my jewel the way he did. I need to know why you taught me that mine was so special? Yet you have always been so willing to tarnish yours with every Luther, Dick or Larry you met. Why isn't your jewel special, Mama? Why can't you be treasured?

"Every night before I go to sleep, I pray to God and ask Him to protect you from all harm. I ask Him to cure your mind and to purify your soul.

"Aren't you tired yet, Mama? Don't you feel like resting, Mama?"

Then Sweets pulled back the covers and reached out for her mother's hands. It brought tears to my eyes as my aunt climbed into bed with Sweets. She placed her head into Sweets' forgiving arms.

My aunt had come face to face with the aftermath of neglect. She was finally forced to see the consequences of her actions. The words spoken in that room changed both their lives forever. I jumped up to hug them both as we all cried jubilant tears of forgiveness. Aunt Jackie was never the same again, but then neither was I.

The next day Sweets was released from the hospital. My father and I brought her home, and Aunt Jackie called like clockwork everyday at five. You could set your watch by the phone ringing. We could tell she was finally trying to be a better mother.

Sweets was leery at first, but she never stopped believing as her mother apologized over and over. Aunt Jackie claimed that she had spoken to the minister at the church down the street from her house, and planned on attending real soon.

The emotional conflicts Sweets had to endure weighed on us all, but we were in it for the long haul. Daddy and I desired peace and privacy, but we couldn't live with ourselves if we didn't try to make things right for her. Sweets was family.

Two or three weeks went by after the incident at the skating rink, and everything seemed to be going great.

My aunt said she had given herself to the Lord, and we were convinced. She invited us over for dinner on the Friday of the following week.

"I didn't even know that she knew how to cook," Sweets whispered to me after accepting the dinner invitation.

"Sweets, can your mother cook?" asked my father.

"Now, Uncle Marvin, I know how you feel about lying, so I'm going to plead the fifth."

"Well, whatever she prepares, we're going to at least act like we enjoy it, right girls?"

Sweets and I shared a nasty expression as we both answered at the same time, "Oooh-kay."

Everything was nice at Aunt Jackie's when we arrived for the dreaded dinner. We looked at each other in amazement, shaking our heads trying to wake up. We didn't know what was for dinner, but whatever it was smelled great.

"Mama, how much did it cost to have someone come over and clean up this house?" Sweets asked.

"Child, I know how to clean up my own house. It didn't cost me anything," Aunt Jackie replied, and changed the subject.

"Well, is everyone ready to eat? If so, then let's go into the kitchen. Oh, by the way, Sweets, here is a card from your father."

"From who?" Sweets asked.

"Your father. After you and Chocolate trapped me in that hospital room, I was forced to do some thinking. Everything you said about me was true. So I called him and invited him to be here tonight too, but he was off working abroad again and couldn't make it back in time."

Sweets was too excited and couldn't wait to get home to read her card, so she opened it in front of all of us. She saw the money first and threw it across the room, angry at being paid off once again. She didn't hesitate to read the message out loud.

With sarcasm dripping from her voice she read, "'Sweets. I'm sorry for not being the father I should have been. I'm sorry for sending you money instead of being there myself. I have been informed about the mishaps in your life and I'm deeply sorry. For years, I've placed financial greed in front of my only child and as I stand in front of you now, I plead for your forgiveness.'"

She stopped reading and looked up at us. "That's just like my father. How can I forgive…"

At that moment Uncle Jimmy walked into the room with open arms. Sweets' jaw dropped. She looked like she had just seen a ghost. Before I knew it she ran across the room to her father.

My father's eyes teared up and Aunt Jackie and I both wept with joy. She had finally made the call she should have years ago. I turned to her and kissed her cheek.

As I looked tenderly into her eyes, I silently mouthed, "Thank you."

Sweets smiled and gazed into her father's eyes with great hope. She didn't love us any less now that he was there, but we could tell a void was filled that had been vacant for much too long.

"Mama, thank you. This is a dream come true. I will never forget this as long as I live."

"I couldn't have pulled it off without your Uncle Marvin. He helped me make the necessary phone calls to your father overseas."

"I thank everyone involved," Sweets said as she held on tightly to her father's hand.

"So, this is the good part," she said as she eyed him skeptically. "Now tell me the bad part. When are you going to leave?"

He looked at her and made a statement that emotionally paralyzed me for several seconds.

"Sweets, I came back for you," he said, confirming the statement as he held up two plane tickets.

Sweets started screaming, "Yes! Yes!" She couldn't stop hugging him.

I was suddenly feeling every aspect of the rejection Sweets must have felt over the years. Instantly I became threatened by the idea of not having her around. Life had always guaranteed me three things: my parents would always love me; one day I would die; and no matter what happened in my life, Sweets would always be there.

I should have known something was different about my own father the past few weeks. His ways had become foreign to me and his daily words of wisdom had been neutralized by something. He was getting himself ready to say good-bye to Sweets, and a part of me felt angry because I hadn't been granted the same opportunity.

Who was I kidding? I could have been given three years to get ready for Sweets' departure and still it wouldn't have been long enough. My father noticed me staring sadly at Sweets and Uncle Jimmy. He got up out of his seat and came over to me.

"Chocolate, we've done all we can. She needs her father, can't you see?" he said as he tried to console me.

"Yes, Dad, I know. But it still hurts to know that Sweets won't be here anymore."

I paused, then said, "I promised God, if He could make Sweets whole again, I would do anything. So I guess it's time for me to allow her to be happy."

"Baby, Sweets will always be with us, no matter where she goes. She's a part of us for life, and don't you ever forget it. You'll be able to visit her from time to time, I'll see to it," he said. I still wasn't consoled.

There I was crying about her leaving me, instead of celebrating with her in her time of joy. I wanted to go to her and congratulate her in her happiest hour, but I couldn't make my feet move. I couldn't take myself out of the equation. I was being selfish and I knew it, but I was too caught up in myself to care.

When Sweets released Uncle Jimmy's hand, she turned and reached for mine. "Chocolate, please don't be mad at me, I just…"

I placed my hand softly over her mouth to stop her from finishing.

"I understand, Sweets. Now go and be happy. You don't have to apologize for needing your father's love. It would be selfish of me to try and come between you and your dad. Besides I've prayed for this reunion for years, and now that God has finally answered my prayers, it would be wrong of me to stand in the way."

"I'm so glad you understand, Chocolate. I love you for that."

I hugged her tightly as if she were going off to war. I didn't think I would ever see her again, but I loved her enough to know when it was time to let go.

"Sweets, be a good girl and don't ever forget me."

She looked at me as if I had made the most ridiculous statement ever.

"Chocolate, what is wrong… aren't you happy for me?"

"Sure I am, Sweets," I said not very convincingly.

After a deep breath I managed to say, "Yes, of course I am," a bit more whole-heartedly. "This whole thing just caught me by surprise, that's all."

She was finally happy for once, and there I was still thinking of me. Now I had to let go for God's sake. This was Sweets' own father, not some stranger who had suddenly appeared on the doorstep. She was in great hands and I needed to be happy for her. I was desperately trying to convince myself of the necessary truth.

"So, when are you leaving, Uncle Jimmy?" I asked slightly off-subject.

"I have to be in Brazil in a couple of days, so we're leaving before morning. We'll keep you posted as we travel, but our next stop is Rome. After that, I'm not quite sure. I'm hoping to have Sweets finish school in Paris."

CHOCOLATE

My heart began to bleed as my soul grasped frantically for composure, but I forced a smile adequate enough to hide the pain I felt.

Darkness had already touched the sky, and I knew after hearing the news that the next time my eyes were to be caressed by sunlight, they would do so without Sweets by my side. I couldn't feel her joy because the thought of living without her was unbearable.

I felt used and emotionally abused, I felt betrayed and robbed, but more than anything, I felt empty. I hurt so badly because it didn't seem to matter much to Sweets. My father and Uncle Jimmy knew it would be difficult for us to part, so they tried to make light of it all.

My uncle said, "Hey, you girls need a break anyway; after all you've practically been together since you two were born."

Until I heard that, I had thought of him as being a bright man. That statement alone brought about serious doubt. It was an oxymoron; it was such a contradiction in my mind. Of course we had been together since birth, and for that reason alone he should have known the degree of devastation our separation would cause.

My father and I went for a drive on the way home, as was our habit when life needed immediate discussion. We went to an ice-cream parlor not far from our house. He often took me there as a reward for an accomplishment, a birthday, or just because. I ordered a triple scoop of chocolate on a sugar cone. Pops got his usual: cookies and cream in a cup.

It was nice out, so we walked for a while in the warmth of the pleasant evening. Like always, he insisted I walk on the inside of the sidewalk, staying away from the street. We headed east on Montgomery and talked, just saying enough to acknowledge each other's presence. I knew my father well enough to know that it wouldn't be long before we talked about Sweets leaving. He was just waiting for the appropriate time to open his bag of wisdom and pour it on.

There was a little park bench a bit farther up the street where I knew the conversation would take place. So I slowed the pace and mentally collected myself to hold on for the emotional ride ahead.

"Let's stop here, Chocolate, and rest for a while," Pops said with no surprise as we approached the bench. "I've got something to say."

"I know it's about Sweets, isn't it?"

"Yes, it is. Why don't you start by telling me how you feel?"

"To tell you the truth, Daddy, I feel a lot of things. But more than anything, I feel selfish and resentful."

"Oh, baby," he sighed.

"I have a father I was willing to share with her."

"Baby, that was generous, sweet and so unselfish. But that's not reality."

"What is reality, Daddy? This pain I feel inside? Is this reality?"

"No, but hurting is. Caring is, needing and wishing is," he clarified wisely.

"I understand how you feel about Sweets, Chocolate. I know you love her, but it's not a crime to be indifferent about separation. You have every right to miss Sweets, but no one who truly loves, places their own wants before their loved one's needs. Our love for her was sufficient for the time, but we could have never filled her need for her father's love.

"Sweets was running on empty and her father's return re-filled her tank with emotional contentment. We did not fail, Chocolate. You see, it was her trust in us that kept the fire of love and hope alive.

"Love is more than a four-letter word, though. Somewhere hidden in the midst of love's forethought should be a certain degree of trust. Never think that love by itself can heal a broken heart.

"I am so proud of you for loving Sweets the way you do. I adore you for learning to share. I love you for caring enough to care, but Chocolate, more than anything, Sweets worships you because you've always been there for her." His words were sinking in.

I loved my father for his timely and gentle way of comforting me. I was blessed by his presence, appreciative for the opportunity to listen, and grateful to have him for my father.

While we were out having ice cream, Sweets and her parents had gone to my house to collect her things. By the time we got home, it was late, but I knew Sweets would be gone. I could feel it in my bones. I understood that she had to leave that way; being whisked away in the middle of the night. I convinced myself it was best for both of us. I couldn't bear to have watched Sweets take her things away.

As soon as we got home, I went straight to my room, unable to even glance into the guest-room. I felt an overwhelming sense of emptiness as I walked back to my room and gazed out of the window. Sweets and I used to stare out of it when we couldn't sleep.

While gazing up at the summer stars, I opened the window to let in the cool night air. The sky wore a blanket of inspired calmness and a gentle summer breeze blew against my frail emotions.

Who was I going to share this moment with? Who would even care?

The darkness impregnated the night and reached my heart. It caressed my woes as tears of emptiness fell. I asked God to take care of Sweets as I had over the years. While I was teetering on the ledge of hope, memories of Sweets and I together dangled before me. No matter how hard I tried, I couldn't extract myself from them. They were hopelessly embedded not only in my mind, but also in my soul.

When Sweets left that night a part of me left with her. I wished I could have made myself fit inside one of her bags. For a while, I felt that what Pops and Uncle Jimmy did that night was wrong. We should have been given a chance to say good-bye to each other. But I could eventually see that the way they handled it was right. Who knows what would have happened if we had the chance to hold on? I probably would have tried to stop the car. I would have grabbed Sweets' arms and never let go. I needed her that much.

I wallowed so deeply in self-pity that my soul became numb and my inner peace turned to anger. Not anger towards Sweets, but towards what was supposedly right. My father said that it was the 'right thing' for Sweets to go, but my selfish voice cried out, 'Right for whom?' I wondered. Surely not for me.

I could have taken care of Sweets. I had done so for years and I was prepared to continue. I cried myself to sleep that night and every night for months after her departure. I cried until nothing else mattered. I slept with my hand on my brush under my pillow. The same brush Sweets and I used for our hair.

I went to bed every night saying, "Sweets I love you. Wherever you are, love me back from afar."

It was the summer of ninety-three when Sweets left my side. We had finished up our sophomore year in high school. That May, prior to her departure, I had my sixteenth birthday. Celebrating hers was weeks away when fate intervened and took her from me. We had so many plans, so many places to see, Sweets and me.

Now she was gone and there would be no one to talk with before I fell off to sleep; no one to nudge through the night as I reached for a more comfortable resting place. There I was, lying in bed with my brush in one hand and memories of

Sweets in the other. I felt the same emptiness I had felt the day after God took my mother from me. I felt a sense of betrayal and began to allow self-pity to overtake me again. Sweets was gone and no one would ever take her place.

Sweets and Uncle Jimmy caught a flight to Brazil early that next morning before the sun had a chance to touch my face. Like a thief in the night, my uncle came and took her away. She was gone and a part of me went with her.

Uncle Jimmy had come for his daughter, my best friend, leaving behind a devastated ball of confusion in the pathetic form of myself. It was all about me and no one else. My wants overshadowed everything else, which included my sense of reasoning. There was nothing sensible about letting go of Sweets. To me, it was like asking a mother to give up her child. I was hurting and what in the world could be worse? The room where Sweets once stored her belongings was as vacant as my heart.

The old cliché, 'you never miss something until it's gone,' had slapped me in the face. My mother had died only four short years before, and now Sweets was taken from me. What was God thinking? What kind of life was this? How could He think that I could withstand all of this?

Sweets was my sounding board and my place of mental refuge. She was such a vital part of my life. I had to devise a plan to lessen the pain. I had to make it stop. Dealing with her absence on a daily basis was not an option.

So there I was, trying to move on, but too afraid to treasure memories. I refused to remember the last time we laughed, knowing that if I did, the recollection alone was enough to keep open the wounds of separation.

I grew tired of crying. My eyes were completely drained. Did I miss my girl? Yes... but how many more times could I summon up tears of loneliness before they were all gone?

A Father's Love

It was not long before calls and letters started coming. The phone rang one day while I was in the bathroom. My father was unusually excited as he walked down the hallway yelling out my name.

"Chocolate! Chocolate! Telephone! There is a call for you and you'll never guess who it is."

I could hear him moving around the house in search of me as he continued talking to Sweets.

"How have you been? Oh, that's great... I'm really happy to hear that... baby, you deserve that,"

I heard the one-sided snippets of conversation.

When I heard him come back towards the bathroom, I finished my business and jumped up to make sure the door was locked. I quickly turned off the light. Pops passed by the bathroom and knocked on my bedroom door.

"Chocolate, are you in there? You have a telephone call!" he yelled urgently.

I heard him calling me, but I was too afraid to answer the phone. I was in no shape to talk. Just knowing that Sweets was on the phone was doing a number on me. I sat on the toilet pressing both of my hands against my ears, trying desperately not to hear any more of their conversation.

"Well, Sweets, I guess she's not here. I looked in her room and she's not in there. I'll tell her to call you when she gets in. I'm sure she'll be happy to hear that you called."

Seconds after he hung up the phone, I unlocked the bathroom door and crept back into my room. It wasn't long before my father back tracked and came down the hallway to check on me again.

He knocked on my door. "Chocolate, are you in there?"

I hesitated before I said, "Yes, Sir, I am."

"How long have you been here?" he asked.

"For a while," I replied.

"Did you hear me calling you earlier?"

"Yes, Daddy, I heard you."

"Then why didn't you answer me, child?"

"Daddy, I didn't want to be here, I mean I didn't want her to know I was home."

"Her… you mean Sweets, don't you?"

"Yes, that's who I mean. I'm not ready to talk to her right now."

"Are you dressed?" my father asked politely. I gave him permission to come in.

The look on his face told me the direction the conversation would take. He sat down on the edge of my bed and stared at me shaking his head. He glanced around the room and noticed that all of the pictures of Sweets had been removed. I had even taken her picture off of my key chain.

"Baby, are you still upset with Sweets because she left?"

I had taken out some nail polish in an attempt to ignore the conversation altogether. I was focused on my toes but I knew I had to say something.

"No, Dad, why would you think that?"

"Come on, child, this is me, not some stranger. I know something is wrong. I'm not blind. I can see the hurt in your eyes from across the room."

"Can you really, Dad? Can you tell what I'm feeling? Or better yet, can you tell me how I'm supposed to turn my emotions on and off like a light switch?" He knew I had given all of this a lot of thought, and I knew he would at least attempt to ease my pain.

"Chocolate, can you imagine what life would be like if there was no you and me? Can you imagine not being able to pick up a phone and call me?"

I knew where he was going and, if my misguided sense of reasoning didn't cause everything and everyone to become transparent, I could have seen that my father was right, again. But at that time I was okay with being selfish. The spirit of selfishness held the spicy appeal of self-centeredness. I had acquired the taste over time so that it was getting easier to swallow emptiness as the days passed.

"I didn't want to place Sweets on the back burner because I *wanted* to. I placed her there because I *had* to."

"Why did you have to, baby?" he asked.

"Why? Because I had to, Daddy. It's easier than remembering Mama. I lost my mother and now my best friend. Now, Daddy, tell me what else does this world want? Does it want my sanity as well? I'm trying not to go crazy, but I'm slipping, Daddy. There are days when I feel like I'm stuck in quicksand and I'm too afraid to move. When you called me a few seconds ago, I didn't move because I was too afraid."

My father reached over and touched my shoulder. I placed the top back on the nail polish and prepared myself for his embrace. The atmosphere was warm and the spirit of bonding had consumed us both. Without saying a word, he spoke to me again. Without looking me in the eye, I could feel his focus.

My father and I began to cry as our worlds connected in a harmonious fashion. He held me close, and I could feel him absorb my pain. I leaned down to take a close look into his eyes, but he dropped his head.

I gently pushed his chin up and said, "Don't worry Daddy, I've got you. Sweets and I will speak again. I know we will, but now is not the time."

He began to wipe away my tears, and not wanting to be outdone, I reached out and began to wipe away his.

"I am so proud of you, Chocolate," he said. "I know that I don't ever have to worry about you making the right decision. You have a great head on your shoulders."

"Thanks a lot, Daddy, but it was you and Mama who helped mold me into who I am. And I won't dare take credit for something my wonderful parents instilled inside of me. I'm sure that I'm going to make some more mistakes in life. And I know you'll be there to help correct them. Right now, I just want to get my feet out of this quicksand. Okay?"

"Okay," he replied.

My father understood the analogy I had just given, and I loved him for always being such a good listener. He had a level of compassion inside that was shunned by most so-called men. My father was in tune with his emotions and he understood the difference between being humble and having humility. Although I didn't see him cry often, I knew that he was capable of conveying his emotions.

When I looked into my father's eyes, a sense of promise was revealed. When I thought of what my father was to me, I was consumed with the thought of being taught, and an eagerness to learn. His strength provided the necessary optimism to cultivate character. My father's love had a way of uniquely dispersing my confusion.

CHOCOLATE

To me, a father is the river that separates right and wrong. His spirit should pierce the misconceptions of the common mind. It is my wish that every child could be caressed by a father's hand. Knowing that he was always there would enable a child to take more risks. A father is a member of the clergy of truth; he is a boulder in the mountain of possibilities. A father exudes strength and exemplifies confidence, and my father, Marvin L. Williams, did just that.

My First Kiss

In spite of assurances to my father, I still needed somewhere to hide and the safest place I knew was inside me. The walls of my emotional displacement were built by endless hours of self-pity. I chose to disconnect, rather than torture myself with glimpses of hope. I was still being selfish but convinced myself there was a direct correlation between the wounds I'd obtained and self-preservation.

Almost a year and a half had passed since Sweets had gone off with her dad, and I was half way into my senior year in high school. Although I hadn't spoken to her in all that time, she was still my best friend.

But Tisha Morgan, the craziest girl I'd ever known, had personally appointed herself my new best friend. I was always quick to remind her that I only had one best friend. Her name was Sweets, and that was final.

I still wasn't into boys the way the rest of my girls, including Tisha, seemed to be. I wouldn't say I was shy, I just never really found boys very interesting. They didn't fascinate me. Besides, I loved studying and doing my schoolwork, and it was important to me that I received good grades.

For whatever reason, boys didn't ever sweat me like they did the other girls. Maybe it was because of the way I carried myself, at least that's what the girls at my school told me.

No one really captured my attention, that is until I met this one boy…

His name was Bruce Emerson, another senior at school. He was a little on the rough side when it came to looks, but he had a touch of innocence that my father would admire. He was always a gentleman and never disrespected me. Even though I didn't like him at first, he grew on me.

One day after school while we were all standing outside waiting for the bus, he smiled a funny little smile in passing. It made me feel strange inside. I had never really given a boy a second look, but this time Mr. Emerson had my attention. He was tall and funny looking at best, but I didn't see anything wrong with saying hello.

I was walking with Tisha, who was boy crazy, and she caught Bruce staring at me. She nudged me with her elbow and said, "Claudia, girl, look. That old ugly boy, Bruce, is staring."

Just as I was about to turn around, she pulled my arm and said, "You can't just turn around to look! He might think you like him or something, and I can't have you going out like that."

"Then why did you tell me to look, if you didn't want me to look?" I asked.

"Well, how else were you going to know he was looking? I just felt you might want to know, that's all."

Bruce had gotten his nerve up to approach us, and Tisha yelled out to him, "No… no you ain't trying to step this way, looking like that, trying to get with something like this." And she pointed at me.

I was embarrassed for him when everyone started laughing out loud. Some of the kids were laughing as if on cue, and others just for the sake of laughing.

Bruce didn't seem to care. He was ready to make his move. He had heard all of the same jokes before, and didn't care what anyone thought about him. He just put his head down and plowed confidently through the humiliation.

He said, "Excuse me, my name is Bruce Emerson. I just wanted you to know that I enjoy looking at you, and I wanted to finally say hello."

I smiled back and said, "Thanks," but by that time my bus had arrived.

Tisha pulled me onto the bus and said, "Girl, come on, you gonna mess around and catch something. You don't even know if whatever that is, has had its shots."

She laughed but I didn't find it amusing in the least. What she did wasn't cool and I needed her to know where I stood on the matter, but I waited until we got on the bus to check her.

"Look here, Tisha, what you did was wrong. Please don't ever embarrass anyone on my account again. All of my life I've been taught to fight my own battles and this is no exception."

"What's wrong, Claudia? I was just having fun. I didn't mean anything by it, that's just me," she said and tried to shrug it off.

"That doesn't excuse your actions. You could mess someone up for life," I said.

She thought I was playing at first, but when she realized I was serious, she rolled her eyes. Deep lines of puzzlement appeared on her forehead.

"Damn Claudia, you're really mad about that, aren't you?"

"Yes, really, Tisha. And the next time you speak for me, I better be too ill to speak for myself. I was taught to treat people like I want to be treated, and I would appreciate it if you wouldn't act that way around me."

Tisha was as ghetto as they came, and she really didn't get it, but she needed to be checked because she was out of order. She had no right to call Bruce ugly; after all, she wasn't the easiest person to look at. She had a nice body and all, but she OD'd on accessories.

She was devoted to wearing matching eye shadow. If she wore orange and blue clothes, her eye shadow was orange and blue. She wore a ring, or sometimes two, on each finger. And she was even saving up money to get a couple of gold teeth. Of course I would never point any of that out, because something told me that she had to already know she was ghetto.

"What's wrong with you?" she asked. "I was just trying to look out for you, Claudia. I mean, look at you - you've got it all. You're smart, you have a great body, and you're beautiful. What chance does he have to be with you?"

I hated her when she got indignant like that. Something was wrong with Tisha, but I was too busy trying to keep myself together to try and figure it out.

"By the way, Claudia, why don't you ever show off your body?" she wondered out loud. "Girl, if I was built like you, I wouldn't be hiding it. Why don't you wear something more revealing once in a while?" she asked.

"I don't feel it's necessary," I said simply.

"You don't feel it's necessary? What kind of answer is that? Is that all you're going to say?"

"What's wrong, Tisha? Is my answer not sufficient enough for you?" She hated when I talked to her that way. I knew that she didn't like it when I used any three-syllable words like that. Even if it was just one per sentence.

"Hey, you don't have to talk to me like you're taking one of those damn I.Q. tests. I am your girl. Make it plain for me, Claudia. You know, make it straight up and down with no crooked lines."

She was actually funny when she got on a roll and the ghetto just started oozing out of her.

"Just keep it real. Ain't no teachers around here, and this ain't no test."

I shook my head in exasperation and broke it down to her.

"I don't have to show my body off to get attention. My greatest asset is my mind, Tisha. My body is a temple, and when I finally reveal it, the person I show it to will be special."

"Damn, hold on one second. I have a thought. Maybe I should have waited to get home and called you, so I could have written all that down," she said.

The bus was approaching my stop, so we hugged each other and said our good-byes.

"Girl, I need to go home and finish studying up for a test. Call me if you get a chance, Tisha."

At my desk I reached for my dictionary, my constant desktop reference. I noticed my junior yearbook and started thumbing through it. I turned a few pages and there he was, wearing repulsive glasses and smiling his funny little smile. It was easy to look past the obvious as I tried to picture myself dating Bruce Emerson, who was one of the most ridiculed brothers in school.

I took the yearbook and held it closer, and then farther away again. I turned it a little to the right and then slightly to the left. Finally I placed a photo of myself next to his.

I said to myself, "Bruce, I'm not gonna be able to do it."

I put the yearbook away, finished my homework and then started in on my chores. My father placed the mail on the kitchen table everyday, and as I set it for dinner I saw that there was a letter from Sweets. I hadn't read any of her letters since she left. So I took the letter to my room and placed it in a shoebox with all the others on the top shelf in my closet.

I prepared dinner for my father that day. He loved my baked chicken and he especially enjoyed the way I seasoned my food. My mother taught me how to cook early in life, and I've been 'burning,' as my father put it, for years. We usually ate around six-thirty after he came home and relaxed while watching the news. I loved watching him eat. It felt good knowing that he enjoyed my cooking.

After dinner that night, while we were still at the table, he said, "So, what has Sweets been doing lately?"

I pretended not to hear him, hoping to avoid the conversation all together. My forever-persistent father reworded his question, "So, Choc, is Sweets all right? Is she doing well in school?"

I didn't want to talk about Sweets. It still wasn't time so I continued to run.

"Would you like some of that cake I made?" I asked.

"There is still a little left? Yes, I'll have a piece." He accommodated my diversion for only a moment.

"Why don't you want to talk about her, Chocolate?"

"Daddy, why won't you leave it alone? Please. I have a lot of other things on my mind. I'm sure Sweets is doing just fine."

"You know she called the other day?" he said.

I had to think of something to get my father's mind off of Sweets and I knew that any mention of bleeding or cramping made him uncomfortable. He evaded any conversation that involved my monthly. I knew, that when all else failed, it was my ace in the hole. He was a private man, and felt that everyone else should respect that as well.

I wasn't ready to discuss my feelings towards the whole Sweets issue, so I said, "I haven't been feeling well, Daddy. It's that time of the month."

Underneath his rough exterior is a gentle soul. He wasn't the kind of man who brought shame on you. He was too modest, and as soon as I said that, the conversation ceased.

"Oh, so that's what wrong? Chocolate, that's okay. I'll pass on the cake… maybe I'll have some tomorrow. Do you have everything you need, baby?"

It worked. I simply smiled at him and pretended to have cramps. I held my stomach and gathered up the plates.

"Chocolate, I'll get the dishes, why don't you go and lie down."

I kissed him goodnight, then turned and walked away, feeling like I had just won an Oscar. I hated lying to my father but I wasn't interested in entertaining the truth.

Distancing myself from emotions was my way of buying time. It gave me another moment to exhale before facing the irrepressible truth of hurt's undeniable reality. I needed to be more in-tune with myself, and feel at one with my spirit-man. That might allow me to deal with the consequences of all of my actions.

I was a fighter who had become too weak to take a swing at my enemies. Somewhere between birth and Sweets' departure, I had lost my identity. I was on the other end of tired and had run out of places to hide.

Surely my father could appreciate that in time, but right now was reserved for me. I knew that one day I would open up each of Sweets' letters, and read them one by one, as if I had just received them. I knew she was safe and she was getting to know her father. Now, I was taking this time to get to know me, Claudia Williams.

No sooner had I closed the door to my room than I heard the phone ringing. It was Tisha trying to get her last bit of gossip in before she went to sleep.

"Girl, what are you doing?"

"Nothing, Tisha. My father and I just finished eating dinner," I said.

"Damn, is that right? I can't remember the last time we all just set down and had dinner together in this house. I mean we all eat the same thing, but never at the same time, at the table like you do at your house."

I knew she wasn't calling to have a family conversation with me and that it wouldn't be long before she introduced the main topic of the night.

"Claudia, can I ask you a personal question?" I knew what was coming.

"Yes, sure, Tisha. Why not? What is it?" I said.

"Could you really ever date somebody like Brruuuce?"

"Well, let me see," I said while I opened up the yearbook. I looked at his picture one more time and reconsidered my earlier declaration.

"Well let's just say, I don't know yet," I replied.

"You don't know? How can you not know as smart as you are? I mean look at him," she said.

"What if his personality outweighs his looks?" I asked her. "What if he treats me like a queen and possesses the charm of a king?"

"What if, what if, girl, what if rocks were bricks, and branches were trees, and lakes were seas, and last but not least, what if D's were B's?" she shot back.

"Claudia, if all of that was true, I guess I could imagine what you're asking me to see, but that simply ain't the case.

"Bruce is through, I mean like the final shot in overtime when the score isn't tied. He's light years ahead of his ugliness and no amount of charm is going to make him a damn king. If you're gonna ask 'what if,' hell, why don't you ask 'what if' he was cute? But he's not now, and he won't be tomorrow, so 'what if' that?

"Claudia, for years I've admired you. I've told you that a hundred times, right?"

"Yes, you have, Tisha," I said.

"I've listened to you tell me at least thousand times that you were a queen, but that doesn't mean that you have to date Kermit the Frog."

I couldn't stand it. She was taking this hypothetical situation to a whole other level. She had apparently given this a great deal of thought and wasn't going to let me go out like that. Tisha was crazy as hell, and as ghetto as they came, but she'd tell you in a minute that she wasn't a fool.

"Girl, I just can't see it, not even with your eyes," she continued. "Do you know why zoo keepers don't feed the monkeys steak?" she asked.

I didn't know where she was going with that one, but I played along.

"No, Tisha, why?"

"Because bananas are for monkeys and steaks are for kings. And I'll bet you'll see Bruce eating a banana before you catch him eating a steak."

It was wrong, but I was enjoying it. I needed to laugh, not at the expense of others, but just because. It sometimes sounded as if Tisha had gone temporarily insane, but her mind was hers to speak and it was funny to hear her get outside herself.

"You are so mean," I said.

"No, not me! The doctor that delivered his ugly ass is mean, and he should no longer have the right to deliver monkeys in this state."

"Tisha, that is so wrong. First you called him a frog, and now a monkey. What did Bruce ever do to you?" I asked.

"What did he ever do to me? I'll tell you what he did to me," she said.

"One morning I was in the school cafeteria just minding my business. I was eating a bowl of cereal and Bruce passed by my table."

"It's a free country, Tisha. He has every right to pass by your table," I said in his defense.

"Yes, you're right, but here's the part that pissed me off. He was so ugly that when he passed by, he spoiled the milk in my bowl!"

"Now come on, Tisha, there's no one that bad looking."

"No one but Bru-uce, that is," she said. "He's so ugly that him and a group of his ugly friends get together when they want it to rain. They simply stare up at the sky, and before you know it, it's raining."

"So what happens to the sky to make it rain when they stare at it?" I asked.

"They make the sky start crying and make us believe that it's rain. Just think, all these years we've been taught that rain was produced by something other than ugliness, but the truth is, it's caused by a group of ugly people."

By that time I was laughing so hard that I had to put a pillow over my head so I wouldn't disturb my father.

"Girl, you're going to make me get in trouble. I've always thought that you were crazy, now tonight I know you are."

"Oh, so you think I'm lying? Then tomorrow I want you to walk up to Bruce and asked him something for me," she said.

"Ask him what?" I said in anticipation of what she was about to spell out.

"Just say, 'Hey, Bruce, can you tell me when it's going to rain again?' And watch, he'll tell you. You see, ugly people know about rain and things like that," she said.

I had laughed all I could for one day and knew that I better go to sleep. I needed to be well rested for school. I said, "Hey, girl, it's getting late, you know I don't stay up late on school nights."

"Okay, Claudia, I'll see you in the morning. Goodnight."

I laughed myself to sleep that night. Tisha really didn't like Bruce but all of this talk about him was sparking my interest.

I saw Bruce after my fourth period class the next day. He was smiling like always, but this time I smiled back. He wore the same horrible green jacket to school everyday. It was so tight that if he were to make a sudden move, the whole jacket would probably rip in two. I was hoping he would say hello, so I could apologize for the mean things Tisha had called him. But as he got closer I started thinking about some of the things Tisha had said on the phone the night before. An uncontrollable grin appeared on my face. The closer he got the harder it became to erase.

I was snickering like a childish fool when he finally spoke.

"Hi there. How are you today, Chocolate?" he asked.

I stopped short and my grin disappeared.

"What did you just call me?" I was stunned.

"I called you Chocolate. Isn't that your name? Isn't that what everyone else calls you?"

"No. Not everyone… In fact, hardly anyone at all. Only those who know me well, like my family and my closest friends. So please don't call me that again, okay?"

"Okay. I'm so sorry," he apologized sincerely.

"By the way, where is that crazy friend of yours?"

I knew who he was talking about, but I wanted to hear what he had to say about Tisha. I paused for a couple of seconds and asked, "Who? Which friend is that? Brenda? Tisha?"

"You know, the one who was with you yesterday. What's up with her? She's always looking at me funny, like I've done something to her."

"Oh yeah, that's Tisha for you. You've just got to excuse her, she was touched as a child."

"Well, why don't I ever see you with anyone?" he asked.

"You just saw me with Tisha yesterday, didn't you?"

"Yes, sure, but I mean with a male."

"And what's wrong with me hanging out with females?"

"Well, you know what I mean…"

Of course I knew what he meant. I could see where his questions were going, but he was running out of rope and I wanted to see if he was narrow minded enough to hang himself.

"Honestly, I don't know what you mean. Why don't you tell me and then we'll both know," I replied.

He stood with his mouth hanging open, wanting to disappear. I'm sure he felt stupid, but what I liked about him was the way he could come back.

"Look, I didn't mean to piss you off, it's just that I like you is all. My friends have all tried to convince me you would never give me the time of day."

"Okay," I accepted his apology.

"The answer to your question is there is no one," I said.

He obviously didn't remember what he had asked me, so I reminded him. "Your question was, 'why don't you see me with anyone,' right? And my answer is because I don't have time for boys right now, my education comes first."

"I heard that. So what if we started off seeing each other in the library?" he grinned.

Now, that was original, I had to admit. I tried to fight back a smile while glancing at his tight green jacket.

"So does that mean we have a date?"

I took a few steps down the hall and tried to ignore him, but he was persistent. He took another shot at me, "Hey, Claudia, I could be your book holder, so your arms won't get tired while you're reading."

That did it. I had never had a human book holder before. So I looked back over my shoulder and said, "I'll be in the library tomorrow around three-fifteen."

He just stood there for a second in disbelief. But before I could turn the corner at the end of the hall, he yelled out, "Yes! You won't be sorry! I'll be the best book holder you've ever had."

For the next month, we met in the library at least twice a week. I never really said much to him; we mostly just smiled at each other. There was something about that green jacket of his that bothered me, though. I was tired of seeing it by then, and was trying to find a tactful way to ask him to remove it.

"It's warm in here, isn't it?" I asked one day in the library. I knew that he heard me but for some reason he didn't answer.

"So, why don't you take your jacket off?" I urged, but there was still no answer. He just sat there with a blank expression on his face.

He finally looked at me and said dejectedly, "I'm not hot, Claudia, and I feel fine, thank you."

Okay, so he didn't like me more than he apparently loved wearing his jacket. I was okay with it; at least I had tried. Maybe he was just one of those cool natured people who felt abnormal breezes.

"Claudia, how long have you been… uh, well, smart?" he asked with hesitation.

"Why do you think I'm smart, Bruce? What is it about me that makes you feel that way?"

"I've been coming here watching you study for over three weeks now…"

"That's actually the point I am trying to make. You have been watching me study, now how smart does that make you?"

He looked at me and shook his head, "What's wrong? Are you angry, Claudia?"

"I'm not angry, I've just been taught that the word 'smart' has been severely over-used. Now if you wish to call me intelligent, I would probably accept it a little better than just being called smart. I study hard to prepare myself for the challenges I'm going to face, and by doing so I eliminate excuses that others use to rationalize their own lack of effort."

He bent down and pulled a pencil out of his book-bag and said, "Hey, man, say that again. Where did you learn to talk like that?" he asked, ready to take notes.

I did what my father would have done at that moment. I simply pulled up the book I was reading and covered my face with it. My actions answered the question as if to say, "By reading."

I sat with the book in front of my face for a few more seconds and then slowly brought it down until our eyes met.

"Girl, you're beautiful. I mean you're not just attractive, you're sweet, you're soft spoken, but most of all you're intelligent." He may not have known it, but he was saying all the right stuff, and I was eating it up, word for word.

"Can I ask you a personal question?" Bruce inquired softly.

"Sure, why not," I said.

"Have you ever been kissed by anyone before?"

"Yes, of course. I kiss my father everyday."

"No, that's not quite what I meant."

"I know what you mean. No, I've never kissed a boy before, but it's not like I haven't wanted to. I'm human like anyone else. The thought has crossed my mind a few times."

"You must be strong, because I haven't ever seen a girl your age who hasn't kissed a boy before."

By that time I was feeling close enough to tell him more about my past.

"Since I was eight or nine years old there has always been someone trying to touch or kiss me."

That made him straighten up in his chair.

He may not have been prepared for my honesty but he kindly said, "Tell me more, Claudia… we have lots of time."

"Okay, Bruce, it seems like you might be a true listener." I felt ready to trust him.

"There was this boy in sixth grade named Russell Madison. He was a nasty little boy, with a penis for a brain. He had to be the horniest boy alive, bar none. He hadn't reached his twelfth birthday and already he was trying to bed every sixth and seventh grade girl he saw."

I interrupted myself and told Bruce that our conversation made me recall how we all thought Russell Madison and Bobby 'I'll-Do-It' Thomas were probably the world's youngest perverts back then.

"That's crazy," Bruce said laughing out loud.

The librarian approached us and warned, "Now, you two, you're going to have to keep it down."

I lowered my voice and continued my narrative.

"At lunchtime they would hide behind the bushes outside the girl's bathroom. They took turns standing on each other's backs while the other knelt down on all fours. All just to peek inside, just hoping they'd get a chance to catch some girl pulling her panties up or down. They would come back into school and give the rest of the perverted little nothings what they called, 'the bush report.'"

"The bush report, what was that?" Bruce asked.

"That meant telling the other boys who had hair down on their privates. It was sad that we couldn't relieve ourselves with any privacy; without being afraid of being watched by the two libido brothers."

My mind jumped back to Russell and the days he used to bring a small mirror to school. He'd tape it on the end of his shoe and walk up to a girl and position his foot just right so that he could see underneath the girl's dress. We hated wearing dresses just for that reason alone. When we did wear dresses, we made sure we wore shorts underneath them.

Russell had a thing for me, I recalled. Every time I would get up from my desk to turn in my work sheets, I could feel his lustful eyes gawking at me. He had the practiced look of a vagrant watching you get money out of an ATM machine. He was always making funny sounds, like a dog in heat, and one day he got up the nerve to speak his peace.

"I was opening up my locker at the time and trying not to hear him," I told Bruce.

"'Hey, Chocolate,' he had the nerve to say. 'I've got this sweet tooth and I need some candy. Can you help me?' I tried hard to ignore him but he was persistent.

"'Hey, pretty girl, can I have a bite of that candy?' I saw that he wasn't about to give up, so I made it easy for him.

"Actually, I don't curse that often but I had a few choice words for him. I waited a few seconds so his friends could tune in and hear their hero get read. I said, 'Look, you butt-hole, this 'Chocolate' is reserved for a real man and since I don't see one around, I suggest you take your funny-looking, no-conversation-having, bad-breath-spreading tail down to the corner store and ask the clerk to direct you to the suckers, because that's exactly what your are.'

"Russell was caught off-guard and never had time to recover. He couldn't move, and just stood there like a small sapling without enough water.

"'Damn, man. She told you,'" said Bobby.

"I reached into my locker, and grabbed my math book then. 'Oh, Russell, just in case you are too slow to remember, the store is that way,' and I pointed out of the school down the road.

"Russell Madison never went there again with me and today we are friends."

I stopped reminiscing for a moment, directing my thoughts to get to a point. Bruce was still willing to listen.

"Bruce, boys, hmm… how shall I say this? Boys have always made me feel like I was a piece of candy in a jar on the top shelf. They were all so very simple, with their one-dimensional comments and their wishful looks. They had me self-conscious about the way I was built. I hated the way my butt stuck out. I wore long shirts so that it wouldn't be so noticeable.

"For so long I couldn't understand why having their attention was so important. It was crazy to see so many girls preoccupied with a need to be seen by the opposite sex. Girls would go into the restroom and stuff toilet paper down their bras. They would bring extra clothing to school in their backpacks, defying their parents for the sake of fitting in.

"Boys made my younger years a living hell. They're the reason we were taught to always cross our legs. I hated the false sense of security they projected and how casual the whole 'hey-come-here-and-let-me-stick-it-in-you' approach was. It was appalling at best and chillingly shameful to say the least.

"My father couldn't have been more right, when it came to boys. I hated God initially for my being born a female. I hated the way society scrutinized our every move," I said.

"Now wait a minute, Claudia," Bruce finally interjected. "Not all boys are the same," he said.

"Okay, you might be right," I was willing to agree to his point at this stage of life. "But I also disliked the fact that the standards for girls were always higher than for boys."

"I can understand that," Bruce acknowledged.

"Isn't it strange how a male spends the better portion of his life attempting to enter a place which had housed his soul for nine months before his birth? Did you ever think of that?" I didn't give him time to answer.

"I've always felt that boys had their place but it wasn't in my conversation, or in my thoughts, and at my age, it surely wasn't in me."

"Woah...Woah," Bruce had had his fill.

"Excuse me for being a male. I just came out of my mother's womb this way, and believe it or not, I wasn't given a choice either," he said.

"I was merely trying to tell you why I hadn't ever kissed anyone and why you've never seen me with a boy," I said defensively.

Bruce looked disturbed. Perhaps I had gone too far. He had probably heard more than he cared to. Maybe he felt that I was a threat to his hormones, and I didn't see him for a while after that.

I went to the library like I always did on Mondays and Wednesdays, but Bruce didn't show up. I admit it bothered me, but I didn't know why. A feeling of blame came over me, and I'm sure Bruce would have agreed. I tried to move on but I just couldn't get him off my mind.

One day while Tisha and I were walking down the hall, I saw Bruce and a couple of his friends standing near the soda machines. They were casually laughing about something. When we walked past them, I turned and looked at Bruce.

I silently said, "Hello."

He looked me straight in eye, yet didn't acknowledge me. Instead, he turned his back on me and continued laughing like I didn't exist.

Tisha saw me say hello out of the corner of her eye and could tell his non-response upset me. She took my hand and pulled me into the restroom.

"Girrrl, please tell me that I didn't just see that. Tell me you didn't get upset that he didn't speak to you." I didn't say anything.

"Well?" she waited.

"Well, what?"

She came closer to me with a serious look on her face. "Do you need to go to the clinic and get your eyes washed out? 'Cause I don't have anything on me to help you right now. No, don't tell me they have gotten to you, too?" She paused for a moment.

"I was just looking at some videos last night on B.E.T. and saw where the 'ugly brothers' had taken over."

I still did not respond to her nonsense, so she went on, "Girl, have you kissed him yet?" I pretended not to hear Tisha drilling me.

"Come on now, shake it off, and let's go to the clinic. We've got to get that 'ugly brothers' mess out of your eyes. I wasn't going to say anything to you, but I was told that you and 'the monkey' were seen in the library several times last month."

I could hardly believe she knew.

"Now don't worry, don't worry, Claudia. I've got you girl. But there has to be a remedy for this," she said.

"But Tisha, I just like him," I finally responded.

She placed both hands over her ears and said, "Noooooooo, no. I'm not hearing this. What is it about him that you could possibly like?" she forced herself to ask.

"Well, if you really want to know, he's..." I tried to explain myself.

"Don't say it, Claudia. Keep it to yourself, girl."

She turned quickly and ran out the door. I ran after her begging her to wait.

"Tisha, wait! Wait! I need to talk to you!!" I yelled after her.

She stopped and said, "Do you know what this is like? This is like giving a jewel to a monkey. He ain't gonna treat you right. He's just going to do you like he does a banana."

"What's that?" I asked.

"Girl, he's gonna peel you back and eat you up, and when he's done, he's just going to throw you in the pile with the rest of the peels."

"Can't you be serious for once? Stop making fun of him."

She saw I was hurting.

"Yes, I can, if you really want me to."

"Okay, now if you were me what would you do?"

"Seek help fast. No, I'm just playing."

But I wasn't laughing, so she got serious for me.

"I would tell him how I felt," she advised.

"Okay, I can do that. I don't have a problem with that. And then what?"

"Monkeys adapt well to their environment. He'll know what to do next."

I looked at her as if to say 'okay, now I've had enough.'

"Okay, okay, I'm through kidding."

I located Bruce in the hall and as soon as we made eye contact, he turned around and rushed to get whatever he needed out of his locker. By the time he closed it I was standing right behind him.

"So I see you're closing everything these days."

He looked at me and responded cynically, "Oh, did your father teach you that too? Oh no, I'm sorry, you probably read that somewhere, after all, you're quite intelligent, aren't you?"

"Okay, so that's what's wrong. You're upset about what I said about boys. That's it, isn't it?"

"No, I'm upset that you wouldn't give me a chance to prove that I wasn't like all those other boys."

I shocked myself as I started kissing him. It caught him off guard, and everyone one else for that matter. Before we could finish, Tisha appeared and saw us. Immediately she fainted. Bruce and I ran over to her, and he and a couple of his friends picked her up. They carried her to the clinic, but no sooner had they laid her on the bed did she come to.

The first words out of her mouth were, "Girl, I thought I saw the strangest thing. It scared the hell out of me."

The nurse and I were wondering what she was talking about when Bruce stuck his head inside the room to hand me my purse. His lips were the same color as mine, because of our earlier kiss.

Tisha noticed.

"Oh my God! You mean I wasn't dreaming? Claudia, how could you? Nurse, what is the strongest eye-drops you have? She needs some of that strong shit," Tisha said pointing to me.

"Young lady! That's the second time you've cursed in here today! You had better watch your language before I send you to the principal's office."

"My bad…" she thought better with that remark and simply said, "it won't happen again."

"Shouldn't you be in class right now?" the nurse asked me.

"I was getting ready for lunch when this happened and I still have a few more minutes before I need to be in class," I replied.

"Well, why don't you say good-byes now and let her rest for a while. She has a pretty nice size lump on her head. She'll be all right, though. I'll call her mother to come and get her."

I walked over and kissed Tisha on her cheek. She dramatically wiped it off her face.

"Eeesh! You kissed him and now you're kissing me?"

I just smiled and shook my head, and walked happily back to class.

The next Wednesday, like always, I went to the library after school to study. I walked over to the history section and reached up to get a book I needed for a report. Before I could touch it, I heard a familiar voice.

"Which book are you reaching for? History before or after the turn of the century?"

I was so happy I couldn't move.

"Where did you come from, Bruce?"

"Does it really matter where I came from? I thought what was most important was that I was here."

There was an air of instant sophistication about him. Within a matter of hours it seemed I had created a monster, a modern day Romeo, a Billy Dee Williams wanna be. Bruce had reached inside and pulled out the confidence needed to destroy my insecurities. He had a newly found swagger, which I found very attractive.

"I'll get the book for you, Claudia. I wouldn't want you to strain your back or anything like that, now would I?"

A few minutes later our destinies were revealed.

"So, are we?" he asked.

"Are we what, Bruce?"

My mind easily drifted away from the school's library. I was thinking about how my mother would have answered that question? She wasn't there but I could often feel her presence, and I needed her wisdom and humble tongue at that very moment. I knew that I cared for Bruce, but I wasn't ready to commit just because of a first kiss.

My father used to say that once a can of fruit has been opened, it was impossible to lock its original flavor back inside. He told me to never show a man anything I didn't want him to have.

Was I sending out mixed signals to Bruce? Was I ready to care for another human being? I had created a situation where I was faced with these important questions, too afraid to lose the moment and too bright to get caught up in the frivolous, potentially dark games of life.

The moment was now and the question was at hand. There was no turning back, so I did what any female with an average amount of intelligence would have done. I got up and ran as fast as I could, holding my stomach and running towards the restroom.

"Are you okay, Claudia?" he asked with great concern.

I looked back and yelled, "Yes, I'll be fine! I'm just cramping real bad, that's all."

There was nothing like faking your period. It was foolproof. When I was brave enough to return, I had just enough time to catch the late bus. I was amazed he was still there.

While I rushed to gather my things, I turned to him and said nonchalantly, "Now, what were you asking me again?"

"Oh, nothing. It can wait I guess," he said as he shrugged his shoulders.

"Are you sure, Bruce? I can stay a little longer and have my father pick me up, if you'd like to talk."

I knew that some boys had a problem talking to young ladies if they knew they were on their period. He was no different than my father when it came to that. I got on the bus and mentally wiped my forehead in relief.

When my bus took off, Bruce just stood there for a few seconds waving like he didn't have anywhere to go. It must have finally dawned on him that he'd have to walk if he didn't hurry up and catch his own bus.

We saw each other as much as time would permit as the year went on. It was April and there were only a couple of months until graduation. After running as fast as I possibly could, I finally slowed down and said 'yes' to Bruce. I became his girlfriend. Tisha never figured out why I chose Bruce to be the first boy I kissed.

One weekend while my father and I were finalizing college choices he asked me out of the blue, "So who's this Bruce?"

"Who's Br... Bruce?" I said. I shouldn't have been shocked that Pops knew about him. "Well he's a boy at school I met a few months ago," I offered.

"Okay. But just who is this boy to you?"

"Oh, Dad. He's just somebody I know, that's all. No big deal."

"Oh, so he's no big deal?"

"Nope. No big deal."

"So why is his name written all over everything in your room?"

I must have written his name on almost every folder I owned. This was going to be a hard one to get out of. I had just had my period two weeks ago, so that excuse was out. No, this time I had to tell the truth.

"Okay, Dad. We've been kind of seeing each other for a while," I confessed.

"Seeing each other? What does that mean exactly?"

"Okay, okay. He's my boyfriend."

"Boyfriend... hmmm... boyfriend... Well, why haven't I met him yet? What kind of family does he come from? And what does he look like?"

"What does he look like?"

I wrinkled my nose at that one.

"Well, maybe I'll ask him to come over and meet you. Would you like that, Daddy?" I said while I kissed him on his forehead.

"Sure, why not? I would love to meet him, even though it's a little late."

"It's a little late? For what, Dad? What are you getting at?" I asked knowingly. "Okay, let me fill in some blanks so you feel better. Here are the answers to your next four questions. Yes. Yes. Yes, and no. Yes, I've held his hand. Yes, I've hugged him. Yes, we've kissed, but no, we haven't 'done it.' I'm not that type of girl. I respect myself too much for that. You should know that about me. Now, are there any other questions?"

"Well, at least you could have allowed me to go off on you, Chocolate. It would have given me some satisfaction," he said suppressing a smile.

"Daddy, I need you to help me decide on a school here."

He was pre-occupied with meeting Bruce, and ignored the issue at hand.

"Okay, what about next Friday? You can cook something and invite him over for dinner."

"Okay, Daddy. Good plan. I'll set it up," I agreed. I gave Bruce a call right there in front of my father.

"Bruce, you've always wanted to meet my father, right? Well, next Friday is your lucky day. When I see you on Monday, I'll give you directions to my house."

"Are you sure he wants to meet me?" he asked tentatively.

"Yes, of course. Your name is Bruce, right?"

"Right."

"You are my boyfriend, right?"

"Right."

"Then… you're the one he wants to meet."

"Okay, then. I'll be there."

"Okay, then. It's our first date."

"Wait just a minute now, you didn't have to call it a date," my father said.

"Dad, really. Your nose is sweating. You must be getting excited. Now you know what the doctor said about your high-blood pressure."

"So, what does this boy look like?" he resorted to repeating earlier queries.

"You've always taught me that looks don't matter, haven't you?"

"Yes, I know I said that. But that's before you told me that you had a boyfriend. Is he short? Is he tall? Is he skinny, fat, dark or light? Come on, Chocolate, just tell me something."

"Dad, please just wait until Friday gets here. I'm sure he won't look any different by then. Besides, you sound like one of my girlfriends."

My hands were full when Bruce knocked on the door that Friday night. Pops let him in and led him to the living room. Seconds later I appeared and greeted him with a respectful hug.

"Hi, Bruce. I see you've met my handsome father."

My father was staring at Bruce out of the corner of his eye, much like a jeweler does a questionable stone. I could feel him appraising Bruce, attempting to see what I saw in him.

"Yes, we've finally met," he said.

"It's Bruce, right?"

"Yes sir. That's right. Bruce Emerson, sir."

"Well, here is the remote to the TV. You can watch whatever you'd like. Dinner will be ready in about ten minutes. If you could excuse us for a moment, we'll be right back."

He ushered Bruce into the living room then turned his attention towards me. "Chocolate, can I see you for a second in my study?"

Oh boy, I thought. Here it comes. Every time he called me into his study it was to discuss something important.

When he closed the door behind us he said, "Chocolate, he must be a very sweet young man."

"Yes, he is, Dad. How can you tell?" I asked.

"Because... how shall I put this? Because, the boy is hard as hell to look at."

"Daddy, that's so mean."

"No, baby, that's being nice. Now if I wouldn't have opened the door and let him in, that would have been mean." He paused for a reaction, but I had none.

"Baby, you kissed him?"

"Sure I did, Pops. What's wrong with him?" He could tell that I was getting upset with his line of questioning.

He avoided a potential crisis by saying, "You're right. I did teach you right, so I've got to live with it."

Before dinner was served I could feel my father staring at Bruce again. When I looked to confirm my senses, his mouth was stuck partially open in amazement. He didn't make Bruce feel uncomfortable, but if first impressions were any indication; he certainly wasn't impressed. And it didn't take long before my father noticed the jacket.

"Claudia, go and check the thermostat. Is it cold in here to you, son?"

"No, sir, it feels great. Why do you ask?"

"Well it might have something to do with that jacket you're wearing. Do you want to take it off?"

"No, sir. I'm fine, thank you."

My father kept insisting that he remove it.

"I would like for you to remove your jacket. In fact, it's a rule in this house, and if you're going to eat dinner with us... the jacket has to come off."

He stood up and reached for Bruce's jacket.

I could tell that Bruce didn't want to take his jacket off, but he did want to stay. He took my father seriously and did something that no one had ever seen him do at school in all four years. He stood up and slowly unzipped his jacket. There was great reluctance with every inch. I could tell this was a very uncomfortable moment for him. No one at our high school had ever seen Bruce without his jacket and I wasn't sure I wanted to. What we were about to see was talked about for years.

The second he took one of his arms out of his jacket, he placed his fears in our hands. He knew that agreeing to remove his jacket meant that he had to disrobe emotionally. His face dawned a menacing look of utter shame. I looked over at my father, who was sitting at the opposite end of the table.

I implored him, "Daddy, look at him... he doesn't want to take off his jacket."

My father placed his right index finger over my mouth to keep me quiet. There was nothing else I could say or do. I knew that Bruce cared for me, but not this much. Though he was just a boy, the stand he was about to take catapulted him into manhood in my eyes.

"What's the big deal? It's just a jacket, and besides it's not cold in here," my father said.

Bruce looked over at me and said, "Claudia, your father is right. It is just a jacket. I'll gladly take it off. Besides, what choice do I have?"

CHOCOLATE

Our eyes met and silently we both began to cry. His emotions were pulling at mine, so much so that they pierced my heart and caused me to wrestle with guilt. I braced myself for what was to come. A tragic part of Bruce's life was about to be exposed.

As my father and I became spectators of heroism, we were also shown the difference between humbleness and humility. By the time Bruce got his jacket off, my father had stood with him. Bruce was emotionally naked, standing before us wearing scars of bravery on over forty percent of his body. Burns that had been inflicted while saving a neighboring mother and her daughter from a burning apartment building when he was only eight and a half years old. Both of his arms and chest were burned severely, but his arms had taken the worst of it.

After seeing the horror and sadness in our faces Bruce broke the silence.

"Can you bear to eat while looking at me? Was my jacket really that big of a deal? I hope that you're happy now. I pray that I haven't caused you to lose your appetites."

"Young man, I'm so sorry... I didn't know. Please forgive me," said my father. "Sure we can eat. If you'd like to... you can put your jacket back on."

Bruce looked over at him and said, "Mr. Williams, I don't enjoy wearing this stupid looking jacket, but it's a special fabric that covers my burns and keeps the light off of them, which is critical for the rest of my life. I took my jacket off because I really like your daughter. I didn't want you to ask me to leave."

My father walked around to Bruce's side of the table and gave him a big hug.

"I'm sorry, Bruce. Can you please forgive me, son?"

"Of course I can, sir," he offered, but he started to put his jacket back on in consideration of us.

"No, Bruce. Please don't! Give it to me and I'll put it away for you." I reached out for the jacket as he handed it to me.

When I sat back down at the table I announced, "Now let's eat."

Bruce looked so relieved. He had finally shed his coat of shame, and my father and I were better for having the honor of watching him do it so bravely. Although Bruce was burned severely over the better part of his body, the best part of him, his heart, was saved.

I went off to college three months later and stayed in touch with Bruce for nearly two years. I shall never forget my first kiss…because my first kiss…was also his.

Crossroads

In the fall I was a member of the freshman class at UC Berkeley in the Bay Area, not all that far from home. Berkeley was just around the corner from Oakland and across the bay from San Francisco. My first year there was spent acquiring the basic courses necessary to graduate, just like all freshmen are required to do. Deciding on a major was premature because most of my friends changed their majors like they changed their sneakers. As a freshman, I had to live in a dormitory, which meant I would have a roommate.

I had never really spent much time with anyone other than Sweets and I knew it was going to take some adjusting. I was nervous but refused to show it. The thought of sharing a room with a stranger was doing a job on my head, but my father assured me it wouldn't be long until I could get my own apartment. That was something to look forward to.

The day Pops dropped me off on campus was a day to remember. The dormitory I was assigned to was like any large apartment building. My room was on the second floor with a balcony, and I could get there by taking the stairs. When

I opened the door to my room, little did I know I had come face to face with trouble.

There she was, in the form of a young woman my age, sitting in the middle of the bed listening to music on wireless headphones. Her legs were crossed and she was wearing a blue and white t-shirt and cut-off blue-jean shorts.

My father and I spoke to her but she never uttered a word in return. Her reasons for not speaking were her own, and it didn't bother us at all. When we saw that she wasn't going to return our greeting we turned to each other, shrugged and smiled.

It seemed as though she had a problem with us being there, but that was a pill she had to digest without any help from the newest tenant. We moved on and left her there to deal with her ignorance on her own. We had a lot of moving to do and it was starting to get dark. It only took a little over an hour for us to unload the car and bring my things in.

While hanging up some of my clothes, I couldn't help but to notice that some of Trouble's clothes were in my closet. I did not mind her not speaking, that was on her, but her clothes being on my side of the room was a bit much. I thought I would be able to take care of that later, though.

I really wasn't ready to deal with her just yet. I was dealing with something far more important; having to say good-bye to my father for the first time. We were not going to be far away from each other, but I hadn't ever been on my own. The only time I had stayed away overnight was when Sweets was here, and I could count those times on one hand.

My father was a proud man who lived like he walked; strong and direct. He had a way of reaching inside himself and pulling out the right words to inspire those he came in contact with. He had beat many odds in life, but he could not hold back tears that were pushing against his soul as he dropped his only child off for college.

He walked back to the truck to get a few more things, and I noticed as he gently wiped away his tears with a handkerchief he always kept in his pocket.

I leaned over the balcony and made a little noise to give him time to get himself together.

"Hey, Daddy," I called down. "Did you see the box that my shoes were in?" I asked trying to ease his mind.

When he heard my voice, he folded the handkerchief back into his pocket as fast as he could. He tried to mask his tears by rotating his shoulders. I wished I could somehow shield his sorrow. But I knew he was also happy for me.

He yelled back to me, "Yeah... it's right here, baby. I was just getting ready to bring it up."

"Okay, then. I'll just run down and get the rest of my hats while you grab the other stuff. I just found the perfect place for them."

"Okay, Choc, I'll be right there. It'll take me a minute though. The truck was making a strange sound and I was just getting ready to check it out..." he mumbled unnecessarily.

My father was never the best liar, but I understood why he was telling this one. I could see by the way his shoulders were swaying that this was going to be harder for him than he imagined it would be.

After taking the rest of my things to my room, I walked my father back out to his truck to say good-bye. I kissed him on the cheek and hugged him with all my love. We were both sad, but my sadness was secondary. What mattered to me the most was my father, the rock of my life.

As we said good-night, I whispered in his ear in an attempt to make him smile, "Now, Daddy, you're not getting soft on me are you?"

He held my shoulders and said, "No, but I'm going to miss not having you around, that's for sure. I was just thinking to myself, that's all."

"Thinking what?" I asked.

"Well, I hope I've prepared you for life. This is it."

I pulled him close for another hug we both so desperately needed.

"Daddy, just look at me. I'm all grown up and it's all because of you. You did well by me and don't you ever second-guess anything. I've got Marvin L. Williams' blood inside of me and that alone has gotten me ready for life. If you want to be afraid for someone, be afraid for those who are foolish enough to become my enemies. Because I am greater than any obstacle this old world can ever place in front of me. Do you know why? Because I am Claudia Williams, the daughter of a king. So tell me old-wise one, what does that make you?"

He stood motionless, smiling the biggest smile he could possibly muster, as I pointed at myself with a sense of satisfaction. His smile allowed me to pivot in the direction of the dorm. I bounded up to my new room two stairs at a time, but reassured him I would call.

"Bye, Daddy! I'll call you when I get all of my classes."

When I got back upstairs my roommate was pacing around still listening to music. She was moving her head from side to side just jamming to some loud Rock & Roll. She turned it down long enough for us to spend two minutes to officially get acquainted with each other.

But no sooner had I walked over to my side of the room did the madness begin. I was already feeling nervous about the whole roommate experience, and now this.

Amy Spencer was a nightmare ready to happen. When I opened the closet door, she began spraying disinfectant towards my side of the room. She was holding her nose as if my clothes stunk. She had crossed the line, and it was time to set some boundaries. I walked over to her and snatched the earphones off her head. I pushed her back to her side of the room and she fell backwards onto her bed.

I said boldly, "Now look, Amy, I didn't ask to be your roommate and I don't particularly care to be your friend. If you have a problem with me, I suggest you take it up with the dorm director. Do you hear me?"

She started acting stupid and tried to make it seem like I was a fool. "What? What's wrong with you? I didn't do anything to you." She was turning redder than a freshly painted fire truck.

"All I was doing was spraying the room. Why should that set you off? So get away from me you nasty nigga. Get away from me. All of you are alike, you think you can solve everything by using violence."

"Oh, so that's what this is all about, my being black?" I asked. I grabbed her arm to help her up, but pulled too hard on purpose.

"Let go of my arm, nigga, you're hurting me."

When she called me a nigga the second time, my grip grew even stronger and I felt a rage rumbling inside my body. I had gone past being angry and I wanted to beat the ignorance out of her. My blood was boiling faster than I could think, so I closed my eyes and let go of her arm.

I took a breath and said, "Look you little witch, let's get this straight. I don't care where you came from and I don't give a damn about where you're going. But you'd better keep your ass on your side of the room, or I'm going to finish this by giving you a strong butt-whuppin'."

I closed my eyes again, hoping to escape the moment. I crawled across my bed and leaned back against the wall to breathe. I was doing all I could to fight off my anger. Amy still wasn't through, though. The anger that I was trying to diffuse had been festering in her heart for years. Her soul was evil and her mind had been washed in stupidity. She hated me yet she had never laid eyes on me. She wanted me dead and knew nothing about the way I lived.

The color of my skin was the line that separated us; a line created by the lack of common sense. Its infinite limit illustrated the enormous amount of ignorance in society. But Amy was relentless in her quest to keep white supremacy alive.

"I hate every last one of you niggas. You can all just go to hell, as far as I am concerned," she persisted.

I needed to know more about her anger, so I just let her display of hatred towards my people continue.

"Come over here and beat me some more, you black bitch. Beat me like my ancestors beat your people. Do whatever you want to me, but no matter how long you beat me, I will never be as black and disgusting as you are."

Her next statement re-ignited my rage, but I fought back my urge to stoop to her level. I grabbed both of my ankles and squeezed them as hard as I could in an effort to remain calm.

"I bet your mama is as dark as your nasty looking father. He has to be the ugliest man I've ever seen."

That made me open my eyes. I waited on God to release my body so that I could move, but her words had temporarily paralyzed me. I wanted her to feel the pain of a mother's death. I needed her to know that her mouth was uglier than my father's skin could ever be. I couldn't get to her as fast as I wanted to. I fought as hard as I could to get to my feet but by the time I stood up I was too exhausted to take a step towards her.

Listening to her degrade my parents was the second worst thing that had ever happened to me. The first was not being able to get to her. Her blue eyes were warming embers of the fire of wickedness, and the boldness in her voice was pulling at the last bit of tolerance I had left. But in the face of this kind of adversity, I was able to summon my father's words of wisdom.

"I am sorry you feel the way you do, Amy. I am also sorry that my skin color threatens you. But I won't apologize for being black. Black is what I am. It is my exterior given to me by the same God that gave you your skin color. Neither color is superior over the other."

"My color is superior," she stated with a toss of her head.

"Oh really? Have you ever taken the time to study your bible?" I asked.

"Yeah, I read it all the time. What business is that of yours?"

"My question was, have you ever *studied* it? There is a difference between studying and reading. With 'superior' status and all, you should already know that, now shouldn't you?"

"I don't need to read a book to know that I'm better than you," she replied defiantly.

"But by reading this one, you might find out that you've been lied to."

"Oh, go to hell, nigga, and leave me alone. Why don't you go back to Africa where you came from?" she spouted ignorantly.

"I've never been to Africa, Amy, and for your information, I was born here in the same America that you were born in."

"So what kind of grant are you here on? One of those that you're probably not ever going to pay back, I'm sure."

"I'm here on an academic scholarship, thank you! And judging by the way you speak, I'm sure that's not your case," I said.

"Well, you little black bitch! Let me tell you something. Most all scholarships are given away by white people."

"Well, if they weren't able to write it off on their taxes, most of them wouldn't be donating money to schools. And besides, for your information, my scholarship wasn't given to me by a white man, thank you!"

She seemed genuinely amazed.

"Well, whoever he was, he must have stolen the money and felt bad about it. So he gave it to some foundation for the poor and underprivileged; one that helps those lazy, unintelligent black kids like yourself just because they're black."

She'd found access to my emotional buttons and she was pushing every single one of them. Her soul hadn't yet acquainted itself with tact and caring. Certainly not for the feelings of a black person, which seemed to be the furthest thing from her mind. A part of me wished I had forced her back on the ground, but fighting her was wrong. Grabbing her had only confirmed her hatred towards me.

She had a hateful look on her face. Her pouty lips were sticking out emphasizing a most unattractive reflection of a prickly, redheaded blowfish. She was an angry, self-centered, southern female. She was a piece of work, and Tisha would agree.

Amy was a problem child but had finally met her match. I assumed something had happened to her early in life that robbed her of her essence. I wasn't about to give her the satisfaction of letting her steal mine. Her backwoods southern beliefs weren't going to cause me endless grief. Her backwater country tail had gotten stuck on the wrong bull this time and she was about to get the ride of her life.

I was born to overcome the greatest odds. I was a disciple of truth and placed on earth to carry a torch of victory over those who proclaimed themselves my enemies. Amy was merely the next hurdle in my life, and I was going to clear any challenges that she was bold enough to impose.

About two weeks passed since our initial encounter, but the friction was still evident. At times it was almost unbearable. Eventually I began to smell a horrible odor that had penetrated the room. At first I thought that maybe Amy had let some food spoil, but for the life of me, I couldn't find it. I thoroughly checked every square inch of our room, but to no avail. Strangely the odor seemed to come and go. Sometimes it was stronger, while at others it was almost undetectable, but no matter how faint, it was still awful.

After a few more days of puzzling and fruitless inspection, I finally narrowed it down to Amy herself. I had done some detective work too. By placing a thread across the inside of the shower door I could gather evidence to back my suspicions. Every time I opened the shower door, I knew to step over the thread to leave it intact. It was still there after almost two weeks! Amy had not taken a shower in days.

I waited for her to come back that day to make sure that my theory was correct, though. No sooner had she stepped back through the door did the odor resurface. I confronted her when I could no longer bear the odor.

"Amy, can I asked you a question? It's bit personal," I warned.

"Sure, it's a free world isn't it?" she shrugged without even looking my way.

"Is there a reason why you're not taking a shower? Is there something wrong that maybe I could help with?"

"No, there's nothing wrong, and I would never need your help, and it's none of your business anyway! Don't you think your questions are a little too personal?" she asked.

"Oh, no, Amy. Frankly, I don't think the question was personal enough considering I've had to smell your tail for the last two weeks."

"What are you talking about?" she sneered. "I don't smell anything," she added.

"Wait just a minute. Are you telling me you can't smell this odor? It's you, Amy. Can't you smell yourself?"

I resorted to placing my hand dramatically over my mouth and asked, "Amy, when was the last time you washed your ass? Of course you know that what you're doing is unsanitary for both of us."

"I don't smell that bad and besides, I refuse to use the same shower that niggas use."

Her smug expression indicated she felt as if she had some scientific data of the grooming habits of black people. No doubt she had extracted her theory from a crazy tobacco spitting redneck, or some tired old backwoods hillbilly with a degree from the School of Stupidity.

"Amy, please tell me you aren't serious. Please tell me there aren't millions out there like you. Tell me that your family is the only group of people walking this earth that feels the way you do," I pleaded. But she just sat there like I wasn't even talking.

I relied on my father's example of calmness and offered, "So, Amy, here's an idea. What if I take my shower and afterwards take some cleanser and scrub the shower from top to bottom. Will you take a shower then?"

She thought about it for a second and agreed, "Sure, I think that might work. I just don't want to catch anything you might have."

"No problem, Amy. I'll take the cleaning products in the shower with me and make sure I wash it each time."

I sounded sincere, but I had a devious plan.

That day I emptied out the cleaning products and replaced them with my own shampoo and conditioner. I set the containers on the shower floor and she didn't know the difference. Of course I cleaned the shower as needed, but not the way I had promised Amy. I knew that I was being dishonest, but the simple plan worked and the problem was solved. Amy was back to taking showers and I was back to breathing fresh air.

College life was different from home life and having Amy for a roommate did not help matters. I felt that God wanted me to try and somehow de-fool a fool, as if that was even possible. I did not have a clue as to how I was to go about it, but I was more than willing to make an impression on her.

My father taught me to lead by example. "How else can we expect to be followed?" he asked.

So I avowed to lead by example, and in everything I did, I did my best. That was at least a start.

When I studied, I studied through the night. Amy would make noises of exasperation as if my night-light bothered her, but I could tell she was actually impressed.

One day Amy answered the phone by pushing the speakerphone feature. From the bathroom I could hear her speaking to her parents.

"Amy, we received your second quarter grades today. After being placed on probation for your first quarter performance, we see there is still a problem. We're going to take you out of Cal if your grades don't improve," said Amy's mother.

"What? You can't do that! I'm doing the best I can. My classes here are very hard and there's no extra time to study. You can't take me out of school," she pleaded. "What am I going to do without an education from Cal?"

Her father's voice sounded stern, "It doesn't appear as if you're taking this opportunity for an education very seriously. Young lady, you are a disgrace to this family. You're never going to amount to anything." His words were so cruel.

Amy got quiet and the conversation became one sided.

"Are you still there, Amy?" her mother inquired.

"Yes… I'm here. Where else would I be?" she replied.

"You're going to be back here at home for good if you have another quarter like this," her father threatened.

"Okay, okay, I heard you. I'll do better, I promise."

I waited for a minute or two to come out of the bathroom after Amy hung up the phone. She was lying across her bed crying silently, trying to hide her desperation.

I approached her and gently asked, "Amy, are you all right?"

"No, stupid girl. Do I look like I'm doing all right? I'm going to have to leave school soon and you'll get your wish."

"My wish? I have never had a problem with you, Amy. You have a problem with me," I reminded her. "Now tell me, why are you crying?"

"I'm not crying… I just have real bad allergy, that's all." Amy was running just fast enough to stay ahead of me.

"Okay then. If you're going to be all right, I'm going to study. Good-night now."

I walked over to my side of the room and studied for a test I had the next day, while Amy got up to take a shower. When she came out of the bathroom she was hysterical.

"You haven't been washing out the shower, have you?" Amy screamed.

"No, I haven't and you haven't caught a thing, now have you?" I replied.

That made her think for a moment. "No, I didn't… did I?" she admitted. I noticed a faint smile for the first time.

When I woke up the next morning I caught her looking through some of my folders.

"What are you looking for?"

"I'm looking for a failing grade, a paper that you've made a bad grade on, something you had to redo, but there isn't anything of the sort." She sat on her bed and pouted. "Hey, you are really smart, aren't you?"

I raised my head and sat up in bed. "No, that's not all there is to it, Amy. I may be smart to some people, but I am also prepared."

"Now what in the hell does that mean?"

"I was taught that there are no 'smart' people, only those who are prepared."

"What? Who taught you that?"

"The man you called 'the ugliest man you've ever seen.'"

She didn't say a word.

"That man you called ugly is one of the most intelligent men alive. He has taught me many great lessons, but one of the greatest of them all was not to fight against the ocean's tides."

"What? What did he mean by that?"

"He said that fighting against the ocean's tide was like fighting against a multitude of people; as soon as you fight one wave another one comes in to take you out."

"So, what does that mean to me?" she asked

"Never take on more than you can defeat, and always identify your enemies before going to war."

"Man, your father's a smart -"

"No," I cut her off. "He's an intelligent man who never stopped turning the pages of empowerment."

"What are his pages of empowerment?"

"Anything written that edified his brain."

"Can you believe that I've never in my whole life received any honors in school?" she asked in a sudden switch.

"Yes, I can tell," I said, thinking there had to be a God in heaven. How else could I honestly explain the humbleness of my tongue? I had to admit I was wondering how she ever got into UC Berkeley in the first place.

"Do you think that maybe I can learn some of the wisdom that you have acquired over the years?" she asked.

"Do you feel that someone my color can teach you?"

The room grew quiet as any answer evaded her. She had to think way too long so I answered for her, "Well, truthfully, Amy, I don't… at least not until you can answer my question.

"When the color of my skin has been exonerated of all forms of negativity, and you have learned to view me as a person rather than a thing, I will help you. When you are able to call me by the name my parents gave me, instead of 'nigga,' I will help you. When you are able to sit down beside me, and expel all forms of racial ignorance, and replace them with empathy instead of emptiness towards my people, I will help you. I will never toil in your academic recovery, until I am sure you are sure of all these things.

"But really, why should I help you of all people, Amy?"

She looked at me with sudden awareness and shame. She grabbed both of my hands and begged, "Please forgive me for the wrong I've done. Knowing you has opened my eyes and shined a light on my dark world. I was taught from birth that colored people stink and that you were all like animals. But since I've known you I've learned what I've been told was a bunch of lies."

"If I agree to help you pass your classes…"

"I will study instead of read, I will research before coming to thoughtless conclusions," Amy blurted out.

"I can see you have something that heals people like me, and besides, your soul isn't angry like mine," she admitted.

"How do you know this?" I asked with interest.

"Because I said horrible things about those that you love, and I lived to talk about it, that's why."

I guess the redhead had a point. She had stepped over the line one too many times and gotten away with it. While crying outwardly for the first time, she presented herself as a human. She was apologizing from the only place that ever mattered to me… her heart.

Her negative, hateful statements were mortifying and so wrong, but I had been handed a chance to renew a broken heart and unveil a shining jewel that had been buried since birth.

What would I have gained by continuing to beat a woman down? Her butt was already scraping the ground. I didn't really ask God for much, but I felt that He might shine a light of gratitude upon my life for this one.

I had learned through the years that a humble man is apt to comprehend life better than a fiery one. My father once told me, "When a man is at war, and about to fall off the cliff, his preference of savior will become broader and he will reach for his, whose hand is near."

Amy was teetering on the edge of a cliff, and though she hated who I was, the fact remained; no matter how black it was, my hand was the only hand available. So she did what any falling warrior would have done. She placed her personal views aside, and saw past my exterior long enough to allow her fear of the unknown to be infiltrated.

She released her grip on 'white power' long enough to grab hold of the truth. No, not the truth of 'black power,' but the power of Divine Intervention.

She had been powerless with hatred and her newfound humbleness provided her a place of refuge. I became her liberator, and my smooth chocolate hands became her hands of hope. Although her mind was filled with blackness, she was willing to wave a white flag, and surrender to her distress.

Over the next few months Amy and I studied together day and night. There were times when she wanted to sleep when there was still work to do. I would shake her tired body awake in order to break her lazy spirit.

"What keeps you going like this?" she asked. "How can you read one book after another and not get tired?"

I pondered the question, as I had never before given it a thought. By way of explanation I told a short story.

"My father handed me my first book when I was one and a half years old. He gave me books before he gave me my toys. Before I could play, I had to stare at the pages. I loved looking at the pictures, but sometimes I got tired of him placing books in my face when I wanted so desperately to play. I did what I had to after a while. I started reading the book, so that I could play. The books never stopped coming and before I knew it, I was reaching for the books instead of my toys."

"Your father is some kind of man."

"Yes he is," I agreed wistfully. "I love him dearly for being not just a man, but for being my rock."

Amy listened intensely as she lay across my bed for the first time.

"Tell me about your mother," she said, but I remembered the mean things Amy had said about her, so I was reluctant.

I felt like lashing out, but I held my tongue. My mother was my heart and the fact that hers was no longer able to beat; it suddenly depressed me more deeply than ever before. I tried to remember the last kiss she had given me and was able to visualize the tender, cherished moment. I mentally placed the kiss upon Amy's face, and was able to open up.

"My mother died several years ago," I said.

Amy paled as the impact of her prior cruel remarks hit her squarely in the face. She tried to apologize for the mean things she had said.

"I didn't know, Claudia. I promise, I didn't know. I'm so sorry."

"Whether you knew or not, it really doesn't matter," I said, not quite willing to believe the sudden apology. But I wanted to talk about my mother at that point so I continued.

"My mother, for your information, was a high-yellow woman with white features. Her skin was just a shade darker than yours."

I could see a quizzical expression develop on her face.

"Yes, Amy, that's right. My grandfather was a white man who loved himself a black woman. My hair came from my grandfather's side of the family, that's why it looks this way. Though my skin is dark, I'm still, to some extent, both black and white. Look closely at our noses and notice how similar in shape they are."

She actually leaned forward to examine my nose. I rolled my eyes.

"Can you ever forgive me?" Amy pleaded.

"Sure, Amy, and so does my mother. She never held a grudge and she never saw a person who she couldn't find some good in. I guess you can say that I somehow adopted her spirit."

"Tell me, Claudia. How did she die?"

"How she died is irrelevant. How she lived is what really matters. She was imperfect and she knew it, but she took her strengths and she stretched them to their fullest. She never hated God for her being born both black and white, instead she cherished being biracial as a gift. She never once denounced either side of her racial background."

Surprisingly, Amy started touching my face, stroking gently with the outside of her hand. She was crying sincere tears of apology.

"I've never seen this shade of white before," she said. "It's more beautiful than mine could ever be."

I closed my eyes as we both lay across my bed in our pj's. We stared into each other's eyes in amazement as our souls began to bond.

How did He know to bring us together? How did He know that we both needed each other? Was this the intersection of truth for both of us? We were standing at the crossroads of life together.

I couldn't help but wonder how critical Amy's presence would be in my continuing emotional growth. Perhaps without each other we would not have ever grown at all?

They say standing at a crossroads is the moment of truth. If our time together offered moments of truth, then the essence of our compassion shall endure forever. Together we buried our fears as we resurrected our hopes.

My father once gave me a speech on intestinal fortitude that was ringing in my ears just then, like the warning signal of a fast approaching train. He said that emotional awareness separates the weak from the strong. It is the staying power of promise that is the ultimate factor, which can determine whether we win or lose.

Amy did it. She won. We stayed roommates for the rest of our freshman year, and she passed every single one of her classes that last quarter with flying colors. For the first time in her short life she made the Dean's List. But after her parents found out that she had befriended a black person, they disowned her and she was forced to apply for grants and loans in order to stay in school. Just before she had all but given up, she received a grant large enough to finish the rest of her college education. Ironically, the grant came through the NAACP.

The Fraternity of the Flesh

All of my female acquaintances either had already had sex or at least been felt on several times, long before I had been kissed twice. There I was, Miss Goody-Two-Shoes, prancing around campus dressed like a boy, wearing floppy scarves and hiding myself under great big T-shirts and baggy jeans. Most of the time, I'd spend my evenings studying, preparing assignments and writing papers. I rarely had to cram for exams.

Like many college students, I was able to manage with only a few hours of sleep. After waking to my alarm, I had just enough time to throw on a pair of loose-fitting sweats or jeans, grab a piece of toast, gulp down a glass of orange juice, and rush off to my first class.

The jocks on campus pegged me as hard-to-get and believe me, I didn't mind. I saw it as a form of respect and was honored by their sentiments. But there were a few young ladies on campus whose monikers weren't so pleasant.

Felicia 'Suction-Cup' Wilson, for instance, apparently earned her name. But she was too ignorant to see having a pet name like that wasn't cool. She was a beautiful sister with a tight body, but unfortunately she did not have a mind to match. Felicia was around five two and wore really cute clothes every day. Her skin was a smooth, flawless almond color, and she wore her hair cut short, feathered close to her head and tapered neatly around the edges. Her personality was suspect at times, but she did have a lovely smile. She was blessed with a set of teeth that could have been shown on toothpaste commercials, but what she was willing to put in her mouth earned her the unfortunate nickname, 'Suction-Cup.'

The campus whore was Veda 'Stick-it' Dickson, or VD for short. She was as nasty and freaky as they came. She was a walking cesspool and was easier to get than a Clippers ticket. No one ever knew her major, and no one really cared. No one had ever even seen her attending class. Veda was always flirting with someone else's man, which often put her on the verge of receiving a beat-down.

Veda was small enough to squeeze through cracks of window openings to unlock a car door. She wasn't bigger than a minute, but she was quick to poke her skinny neck in harm's way for a shot at getting some stray dick. She was rather hard on the eyes, but had a great body to enhance her easy reputation. Some of the guys even called her 'Butter,' which meant that everything looked good on her, *but* her face.

Veda wore her hair up in a bun sometimes. Rumor had it that was only on the days when the top of her head wasn't sore from banging against a headboard. She knew dick better than Sommore (a.k.a. Cookie, a.k.a. Queen of Comedy) knew dick. When she wasn't eating up sex, she ate food. The saddest part was that she looked like she hadn't eaten in days.

Veda had an apparent disregard for her own life, for she allowed her body to be the designated dumping ground for hormonal collegiate waste. The brothers passed her around as if she was a party favor, but she didn't care. She just wanted to lie on her back so she could say, 'VD was here.'

I didn't want my first time 'doing it' to be with a stranger. It was important to me that whoever I slept with at least cared about me. In both Felicia's and Veda's cases it didn't seem to matter.

I discovered all I needed was an interesting conversation and mental simulation to whet my sexual appetite. But the brothers were having none of it. Most of them were away from home for the first time and were not trying to hear, 'slow down.' They couldn't care less about having a conversation, let alone an interesting one. Their hormones were racing and they knew there was a sister around the corner or up the street, who was prepared to lay down and open her legs at the first sound of 'hello, girl.'

Why would anyone want to get to know me, I often wondered. I wasn't easy and I surely wasn't fast. I was a social, sexual outcast. Getting to know me meant you had to mind your P's and Q's. Dinner, a movie, lunch, or even brunch would have been a good start. But any of that meant spending the two things that most of the brothers on campus didn't have: money and time.

I knew early on that I wasn't their first option, and I was not about to settle either. There were those who tried to date me, but when I realized that their definition of having a good time was just a prelude to getting between my legs, all the lights of innocent flirtation were turned off and the party was over.

Unlike many of the other young ladies on campus, it was easy for me to resist the brothers' advancements. After all, I was a sista who was going places and I didn't need anyone to validate who I was. It wasn't hard to pick up and move on. I never allowed my future to be caught up in the moment. So if things ever got out of hand, I just grabbed my car keys, threw my purse over my shoulder and left the scene of the potential crime.

I would have loved to have a special someone to share those exciting college years with, but I held fast to my convictions, and refused to be desperate. I knew how to entertain myself, how to run out and grab a movie or lunch on my own. It was enjoyable for me to pick up a book and read through the night. My social life was gloomy, non-existent in fact. At least I was intelligent enough to know not to play Russian roulette with my life just to say that I had a good time.

I was on top of the world, and at age twenty-one I was ready for my senior year of college. I was basking in the light of my accomplishments and living life to its fullest, with only one kiss to speak of under my belt.

Of course I wasn't the typical female student. My hair wasn't full of pastelle colors, my body didn't have multiple piercings, and I didn't worry about fashion. I was still driven by my beliefs.

I was a 'total square' as the sistas put it, but occasionally I would set my studies aside and attend a fraternity party or two. Frat parties were plentiful during football season, but I wasn't really into sports anymore, and being around crowds of people was never really was my thing.

My friends told me I was boring. I agreed I was a little dull at times, but I didn't care. What I did care about was being successful in life. When the time came for me to celebrate, I knew I would be more than ready. I was aware of my surroundings but I was more aware of my goals. Being withdrawn from the scene was a personal choice. Dating and having fun had its place but I had to remain focused.

CHOCOLATE

Eventually there was a guy on campus who did pique my curiosity. However, not even he could lure me away from my studies. But I followed his progress at Cal, and knew he was accumulating great stats his senior year.

His name was Raymond Clemmons, a better than average-looking brother with an enticing smile and a gorgeous set of teeth. He was too cute for his own good. Raymond had to have been at least six-foot-five, because even when I wore heels he was still several inches taller than I was. He was the most popular athlete on campus: a three-time All-American basketball player with a possible future in the pros.

He wore a ball-fade that was always perfectly groomed. There was never a hair out of place or a line out of sync. He wore his jeans like no one else, and that brother knew how to walk. Always moving around like a proud peacock. Raymond Clemmons was a ladies' man... a real looker. His skin was a deep brown, passionate, smooth, come-and-touch-me color that left an impression with onlookers. I found I was no exception.

I was too nervous to say hello to him at first, but he might have known that I had a thing for him. I settled for admiring the brother from afar, but I didn't feel I would ever be his type. He always seemed to be checking out someone who was mentally incapacitated. The majority of the sistas I saw hanging on his arm also seemed to be suffering from a lack of moral awareness. I didn't want to be mentioned in the same breath with those bimbos, so I stayed where I was.

Even though I saw him as any other young lady with better than average eyesight did, I knew the distant view was much safer. I'd rather run home and take a shower than to publicly degrade myself. But I wished that he would at least try to get with me once, so that I could turn the brother down.

I was told he was a business major, and I took offense, being that I was one myself. I heard he couldn't mind his own business long enough to manage his own affairs. He was going to need a major attitude adjustment just to handle his major. I never saw him with a book in his hands the whole three years I had been there. Many women ran after him without caring if there was a notebook or pen in sight.

Raymond used his good looks to hide any inadequacies and he paraded around campus like he owned it. Originally, Raymond was from Washington D.C., and he was proud of it. There wasn't a time I saw him that he wasn't telling whoever would listen about the 'Chocolate City.'

He had a more than intriguing up side, but with it came his downside… and man, was it a slippery slope.

The Fraternity Party

There was an annual spring 'seniors only' fraternity party a few of my friends were planning to attend, and I had been invited to come along. I didn't want to go at first but it was the end of another year, the end of my college experience, and besides, I wanted to see Raymond in one of his famous elements: the party scene.

He was tall, dark and handsome, just my type, so I took the sistas up on their invitation. I never disclosed my preferences, and no one ever knew I was digging him.

I needed to get new shoes to go with a nice blue outfit I bought a few weeks prior to the party. I braved the Bay Bridge to shop in The City.

Friday afternoon on Powell and Geary Streets proved to be a poor choice for last minute shopping. It turned out there was a Warriors playoff game that night, and traffic, not to mention parking, was a nightmare. Every street and all the stores were overcrowded, but I needed those shoes. I raced from Macy's to Saks to boutiques like I was O.J. Simpson running through airports.

When I finally did find the pair I was looking for, I noticed an attractive Italian man staring in my direction. He must have been in his mid-thirties. I couldn't quite tell.

After the shop cleared a bit, it became more and more obvious that the person he had his eye on was indeed me.

I braced myself just before he spoke to me.

"Excuse me, Miss, please. I'm sure you get asked this all the time, but I'm going to ask you again. Are you a model?"

I knew I was harried and looking a mess in my sweats, and he had the nerve to ask me such a crazy question. I was irritated but did respond.

"No, I'm not a model, but thank you for the compliment," I replied modestly.

At that moment the clerk announced that the shop would be closing in fifteen minutes. I had my purchase and somewhere to be that evening, so I tried to leave, making it clear that I was in a hurry.

He was persistent and the questions started flying. I bit my tongue to keep from cussing at him. I did not want to embarrass either of us, so I moved towards the door trying hard to avoid him.

"How do you keep your skin looking so soft and clear?" How did he get so personal so fast? I looked at him and shook my head from side to side.

I took just a moment to say, "Look, Mister, what's your angle?"

He smiled and handed me his business card.

"I work for a reputable modeling agency here in San Francisco. If you are ever interested in some work, just give me a call."

I was taken aback.

"You haven't even asked me my name," I said shyly. "How are you going to remember me?" I asked.

"My name is Vince, and believe me, Miss… I will remember you, don't worry. Just call me."

There was something about his eyes; something dangerously alluring that drew me in. He never took them off of mine while we talked. I noticed he wore a beautiful black Italian merino wool sweater and a gorgeous smile. He was clean-shaven and wore his black curly hair cut short and neat. So smooth.

I had never thought of myself as a model but who knew what my future entailed?

I made my way back over to Berkeley, after much silent speculation in the car. Back at my apartment, I placed Vince's card on the refrigerator door.

I had about two hours to get ready before the girls would be back for me and we'd set out for the night. I set out my clothes and ran my bath water. I wanted to relax and have a glass of wine before I left for the party. By the time my girls got there I felt I was dressed and ready to impress. It had been a while since I had hung out with them, and I was about to come to grips with just how long that had been.

Tina and Mia, two sistas I had met early in our junior year, were lots of fun to hang out with. When we did get together we had a ball. We always waited until late so that we could make our grand entrance.

When they knocked on my door that night, I grabbed my purse ready to go. "I told you I was going to be ready, but you two didn't believe me."

They stopped dead in their tracks and stared open-mouthed. Together they said, "Oh, no you NOT."

"No I'm not what?" I asked innocently enough.

"You are not going to go anywhere with that mess on. What are you thinking? What are you trying to do, make everybody around you over heat?" Tina said sarcastically.

There I was, thinking that I was looking like a brand new nickel, while they made me feel like an old tarnished penny. I really thought I was looking good until Mia busted my bubble.

"Girl, you are one of the prettiest sistas on campus, but nobody ever notices you. You're always covered up with a sweater like that, and wearing those clunky glasses on the end of your nose. Don't you have some contacts or something?" Mia asked.

"Claudia, this doesn't make any sense," Tina agreed. "Why are you wearing this dowdy outfit? You've been hiding your figure much too long, but we know what you've got. I try to tell people that you are one of the most attractive sistas at school, but…"

"Girl, you don't have to tell me that. I'm already your friend," I said with a smile.

"For real, girl," she acknowledged. "But we're going to show them something tonight. Even if we have to get there just as the party's over," Tina said.

They both walked into my apartment and Mia took me by the hand. "Now come on, girl. Take us to your closet and let's make their eyes pop out of their heads. Let's… put it on them."

They weren't loose like a lot of the others sistas on campus, so I felt it was okay to take their advice. But I also felt that I had to proceed with caution. I agreed to go with it.

"Okay, my sistas, but let's not overdo it. It's been a while since I've been out and I don't want to send the wrong signals," I said.

"We know who you are, Claudia. But damn, girl… if I see another book in your hand before I see you with a man, I will know the world is coming to an end," Mia said.

"Yeah… it's a little too late in the evening to worry about all of that. Besides, we're your girls and we wouldn't let anything happen to you. You know that, so loosen up and let's live a little."

I felt like an alien.

"What's that you got on anyway? Is it a sweater or a small blue bear? Don't you know it's almost summertime? And here you are wearing a whole bear. Come on, girl, you're going to make them turn on the air-conditioner. I mean, you are making me hot just looking at you."

They led me into my bedroom.

"Come on now. Let's get this party started."

They both decided that the pants I was wearing were fine, but that the oversized blue chenille turtleneck sweater had to go.

"Claudia, is there anything in this closet you feel is just a little too tight for you?" Tina asked.

"Yes, I have a few things in here that are too small."

"Okay. That's where we'll start. Now if you've got *a lot* of things, our search will be easier."

I was okay with all of the shots they were taking. I really didn't care one way or the other how they felt about the way I dressed. But if this was going to get them off of my back... then so be it. I would play along.

I opened up my closet and reached for a red blouse I had bought last year. It seemed to show every calorie I consumed, and I thought I looked like a stripper when I wore it. I never knew why I bought it in the first place, but it was the first thing that came to mind on this occasion.

As I pulled it out, Mia said, "Girl, you did not have *my* blouse hanging up in your closet."

"No, this is not yours," I replied at my most gullible. "I've had this for over a year," I said.

Mia looked at me as if I was completely hopeless.

"Claudia, girl, I was just playing with you. But I do have a green one at home just like it, that I wear as often as I can."

"Oh, yeah." I almost got it.

"Yes, that's right. If I could, I would wear it everyday. The brothers like it, and so do some women. There. I'm not ashamed to say it; I get the eye from some sistas. So you know that I have to be careful where I wear it, cause you know I'm strictly-dickly."

Mia always said some of the strangest things, but you had to love her for her organic ways. She really spoke her mind, and she was always keeping it real.

She was the funniest person I knew and I wasn't about to let her waste her talent. So when she was around, I treated her as if she was a world-renowned comedian, turned her on high and got my laugh on.

Mia had missed her calling, but she never missed her cue. She had a knack for knowing when to bear down on you, and tonight she was in rare form. Without an invitation she poured herself a glass of wine. Everyone knew that after she started drinking she was bound to say almost anything.

"Girl, if you know like I do, you'd put that blouse on and start to stepping, cause ain't nothing better than being an eye-popper."

"An eye-popper? What in the hell is that?" Tina asked.

"Well, have you ever seen the eyes of a man who has just seen the woman of his dreams?" she asked.

Tina replied, "No, I haven't."

"And I haven't either… that's because I wasn't talking to you, Tina, I was talking to Claudia. This is an A and B conversation and I wish that you would politely C your way out of it."

I was feeling good after having a few glasses of wine myself, and I agreed to put the blouse on. I saw that they were right. It did fit me well. It was time for me to step outside my comfort zone. I needed to let my hair down, so to speak.

I walked into the bathroom to seal the deal. I stood in front of the mirror, staring at Marvin L. Williams' only daughter, as she stared back at me. I lifted my chin and pushed in my stomach with both of my hands on my waist. I was feeling something I had never felt before, smiling a smile I thought would never grace my face. But much to my surprise… there it was. Sexy outer confidence.

There was a knock on the bathroom door.

"Girl! Brang your tail out of there, and let's go party!"

As I reached to open the door that separated the present me from the person I was about to become, a part of the old me fell to the floor. I gingerly stepped into a world that had never known Chocolate… but was about to meet her for the first time.

When I opened the bathroom door, Tina and Mia went crazy. "Who in the hell is that?" Mia asked as she glanced over at Tina.

Tina jokingly replied, "Girl, I don't know who that is, but I'm glad I've got my man pecking like a hen already, or I'd be in serious trouble."

"Okay, Claudia. We now know that you can get cute, so those glasses have got to vacate your face," and she grabbed my glasses off my face. "Now go and get your contacts before you run into a wall or something."

I was a step ahead of them. "Oh, I've got my contacts on, thank you."

"Can't nothing stop this train but the tracks, and they've all been bolted down, so let's get moving," said Mia. We all gave each other a high five and reached for our purses.

I hadn't felt that cute since I was eight years old, when my mother made a beautiful blue dress for me at Easter. Or was it the last time Sweets and I did our little thing at the skating rink? It really didn't matter. What did matter was right now, and boy was I feeling right.

Tina and Mia were also very pretty girls. They were both lighter than me, but I was in love with my chocolate skin. I was convinced, that if nothing else, I had an inner beauty that could surpass the prettiest of them all.

Tina was about five-four and had a walk that the brothers called magical. She was average in color and had a set of eyes that ignited a man's libido. She didn't wear makeup, and didn't need to. Her enormously bubbly personality shaped her character. Her skin was unblemished and its warm-butter color was soothing to the eyes, so the brothers said. She had a nice shape and wore name-brand clothes, or she wore nothing at all. I loved being around her because she knew when to say no.

Mia could also be considered naturally beautiful. She was just a hair taller than Tina and had a striking body. She had a beautiful grade of hair and was not afraid to alter it on a whim. I could tell brothers on campus loved watching her.

Mia was always so cheerful, so outgoing and so full of life. She was a journalism major who was born to make people laugh. Everyone knew not to mess with her, as she was verbally gifted and could out-cuss anyone. We all loved her because she stood up for her rights; she was not afraid to fight for whatever she believed in. We all loved her because she wasn't afraid to love herself. With her around we knew if we did nothing else, we knew we were going to laugh.

But there was one drawback - she had very little to mention. She was a sister with no behind, and she was mad at God for not giving her one. She felt she had a right to have a butt, because as she put it, 'the white man had taken everything else.' I never thought her butt was too small, but being around Tina everyday had to give her a complex.

So there you have it. My girl Tina had a body that had the guys going crazy, and Mia had everything but a butt.

When we got to the party, it was rocking. The music was loud and the stage was set for our more than fashionably late entrance. Mia went in the frat house first and then Tina. I was not in any hurry. In fact, I was feeling a little nervous, but arriving late suited my style.

As my eyes adjusted to the dark room, I noticed that all other eyes were on me. It felt good and strange at the same time. I craved the attention, yet I wanted to run.

That didn't last too long, though. My emotions were like a bucking horse for the first five minutes but after a couple more minutes of intense interest on the brothers' parts, I was feeling good about Claudia Williams. Let me stop lying. The wildness of the bucking horse had been tamed, I was caught up in myself, and loving it. I took it all in and felt worthy of all the attention that was bestowed upon me.

We made our way to the kitchen area and poured ourselves a drink. A brother named Darien, who I had seen many times on campus, came over to us and spoke to Mia.

"Hey, who's your friend? Ain't someone gonna introduce a brother to this fine sista?"

Tina looked at him and said, "Hell, you pass by her everyday in the student center on campus, and you have never spoken to her."

He was drawing a blank.

"Nigga, you must be blind. Please tell me that you're playing. You've got to know who that is. I mean, how can you not know? You practically gave her a nickname."

"Gave her a nickname... I gave her a nickname?" His brain was in reverse at a mile a minute.

"Not me, girl. You've got your people mixed up. I've never seen her before in my life."

Mia called me over to help him recollect.

"Hey, Books! Come over here."

Books! I knew that nickname. A nameless, no-brain fool and his brothers, who were only in college because they could play sports, had called me that a few times around campus. I recalled hearing it as I walked across the quad to my Business Administration class usually on Tuesdays, but it was always harmless. I had never even bothered to identify the individual who started it.

As I was hailed by Darien's pet name for me, I could see disbelief oozing from the corners of his mouth. I had never seen a black man turn so pale. He was feeling low about his decision to mock me for seeking a higher education. Right then he knew his insults hadn't shown his brightest moments.

I could see that's what a fool looks like when he's caught red-handed. I walked over and held out my hand to shake his. He slowly gained enough composure to close his big mouth.

"Hi there, I bet right now you wish you were a librarian, don't you?"

He still didn't get it. Despite what was already a seemingly embarrassing moment, the fool in him was still alive. He had yet one more ignorant statement, and showed his true color - and pale was far from it.

"No. Hell no. That ain't Books!" He was stunned.

I knew that I could always count on Mia to handle things like this. It was her birthright, and she was forever ready to P-A-N-I-H-P (put a nigga in his place).

"Look, black man. Her name ain't Books! And that's that. Now why don't just go down to the library and read one on ethics, and while you're at it, grab yourself a twelve-pack of mints, 'cause that shit that's coming out of your mouth has created a disgusting o-deer up here." Her quick tongue took him aback.

"Don't look at me like you never knew you need a Tic-Tac! Boy, it smells like someone just busted you in the mouth with a wet cow patty. Now go on… get away from her before you get booked by the police for eating ass."

Mia was so wrong just then, but she was as funny as they came. All Darien could do was take it. He knew Mia had exceptional skills and he didn't stand a chance. So he did what everyone else was doing at the time… he laughed at himself.

I walked closer to Darien to formally introduce myself.

"Hello there, Darien. My name is Claudia and it's nice to finally meet you."

"So, you don't say… well… all right then," he stuttered.

"Books is it? I mean, uh, Claudia? I hope that you girls enjoy yourselves," he said and walked away.

Mia yelled out, "Hey Darien! No bad feelings right?"

He didn't look back but she continued, "Don't forget - if you ever get some time, take a few minutes out of your day and read one, or two, or three."

That made me cringe.

"Come on now, Mia. That's enough. He gets the message. I thought you were a little hard on him."

"No, not at all. What he needs is a mouthwash, but only after his ass chews on a bar of soap. Claudia, it's okay to bear down on a fool, 'cause in most cases he just reaps what he's sown anyhow."

I took her advice with a grain of salt.

It didn't take long before I saw Raymond Clemmons, the real reason I agreed to come to the party. I had been scanning the dance floor where I noticed both Felicia and Veda making their moves. When I finally laid eyes on Raymond he was out on the floor too, dancing with a full-fledged hood-rat. He was out there with his fine self, dancing his tail off. My eyes rolled back as I wistfully caressed his strong arms from across the room.

Mia was so nosey she couldn't hold water, not even if she was a swimming pool. She was the last person you wanted to tell a secret to, but for some reason she was always the first to know. While I was admiring Raymond's arms from afar, she must have been watching me. Before I could blink she was in my ear with her latest discovery.

"Now child, that's a hound-dog that ain't worth hunting. Don't believe all of those stories about the hands and the feet. I don't know where all of that came from, but believe me, in his case that shit ain't true. He is the worst kind of dog in the world... a dog without a sense of loyalty."

I listened to her. My Daddy had told me about those kinds of dogs. He said as soon as I was able to hold my head up, never look down at one or it was going to bite me.

"...And if you don't believe me, look at my ass," Mia continued to prove her assessment of Raymond was true.

"I had more ass than this before I met him, now look at me. He's a dog without compassion, the kind that digs a hole underneath the next-door neighbor's fence and eats wherever he can. Believe me when I tell you, Claudia, that this world would be a better place if they would have just put him out of his misery at birth."

Something bad had obviously happened between the two of them. I didn't know what I had been feeling for him, but after Mia's tirade, the notion of being touched by him was gone forever. I might have been out of my element but I was still clothed in my right mind. Raymond was fine as hell but he was not break-my-heart fine. No one was.

Shortly after Mia deflated my craving for Mr. Clemmons, we went back to the kitchen for another drink. The pain in her voice was vivid enough for us to take leave of the dance scene. Within no time Raymond Clemmons appeared in the kitchen to check things out.

I finally found myself face to face with what I had thought was a heartthrob. He was even better looking up close, but now I was seeing him in a whole new light. Though I had seen him what seemed like a million times around campus, we had never talked to each other. But this time he finally spoke.

"Hello, pretty ladies," was all he had to say. Unfortunately for him, anything he might say would bring Mia's dog theory to the surface.

She immediately started firing her famous verbal flames.

"Black man, how do you know what a lady is? You've never had the pleasure of coming out of one." Even I was confused, but I knew it was a low blow.

I almost felt badly for him until he started in on her.

"Bitch, take your no-ass-having tail to see the wizard. I heard that he has a ass on hold just for you."

By that time the whole kitchen had grown quiet enough to hear a church mouse tapping on the ceiling. Mia had been on a roll all night and, since she was my girl, I had to believe that she definitely had one more in her. Raymond had a following too, and I could tell that this round wasn't going to be the piece of cake that the first one was. This time Mia was going to have to bring out the heavy artillery.

There were times when I saw her down, but I never saw her out. Mia needed a big one, and after loading up with a swig off her drink she went for the jugular. My original estimate of six-five was accurate and I could see Raymond was built like Mount Everest, but Mia's next blow damaged his ego and sent his reputation into shambles like an avalanche on K-2.

"Oh, so you gonna try and clown a sista now, right? Well, okay. Since we're both in need of the seeing the wizard, why don't we both share the cab fair, shorty. And you know what I mean by that," she tried to spell it out for her audience. "You see, I hear the wizard's got at least one spare dick lying around that you can at least see. Because the last time I tried to see yours, it looked about as small as your baby teeth."

That comment sparked mayhem in the kitchen. Random people were literally rolling on the floor or running over to Mia giving her high-fives.

Veda and Felicia had joined the kitchen crowd by then. They smiled at each other and nodded knowingly. I looked around at the sea of unfamiliar faces, and I caught a glimpse of two hecklers who were spouting nonsense reminiscent of Russell Madison and Bobby Thomas from junior high.

It was painful to watch a man who stood so tall, fall so fast. But I must admit, I had no problem enduring it. From what I could tell her verbal barrage was just, but I hated that he had to learn from the way she dished it out. I was convinced, after hearing those two carry on, that saving myself for Mr. Right was still the right choice.

Raymond was humiliated in the worst way. The size of his private property had been exposed and the lack of its development over the years had been tallied up and put on display. Even though he was a few inches smaller than many thought he'd be, he was still determined to hang on to the last bit of pride he could muster. Even though he was indeed down for the count, in his own demented way he was certainly not out.

As Mia continued to accept congratulations for slaying the biggest bull in the arena, Raymond had to swing one last time.

"Oh, now that was cold, girl. Why you want to clown a brother like that?"

Mia had gotten the better of him, so he did what he knew best. He walked over to her and pushed her in the face with the palm of his hand as if he was handling a basketball. He barely had time to pull his hand back before a couple of brothers grabbed him and escorted him to the door.

Mia, a woman who prided herself on never being outdone, was not about to take that shove lying down. In fact, she had the nerve to following the escort posse outside. She never stopped talking a gang of stuff.

That was until Raymond broke loose and ran back towards her. He was obviously still pissed off about the short dick jokes. He ran as fast as he could, but only made it to the front door. Luckily for everyone involved, one of the escorts Raymond slipped away from caught him on the porch and took him down to the floor.

Mia was mad but she wasn't mad enough to strike out here. And she was no fool. She ran like her soul was on fire. She looked like Florence Griffith Joyner winning a gold medal at the Olympics. In the three years I had known Mia, I never saw her move so fast. Her knees were up and her arms were pumping like a machine. She wanted no part of the ass-whuppin' Raymond wanted to deliver. She moved too damn fast to realize that she could have quit running a block sooner. By the time she stopped she had gone through the frat house, out the back door and halfway down her second block.

It was not really funny, but we couldn't stop laughing. By the time she had caught her breath and made it back to the house, Tina and I were sitting on the porch still fighting back laughter.

"I know you two aren't laughing at me," she dared. "Why didn't you come looking for me?" she wondered feeling a dash of betrayal.

When we went to breakfast later that night we were still laughing and carrying on. Mia had heard her share of it and did not think it was right for us to continue laughing along with everyone else. But we knew if it had been me or Tina running down the street, we'd have to peel what little butt Mia did have off of the floor. She'd be laughing more than anyone.

"To be honest with you, girl, we just stopped laughing a second before you got back to the frat house," I explained at breakfast.

"That had to have been the funniest damn thing I have ever seen in my life. Mia, you are my girl. But I have told you about cracking jokes on people two and three times larger than yourself. You had already embarrassed the man enough when you had to go and follow him down the hallway."

"I wasn't just going to let him push me in my face and get away with it," Mia said defensively.

"Yeah, we saw you. You really showed him. Girl, I bet you he ain't never gonna ever mess with you again after that beating you put on him."

"That ain't funny, I was running for my life," she said.

"No, Raymond pushing you in your face wasn't funny. But all that running you did, Mia, come on now. That was classic. And I'm taking that moment to heaven with me," I said with admiration.

"I never knew you could move like that, girl," said Tina. You could be late to nothing ever again. Child, you've got some Flo-Jo in you. When I saw you moving like that I felt special," Tina said.

"Why did me running for *my* life make *you* feel special?" Mia asked.

"I felt special because of all of the fame you're going to get. Just think, all this time I thought that you were lazy, but now I know that I was wrong about you. You're a Flo-Jo stunt double."

After all that I was still glad I went to the party that night. It gave me a chance to see Raymond for who he really was. I hadn't known that Mia and him had a thing for each other, but after seeing his true colors it was all a moot point. Besides, the second I found out about him and Mia dating sufficed as a deterrent from ever having any romantic dealings with him. Raymond was definitely out of my system.

No woman should be exposed to any degree of public humiliation, or barrage of degrading remarks, or other personal insults and verbal abuse. That type of treatment is wrong in every sense of the word. It's a real no-no, a definite hell-no. Period. I didn't know who Raymond's next victim would be, but it wouldn't be Tina, or Mia, and it certainly wouldn't be me.

In spite of the potential for bodily harm and emotional trauma, I had not laughed that much in years. It was great hanging out with the sistas for a change. It gave me a chance to go through my closet and let down my hair at least.

If ever my father were to find out about that night, and the poor treatment we received from a brother, he would have something to say right on the spot. He would have been disappointed that we had put up with it for as long as we did, but he would be proud that I walked away.

By the time I got home the sun was coming up, but I was too tired to do anything but sleep for the rest of the day. I did, however, take the business card I received during my shoe shopping expedition off the refrigerator, and place it next to the phone near my bed. I pinned my hair back up, and brushed my teeth. My soul embraced slumber as soon as my head touched the pillow.

Reinventing Myself

I had slept over twenty-four hours and when I woke up early the next day I felt different. It was as if my life had undergone an emotional metamorphosis. I was excited to get to know the person I could become. I had thrived on the attention I received at the frat party; it had felt great to be noticed. The thought of a man's hand reaching for a touch of my skin excited me.

Could I be the next cover model? Did I have what it took to be a diva? Could I be divinely enticing? Who knew? I pranced around my apartment with an attitude about myself that could have brought a whole new meaning to the word arrogant. Just swapping facial expressions at the drop of a hat, like I was somebody, made me look at myself as a new person. I did little turns like I had seen models do on the runway. I was feeling good about being me, and I was bringing it.

I even imagined myself receiving my 'model of the year' award. I was at the gala accompanied by the greatest companion in my life, my father, who was seated in the front row of course.

"Ladies and Gentlemen," the emcee began, "the winner of the 'model of the year' goes to… who else? None other than the diva herself, Miss Claudia Williams." I imagined the applause from the adoring crowd.

The evening wouldn't have been complete without my award-winning acceptance speech. I stood in front of what seemed like millions of fans, just giving them what they came for. Imaginary microphone in hand, in the form of a mixing spoon, I addressed them as I stood half naked in my bathroom. With plenty of attitude, ugly as it was, I was too cute to stop the madness.

"Well, I'm deeply honored to be receiving such a prestigious award. First of all, I would like to thank all the little people. Come on… let's face it. Without anyone to walk on, there wouldn't be a stage. Daddy, wherever you are, could you please come up here and get this award, because it's getting a little too heavy. Well, I guess that's it…"

I paused and batted my eyes and put my lips into a baby's pout.

"Oh yes, to all of the other contestants, do try hard to get some companionship, because I hear that it gets very lonely down there on the bottom. God bless you all, and good-night." I blew a few kisses into the mirror.

It was funny carrying on like that, and I wondered where the ridiculous sentiments had come from.

By the time I was finished with my early morning reverie, I had tried on several dresses and only God knows how many pairs of shoes. Was I really good enough to be a model? Well, there would only be one way to find out.

After giving my never to be infamous speech I stared at the mystery man's business card on my nightstand. I actually thought about calling him, but who was I fooling? I was no runway model. I was Claudia Renee Williams, a.k.a. Chocolate! Just another studious sista from around the way. I placed the business card back on my nightstand.

I had a pretty face and an okay body, but I couldn't compete with the truly beautiful women. Maybe I could out-think most of them, but out-walk them... noooo. I could easily dismiss the idea, as I thought of myself as just a bit over-educated for this overly vain, self-centered life-style.

I set it all aside eager to get my real day started. I needed a few things from the grocery store, but unfortunately the one near my apartment was under construction, which meant that I would have to drive. I knew if I didn't go early I wouldn't get there at all. The store I headed to was actually in Oakland, but before long I pulled into the still empty parking lot.

Destiny had its own appointments and who was I to stand in its way? Little did I know I was about to come face to face with a factor I could not reason with. When destiny is in question there is nowhere to hide. My father had taught me that years ago, and its truth was about to come to light. I was about to be presented with another crossroads in my life.

I had been taught about the authority destiny possessed, and now more than ever it was about to be revealed. I had faith in what was yet to come; it was deeper than yesterday and stronger than tomorrow, and I knew faith had a way of transcending our fears and reconstructing our hopes.

All I wanted to do was avoid construction and beat the rush. That's all. I didn't want to ponder over the what if's or the maybe's of life. I just wanted my apartment to smell fresh. My shopping list consisted of scented candles, a new toothbrush and a few toiletries. That was it. I could have gone a dozen different places but I had to go to that particular store, to manifest life's next quest.

I was merely a passenger on board a vehicle unaware of its destination, and destiny had to have its way. Why couldn't I just have been allowed to go in the store, get the few items I wanted and leave? Why? Because that's not the way it works.

All I wanted to do was pick up a few things and jet back to my little apartment, perhaps to continue mimicking models. I didn't know. But I soon realized my date with destiny was much more important.

Destiny was about to introduce itself and indeed, it tapped me on my shoulder as I entered the store. I had only walked down two aisles searching for the items on my list, when I heard a vaguely familiar voice behind me.

"Good morning... I bet you thought you'd never see me again."

It was Vince, the man from the modeling agency in San Francisco.

"I really think you'd look magnificent on the opposite side of a camera. I mean, look at us. Here we both are, in this particular grocery store, early this particular morning. Don't you believe in destiny?"

I didn't know what to say, but I absorbed his every word.

I had to admit I did ask myself why were we both there at the same time. I had never even gone to that store before. Was it just the coincidence of abrupt construction? The all too late night Friday frat party? The breakfast with the girls 'til 6 am? The need to sleep all day Saturday? Only God knew what brought us both there that Sunday morning.

"So, all you want me to do is pose for a few pictures and you'll leave me alone, right?" I asked.

"Right, that's all. If you don't like it, you're free to go... I promise."

I pretended to consider the offer for a moment before I agreed, "Okay, where is your studio?"

"It's in the city, off Market. I can give you detailed directions. When are you available?" he asked.

"My last quarter is over, except for finals, and I graduate in a few weeks, then I have the summer off. Tomorrow I have no classes, so my schedule will be open after that."

"Why don't you come by the studio tomorrow, Monday around eleven o'clock? Traffic will have died down by then and the ride over the bridge will be less congested."

"I'll be there. What do I need to wear?"

"Are you sure?" he asked.

I nodded like I knew what I was doing.

"Wear whatever you'd like. I'm sure whatever you choose will be fine. Here's my card again, just in case you lost the first one," and he reached into his jacket for his card case. "So I'll see you tomorrow?"

"If I say I'm going to do something, I will. Just make sure that everything is on the up and up."

"Of course. By the way, I never caught your name," he said.

"I never threw it to you, but it's Claudia Williams. And yours is Vince, right?"

"Oh, and you can think, too. Great," he said with a grin.

"Does that surprise you?"

"No, it doesn't really surprise me, but after you meet a couple of the models, you'll more than understand why I made the statement. Beauty *and* brains. It certainly is refreshing." More grinning ensued.

"Okay, then. Monday at eleven, right Vince?"

"Right."

"Then I'll see you there. I have a lot of things to do today. Bye for now."

Now, here was a man able to see past my funky rimmed glasses, which clung to the end of my nose. If he could see past my grungy bun, past my wrinkled T-shirts and baggy sweats; surely I could show up for a photo shoot.

As I was walked to the checkout stand, I passed the magazine display. I stopped to peruse fashions for the first time in my life. There were so many publications, all with so many beautiful faces on their covers. I adored them all. Many of the magazines, though published in the states, were still foreign to me. Not once had I allowed myself to think past my studies, but I was smart enough at that moment to know, that if I could pull this one off and sustain the knowledge I had acquired, I would be unstoppable.

I grabbed one magazine after the other and added them to my cart. I must have selected at least a dozen. Just as I was ready to pay, Vince walked towards me again. There were a few magazines that had yet to be bagged and I didn't want him to catch me buying them. I could see my balance due and threw more than enough money towards the cashier. I grabbed my bags and hurried out of the store.

"Hey, laaady! You forgot your change!" he yelled after me.

"Keep it, it's yours," I called over my shoulder as I rushed out the automatic door. I looked back and waved to Vince, shoved my furtive purchase into the backseat and drove off. I breathed a huge sigh of relief and was so glad I didn't get caught with the magazines.

When I got home I called Tina. She was always easy to talk to and she actually listened. I was so excited; my heart was beating faster than I could think.

As the phone rang I thought of the many bad stories I had heard about young ladies who were approached by men claiming to be modeling agents, or any number of things. The girls would get lured into a bad situation and before families knew anything, their daughter had been exploited. I didn't want to become a victim, but I was so intrigued.

Tina did not answer her phone and I needed to talk to someone. Her answering machine picked up, so I left her a message.

"Hey, girl, if you're there, please pick up. I have something to tell you. Oh well, just give me a call when you can. Bye."

As soon as I put the bags down on the table, I headed into my room towards the closet where I kept an old make-up bag that used to belong to my mother. It was something my father thought I should have after she had passed. I never knew why, I wasn't real big on wearing make-up, but it was going to come in handy now. I went back into the kitchen and spilled the magazines out on the table, and poured through them searching for 'a look' that best suited me.

There were so many choices, so much to peruse, and each page I turned showed me something new. I was searching for 'a look' with particular specifications. I needed a hairstyle that made a sane man go insane, and a dress that would make a liar tell the truth. With every page, I could feel my confidence growing.

My mother was the most gorgeous lady most of this world never had the pleasure of seeing, and now I might be given a chance to carry on her unfulfilled legacy. Who was better suited to do so than I? I was her beautiful daughter, Chocolate, and it was about time I recognized just how beautiful being black really was.

The world had moved for years without me and now I was ready to evolve along with it. Could I comb my hair in such a way that heads would turn? That was a question society would have to answer.

No one knows where their blessings are derived, but when they manifest themselves, we must be prepared to receive them. I was prepared.

I took a break from the magazine search to do my daily workout and finished up with my usual hundred crunches. I spread the magazines around the living room floor and ate a big bowl of fruit for breakfast. Narrowing down the hairstyles and mulling over the top five outfits was quite fun. But I still hadn't shared my news with anyone.

Finally the phone rang and it was Tina.

"Girl, I'm so glad you called back. I've been waiting on you forever. Guess what?"

"What? What's up girl? Are you getting married? Wait. I know. You finally had sex," she said with a laugh.

"No, Tina, of course not. You know I'm not getting married, and you know I'm waiting for Mr. Right. Now stop playing and listen," I said. "You won't believe what happened to me today."

"Just try me."

"You remember the other day? Friday, the day of the infamous frat party when I told you I got a business card from that modeling agent in San Francisco?"

"Yeah, what about it? I thought you threw it away. Did you go and search through the dumpster to find it?"

"No Tina... nothing like that. I thought about tossing it, but I kept it on my fridge. I picked it up this morning and it made me wonder about possibilities. Then check out what else happened."

"Okay, what? What else happened?"

"I got up early this morning and needed some things from the store."

"If you mean the one around the corner from your apartment, it's closed."

"I found that out just today. I wanted to go there of course, but since it's under construction, I had to drive into Oakland." I paused for a second too long and could tell that Tina was getting a little impatient with me.

"Look, Claudia, I'm not trying to be funny, but when I heard you say that you needed me to call you, I hurried to my phone to make sure everything was okay."

"Just listen, Tina. I'm getting there if you'll let me. Please."

"Okay, but get to the point."

"I went to another grocery store like I said, and guess who was there?"

"Nooo, nooo, no guessing. You just tell me. Who was there?"

"The man named Vince. The guy from the modeling agency. The business-card-Vince from the shoe store." I explained every which way I could think of. I think she got the drift.

She did seem to get excited for me. "What? What's that girl? You're gonna be a star! I told you that you were beautiful! You go ahead with your bad self and do the dang-thang."

I wanted to tell the whole story before she was too over the top. "So, Tina, he walked up to me and asked if I had changed my mind about modeling. I really don't remember exactly what I said word-for-word, but I will tell you that I have a photo shoot tomorrow, on Monday at eleven."

"Oohhh, Chocolate. I'm so happy for you, you just don't know," she cooed.

"So that's why I called you, Tina. I need some pointers."

"Chocolate, you don't need any pointers. You're so beautiful, girl. All you need are cameras and lights pointed towards you, and as far as I am concerned... it's money.

"You're the most beautiful woman on campus. Girl, just do what comes natural. Go out there and walk like your mother used to when she wanted Uncle Marvin to handle his business."

My heart tingled when she said that.

"I know it sounds a little ghetto, but hey, Claudia, you know what I'm saying. If they're going to pay for it, just get your change off the top."

"What does that mean, Tina?"

"Chocolate, it's not time to act naïve. This world is riding on a sexual high and you've got to learn how to put in, without putting out. A strong, beautiful, intelligent black woman can at times be one of the rarest gems on earth. You exude beauty, and your intellect exemplifies your emotional wealth."

By the time she had finished, I felt like I could walk on water. The fact that it was going to be a stage I had to conquer became secondary. I needed a friend's blessing and I knew that if my potential pursuit were laced with bad karma, she would be the first to tell me.

"Thanks, Tina. I knew you'd know what to say."

"The truth is easy to speak, Claudia. Just wait until you ask me to lie."

Early the next morning my feet hit the floor running. I was moving with purpose towards my next quest. I woke up knowing that I needed to be better than my hopes, and I moved across the room as if I was floating on a promise from God himself. My fears had been pacified by Tina's confidence in me, and my goal was to be all that I could be.

It was tough to select a wardrobe for the day, but I took a few blouses out of my closet that I thought would do. I also found a dress I had bought from a waterfront boutique several months back, and selected two pairs of shoes that helped magnify my luxurious stroll.

When I arrived at the agency there was no one in the foyer. I imagined twenty or more others just like me sitting around waiting for the opportunity to make fools out of themselves. But to my surprise I was alone. I felt like time had suddenly stood still. My heart was beating twice as fast as a second-hand on a clock. I was way past nervous and all I could do was breathe deeply. I continued to picture over-exaggerated runway smiles, but the visions didn't help me relax.

Within a few minutes the receptionist came out and said, "Welcome to Dramatic-Impressions, Incorporated, home of the most beautiful models in the world." She sounded like a recording, but the smile was real as I turned around to address her. I remembered to smile too.

By the time my eyes had focused, I found myself staring at what I thought was a model. She was a beautiful brunette with an award-winning smile. As I walked closer to her, I could feel her exude confidence. It was as if God had shown me an image I desperately needed to embody in order to accomplish my mission.

I closed my eyes and willed my soul to reach across the room, inside the receptionist to extract the confidence necessary to overcome any obstacle. Her self-assurance was a sign I needed to read and adhere to. I was not about to leave another of life's daily clues unread. I thanked God that I didn't miss the writing on the wall.

"You must be Claudia, the young lady Mr. Morelli is expecting… If you'll just have a seat, he'll be right with you."

"I don't know the photographer's last name, but his first name is Vince. I'm here for a photo shoot."

She smiled with a bit of a laugh, finding my reply somewhat humorous. She only repeated, however, "Mr. Morelli said he'll be right out."

I grabbed one of the magazines lying on a table near the front entrance and sat down to wait. I began leafing through the pages admiring the beauty of the female form. I was lost in daydreams trying to imagine my 'look' when I heard his voice.

"Hello, there. Soooo, I see you actually made it."

"Yes, your directions were easy to follow."

I appraised his appearance and commented, "You're not dressed like a photographer." Something was out of place. He was wearing a brown three-quarter length tailored Italian suit, with a pair of seven hundred dollar shoes on. He stood in front of me with a charming smile.

"And, you're not dressed like a scared little school girl either," he replied as he watched me watch him.

"You're not a photographer, are you?"

"No, I'm not the photographer. In fact, I own this company."

"Why couldn't you just tell me that from the beginning?" I said.

"What? And miss seeing the look on your face just now? No, I wouldn't have missed this moment for the world. You are priceless." I couldn't believe what I was hearing.

"Come with me and let me show you what I have in mind for you."

I set the magazine down, grabbed my purse and all of my things and followed him through a set of glass doors. I was wearing a cream colored two-piece outfit, but not enough confidence.

When I stepped into his office, I noticed the décor was so elegant and classy that my heart began signing contracts that weren't even on the table yet.

"You can put your things over there if you'd like," he offered and gestured to a corner chair.

I wasn't nervous; at least that's what I kept saying to myself.

"So that's what was underneath all those baggy clothes," he said as he appraised me from head to toe.

"Let me start by telling you a bit about my company to set you at ease here. Did you know that Dramatic-Impressions is the fifth largest modeling agency in the world?"

"No, I didn't realize that," I responded politely.

"Well, seeing that you are a college student and all, I thought you would have at least checked us out."

"I've been b-b-busy," I stammered. Of course I should have checked out the company. I knew better than to take something like this at face value.

"I've been taking finals and finishing the quarter. I really haven't had time to do anything else but study," I said by way of explanation. He paid no attention.

"I need you to take off all your clothes," he instructed with a straight face.

"What?" I wasn't sure I heard correctly, but if so, I was shocked by the demand. Many things fell into place. I could see what all this was about. I should have done my homework.

I became defensive and asked, "What is this anyway? This is all about sex, isn't it?"

"Yes, and no," he responded in a straightforward, businesslike manner.

"Yes, this is all about sex, but no, I don't want to make love to you. I want the camera to do that. Here's a swimsuit I'd like to see you model. The dressing room is over there." He pointed across his massive desk to a door leading, hopefully, to some privacy.

"But, I brought some of my own clothes to wear," I said.

"I'll buy you a whole new wardrobe if you can wear this like I think you can. Now go and change in private." He held the tiny suit out to me.

I remembered a simple statement my father once told me, "Never let the world see you with your pants down." But he also admonished me to remember that whatever I did, I must deal with the consequences of my actions.

I thought about his wisdom and pulled myself together enough to ask myself a few hard questions. What exactly was

I doing here? Was I looking for some sort of validation or was I on a lark? Was I looking at an opportunity or setting myself up for trouble? I thought I had a chance to become a model; I had even been encouraged to go for it. If I left now, I'd never know. Had I come this far just to turn around and walk away? What would my mother have done in this position? I wished so hard for a sign from her, but I felt like I was on my own.

The man just wanted to see me walk around the room in a swimsuit, I reasoned. That was relatively harmless. I convinced myself I could manage that. I started thinking about money and my pride left the building. I chose door number one.

I took the two small white pieces of fabric dangling from his outstretched hand. I had never worn thong panties before, but it wasn't hard to figure out. I played around with them for a minute and got everything adjusted, top and bottom, front to back.

I came out of the dressing room like Tina had instructed. She had said, 'learn how to put in, without putting out,' I recalled. I exited the dressing room and entered his office like I knew what I was doing. I walked to the outer door and back down the center of the room with a barefoot swivel. Adam's eyes grew wider with every step. When I turned around I made it last for nearly twenty seconds. He couldn't pull his eyes off of my behind. I finally stopped a few feet from his desk and placed both of my hands on my hips.

"Well, what do you think?"

He exhaled audibly, wiped his brow, smiled, and then reached over to buzz the office intercom. "Everyone, come in and meet our hottest new star," he said without taking his eyes off me.

My half-naked body was exposed for all to see. My air of confidence was waning as everyone gathered around me. I began to feel cheap. I was not able to think about how much money I might be worth in the years to come.

"So, what would you like to be called?" asked the beautiful brunette.

I snapped into my current role and didn't hesitate for a moment. "Chocolate. Just call me Chocolate."

Mr. Morelli walked from around his desk and said, "Ladies and gentlemen, meet Chocolate!" Mr. Morelli was proud to introduce me to the staff at Dramatic-Impressions.

He paused to let my own dramatic impression sink in.

"This calls for a celebration," he announced.

Suddenly there were people rolling in carts of champagne, music started seeping through the walls, and I was being congratulated by some of the 'beautiful people.' I couldn't believe that it was all happening to me.

Ironically, Mr. Morelli was my instant confidante. I held his arm and whispered, "How did you know I was going to say 'yes'?"

"How could you not?" he said confidently. "Do you think I just happen to keep cases of chilled champagne on hand? No, I had to believe in my hunch. Every once in a while, a millionaire has to do that you know," he said and winked.

He reached inside his jacket and pulled out an envelope with a check in it. As I opened it I had to blink to read correctly. The check was in the amount of twenty thousand dollars!

"What? Who is this for?"

"Now, Chocolate, you don't think I'd ask you to wear that swimsuit for nothing do you? Not bad for one day's work, wouldn't you agree? Why don't you just run out and get yourself something nice to wear to dinner tonight. The place I'm taking you to is… quite lovely actually, and the food is beyond compare. I'm sure it will meet with your satisfaction. I'll have a contract there, ready for you to sign."

He noticed my hesitation. "You do want to model, don't you?"

I was in shock, trying desperately to remain calm. It was all happening so fast. I needed to collect my thoughts, so that I could truly appreciate what had just taken place. I was so wrapped up in the moment that I almost forgot where I was. As I blinked again, to see if the situation was real, Mr. Morelli was still standing there.

He had to repeat the question I was unaware he'd asked.

"Is that a 'yes' or a 'no'?"

"Yes or no?" His words flooded my mind at once, but I was so dazed.

"Well, Chocolate? Do you accept my offer?" I nodded slowly, not quite sure what it was I just agreed to.

"Look, you can hang out here at the studio as long as you'd like. I have to take off and handle some other business this afternoon."

"Yes… I mean, I guess so. Sure. Thank you, of course," I said breathlessly.

"I'll see you later on tonight then," he confirmed with a sharp nod.

"Where is that exactly?"

"Just give the receptionist your home phone number on your way out and I'll call you with the particulars a little later on."

"Sure, I'll do that. Thank you." I still hadn't caught my breath.

"Okay, then. Dinner will be at 8:00. Be sweet and enjoy yourself in the meantime. Bye now." With that, Mr. Morelli was off and I was left to my own devices at Dramatic-Impressions, Incorporated.

With Vince gone, I was uncomfortable staying on my own for any reason. I went back to the dressing room and put my own clothes back on. I looked in the mirror and shook my head, bringing my thoughts back down to earth. I had to get home.

An inconspicuous exit would be difficult, as I had to pass by my cheering section. The staff was still in the party mode, and I thanked everyone as I walked towards the front door. To my surprise and relief they gave me a rousing round of encouragement. I was able to smile as I gave the receptionist my home number and hurried out the door, down the corridor to get the elevator.

A gentleman was kindly holding the elevator open for me. I could see his lips moving, but I couldn't hear him. My brain was on overload from all the excitement.

"I'm sorry, what did you say?" I asked him.

"I said, you dropped your envelope, miss."

I was horrified when I realized it was the envelope I had just received from Mr. Morelli. The twenty thousand dollar check!

"Thank you, so much, sir. You really are a very kind man."

He handed me the envelope and I gave him a grateful hug.

He was an older freckle-faced Caucasian, who at first glance appeared to have an honest soul. He wore his smile much like he wore his suit, high and extremely tight. The man's pants outlined his private area, revealing much too much detail. When he saw that I noticed, he smiled. Egads! I had three more floors before I could exit at the lobby.

Freckle-face leaned towards me, still smiling tightly. His freckles appeared to be moving and one of his eyebrows was raised up higher than the cuffs on his pants. We were standing side by side not more than a foot apart. The elevator wasn't moving fast enough for me and I could feel the man inching closer. I tried not to look at him and placed my focus on the numbers of the floors as they flashed.

"So, are you married?" he asked. I couldn't believe that we had only descended to the second floor.

I was fast on my feet, and said the first thing that came to mind. "Yes, I am. In fact, my husband works here in the building."

That made him straighten up. He inched his way back over to the far side of the elevator, but had a few questions. "Oh really? What floor is he on? My office is on the top floor, I might have seen him around."

His breath was atrocious. It was enough to curl anyone's nose hairs and it caused my eyes to water.

"What does he do here?" he persisted.

"You mean you don't know Lester?"

"No, I've never heard of a Lester here."

"Lester, the big black guy on the ground floor. He wears the blue suit... you know, the security guard."

The elevator grew quiet as we reached the first floor. You could have heard a rat breathing. In fact, I thought I did. A freckle-faced rat.

Just as the elevator door opened at the lobby, I asked, "So, would you like to meet him?"

"No... not today. Maybe I'll meet him some other time, when I'm not in such a hurry, that is. Better yet, let's just forget that this whole conversation ever took place. Your husband might be a little irritated today and I'm sure he's very protective of you."

Was he transforming from a rat to a mouse?

"I'm sorry for my behavior, miss, please forgive me."

"Okay, sure. I understand."

I tried to pass it off as inconsequential so I could make a quick get-a-way.

CHOCOLATE

Freckle-face was out of the elevator first and purposefully avoided the security guard. I looked over towards the guard booth and blew the brother a kiss for good measure. He must have thought I was crazy. He looked back over his shoulder to identify the lucky recipient of the kiss, and by the time he turned back to the front entry, I was gone.

He might have heard me, though, as I jumped in my car and screamed, "Yeeeeeeessssssss…" at the top of my lungs.

I couldn't quite believe that I had just become a model for a top agency. Models from Dramatic-Impressions were in all the magazines and I tried to picture my face and body right there with them. It certainly was an exciting proposition.

I thanked God for blessing me the way He just had, and smiled upwards to my mother in heaven. I knew she had something to do with everything in my life including what had just happened. But my biggest worry was still on my plate. I wasn't sure how my father would take the news of hearing that his daughter was now a model.

I hadn't mentioned anything about it before hand because he might have discouraged me from going. Perhaps he would see it in a different light now that I had made it. Regardless, this would be a hard pill for him to swallow. His biggest worry would be my education. I only had two more finals left and I knew I would finish with flying colors. Nothing could prevent me from graduating on time. I headed for his house on the way home, but without giving him the benefit of a warning phone call. Part of me hoped he wouldn't be there.

On the drive home my hands were shaking on the steering wheel but the traffic was light and my crazy high never posed a threat. It was about three o'clock when I pulled up in front of my father's house. I knew he was there because his truck was parked on the side of the house. I pulled into the driveway – the visitor's parking spot.

I walked inside and yelled, "Daddy, where are you?"

"Back here!" he called from his study.

When he saw my face, he knew I had news.

"So, what's troubling Daddy's little baby now?"

I hadn't realized I was worked into a state of such confusion. My mixed emotions were running high and my face was easy to read.

Before I could open my mouth, tears were streaming down my face. He got up from his chair and put his arms around me.

"Child, what's wrong? Is it something about Sweets again?"

"No, Daddy, nothing about Sweets. I've just got something to say and I don't really know how to tell you."

"Just tell me, Chocolate. I'm your father. And we've been through this same scenario before. You know that whatever it is we can work it out."

For years I had spent countless hours studying and grooming my mind, in complete disregard of my outward appearance. I had been so deeply consumed with trying to better my education that I had forgotten how God had blessed me on the outside. When most of my friends were dating, I was researching and rambling through notes, attempting to build up an educational foundation for my future. I never complained, I just kept on reading. It was my passion.

My father was my example of greatness. I wanted to become a mirror image of him. Not only did I watch him read, I watched him accomplish his goals through hard work and perseverance. I often saw him study through the night.

When he viewed my report cards as early as grade school, the look in his eyes was priceless. Letting him down was never an option; he demanded my best and my obedient spirit was always willing to meet those demands. I did all I could do to stay on the honor roll, because to do so honored my father.

I knew I was being somewhat rude at the moment, as my father and I hadn't seen each other in quite sometime. But all of the excitement had me feeling selfish. I needed my concerns to be heard and that was all there was to it.

But, I had rushed into his house without knocking or even saying hello. So I slowed down for a moment to display some common courtesy.

He and his new lady friend had taken a cruise early in the spring, and since their return we had continued to miss each other like two ships that pass in the night.

I managed to remember that tidbit and finally asked him how their cruise was to get the niceties out of the way. But he knew from the sound of my voice, I wasn't really very interested. I had to at least pretend I cared, and he pretended not to notice my indifference.

As he rambled on about their trip, I sighed and nodded at appropriate moments for good measure.

"Oh, baby, it went fine. We had ourselves a great time. I had never been on a ship that large before, and our stomachs felt a little queasy at times, but overall it was fun. Nicole really enjoyed herself and told me to say hello next time I saw you. She says, 'thanks for sharing your father.'"

"That's great, Dad. I'm happy you guys enjoyed yourselves, after all, it has been some time since you have gone on a vacation." We shared a moment of rare awkward silence.

"Dad, of course you know I graduate this quarter, and I've been thinking about what my options might be."

"Well, baby, I thought that we've already decided that you were going straight on to grad school."

I did know that was his plan for me, and I admit it was mine as well.

"But what if I don't want to go to grad school right now, and I want to pursue a career?" I asked evasively.

"I'm sure we can sit down and work it out."

"Not necessary, Daddy. I've already figured it out for myself." I could see by the look on his face he didn't like the direction the conversation was going, but he sat there and took it all in.

"So, Chocolate, what career have you chosen?"

"Now, Daddy, before you interrupt me, please just let me finish. Okay?"

"Okay, baby, go right ahead. I'm listening."

"Before you say anything about school, please believe me... no matter what I do, I'm going to ace my last two finals, and I know I'll graduate with honors. But... I want to be a model."

The room grew calm, and I expected the worst of storms. Neither of us said a word for a few seconds.

"Well, what do you think?"

He looked up at me and in a playful voice said, "Baby, I think you would make a great model. You're so beautiful, just like your mother was. And you're smart, just like me," he added as his grin widened.

"Now, is that what you are so worked up about? You're a grown woman, Chocolate. I know I've taught you enough about life to make rational decisions."

The burden of doubt disappeared and I heaved a huge sigh of relief. I never wanted to disappoint him and knowing I had his blessing meant the world to me. I jumped up and ran to him, just like I did when I was little. My tears were gone, I had a huge smile and I was ready for a hug from Pops.

"Oh, Dad. Thank you, thank you. Your positive support means everything to me, and you've got to know I wouldn't do this without your approval. Thanks, Dad," I said.

He looked down at me as we hugged and said, "Claudia, don't worry about me. Go and be the best model this world has ever seen. Know that whatever you do, my love and support will be with you."

"Oh, Daddy. You don't know how good that makes me feel. I never want you to look down on me."

"Baby, listen. You've given me twenty-one, oh, twenty-two now, of the greatest years a father could ever have. It is a joy to be your dad and an honor to be loved by you. I know how blessed I am to have a daughter like you, and I wouldn't trade you in for anything in this world. Do you hear me, Chocolate? Nothing could ever replace you."

"Well, in that case, Dad. Let me tell you the rest of the news. Today I went to a modeling agency and landed a job right on the spot." I reached into my purse and pulled out the twenty thousand dollar check.

"Look at how much money I earned today. In just one day!" I was still in a state of disbelief, and was trying to convince him as well as myself.

I handed him the envelope. He fumbled with it but extracted the check. When he saw the amount for himself, he nearly fell off his chair.

"Chocolate... twenty-thousand dollars in one day? You have to be kidding me! Are there any modeling jobs for old dads my age?"

"No, Daddy, I don't think so. But if there were, you'd have one in a heartbeat."

We hugged again in mutual admiration with arms full of love.

"I'm so glad I came by, Dad, and that you were home. I wish we had talked about this sooner, but I feel so much better now. But, I've got to run. I have to go shopping and get myself a new dress to wear tonight."

"A new dress? All those dresses you have in your closet and you've got to go shopping? Look at you, that money is already burning a hole in your pocket, and you haven't even had it for twenty-four hours. Tell me, Chocolate, why do you need another dress in such a hurry?"

"My boss, the owner of the agency, is taking me to dinner so I can sign the contract." I thought this might be the moment of truth for him.

"Would you like to come?" I added as an afterthought, but it was a sincere invitation.

"No, of course not. But, Chocolate, that was awfully considerate of you. Besides, tonight is the night Nicole and I sit around and watch movies," he said. "And you, this is your night."

He held me at arm's length.

"Just look at you, my beautiful model you. You go ahead and have fun, and don't spend all that money in one place... you hear?"

While I was shopping I found a beautiful 'little black dress' with spaghetti straps. The neckline enhanced my shoulders and the bodice pressed intimately against the rest of my anatomy like shame embraces a sinner. It really fit me quite nicely. I picked up another pair of shoes to match and felt like Imelda Marcos.

By the time I got home it was already six o'clock. The first thing I did was check my messages. Mr. Morelli had called and said that a limousine would pick me up just before eight. I had never ridden in a limo before, but I figured there's a first time for everything.

The black stretch limousine pulled up in front of my apartment at exactly seven fifty-five and I was ready. By the time I reached the sidewalk the driver had opened the right rear door. He waited patiently while I climbed in and then closed the door behind me.

A complete stranger was treating me like a queen. But I felt like the queen I was born to be; sitting in the back of that plush limousine like I was somebody. I felt like new money in that lovely little black dress. My purchases had barely put a dent in the twenty thousand dollar paycheck.

After I was comfortable and we had almost arrived at the Bay Bridge tollbooth, the driver lowered the partition and his voice spoke over the intercom.

"Would you like a glass of wine while we ride, Miss Williams?"

I unnecessarily leaned forward to speak directly to him through the partition, "Sure, yes. Of course. Why not? I would love a glass of wine. I mean, thank you so much." I could see the driver break a slight smile through the rear view mirror.

Before I could lean back a small door slid open midway along the seat in front of me. A nice bottle of white wine was chilling in a bucket of ice. All I could do was smile and pour.

Somewhere between dreams, I had awakened to find a reality where good things still do happen to good people.

The ride into San Francisco was pleasant and seemed to be much shorter as a passenger sitting in luxury. Even though I knew we were headed into the city I wasn't sure of our exact destination.

When we arrived, I was expecting the driver to open the door, but much to my surprise, Mr. Morelli did the honors.

He was wearing yet another beautiful Italian suit, this time it was all black. When he saw my dress he said, "Good evening, Chocolate. I see that great minds really do think alike."

I could feel a little-school-girl-crush come oozing out of me as he held his hand out for me. I tried to reach for it, but I just couldn't move. I was desperately trying not to appear overly impressed. The dreamy scent of his cologne wafted my way and it overwhelmed me. I couldn't suppress my emotional reaction any longer, and before I knew it my hand was wrapped tightly in his.

As I climbed out of the limo, I knew one thing for sure: I, Claudia "Chocolate" Williams, was with an extremely handsome man, and loving it.

"Well, Chocolate! You look absolutely gorgeous," he said as I stood up.

The compliment went to my head. "Thank you, Mr. Morelli. I was hoping you'd like it," I replied referring to my dress of course.

He shook his head and said, "Mmm, mmm, mmm. Like it, Chocolate... I love it."

"Would you like to go inside?" he asked, and offered me his arm.

I realized we were standing at Number One Nob Hill, one of the most posh addresses in all of San Francisco, the Mark Hopkins Hotel.

We entered the grand lobby of the historic San Francisco landmark and made our way across to the elevators as all eyes were upon us. Mr. Morelli held my hand as we boarded the elevator. His eyes offered me his undivided attention as we ascended. I had never encountered such personal care before. I had barely held hands with another man, and was feeling absolutely giddy. I stole a moment to glance down at our hands, smiling inside as ideas of what if's surfaced once again.

The restaurant was on the top floor of the hotel. As we got off the elevator I felt as if I was on top of the world, and indeed I was, there at the legendary Top of the Mark, the most elegant restaurant in all of San Francisco. I was in need of a good pinch or an elbow nudge, something... anything to let me know I wasn't dreaming again.

The two glasses of wine I consumed in the limo had me feeling rather mellow... and a bit frisky. But I was not going to come unglued. I was a Williams girl. I was taught that if all else failed, I was supposed to act like I had been there before.

Though I had never seen this side of pleasure, I was not about to reveal that to a soul. After all, this was my night. It was as if God had given me a day-pass to heaven, and was showing me the respect my eyes thought they'd never see.

Who would have ever known that I would stumble upon such a man in a shoe store of all places? And I really was just minding my own business, on a mission when I went into that grocery store. Was that just yesterday? My intention was just to pick up a box of matches, a candle or two and a few other personal items. But look at destiny, it wasn't even on the shelves and somehow ended up in my basket.

There was destiny standing next to me in the form of a six-foot one Italian gentleman with strong firm hands and a soul to match. I felt as if I was holding hands with the inevitable.

My quick recollection of how we met and thoughts of what was to come stopped abruptly as the elevator arrived at the restaurant. The panoramic view was stunning. The city lights were another kind of pretty I had only seen in the movies.

"Well, this is our floor. Follow me, Chocolate," he said as he led me by the hand. I was beginning to see how important and respected Mr. Morelli must have been around the city. So far, everyone seemed to know him.

When we first walked in the restaurant, I saw people wave at him from across the room. Just before we were seated, a gentleman at the next table smiled at Mr. Morelli and nodded in my direction.

I heard him say, "Well, Vince, I see you've gone and done it again."

Mr. Morelli quietly answered with a grin, "Some people are born smart John, I just happen to be lucky."

I couldn't help but over-hear what they said, and I let go of Mr. Morelli's hand. I reached out and touched his arm to bring his attention back to me. He turned and our eyes met again.

"My father has always told me, it's better to be lucky than smart."

"Well?" he said.

"Well, what?" I replied, blushing out of control.

"Well, is he right or is he wrong?" he challenged.

I knew my response would be appropriate, so I waited to answer him after he pulled back my chair and I was seated.

"Well, Chocolate? Is he right or wrong?"

"Mr. Morelli, my father is always right." Without asking, I took the lead and said, "I would love a glass of wine."

"Oh, Chocolate, I'm so sorry. Where are my manners? May I suggest, however, a martini? The Top of the Mark has a famed list of over 100 mouthwatering martinis to offer."

Before I could reply one of our three waiters, who had been standing adjacent to our table, came near as Mr. Morelli made a simple gesture. "Excuse me, could you please recommend a special martini for the lady? And a bottle of your best white wine with dinner."

We sipped our lovely martinis, and enjoyed the view as we perused the menu.

After we ordered, the wine steward was back with the wine. Mr. Morelli appraised the selection, and nodded to the waiter, who effortlessly uncorked the wine. He offered Mr. Morelli the first sip, and again he nodded with pleasure. My glass was filled with a slight turn of the bottle to prevent any drips. The wine steward wrapped the bottle in a white linen cloth and set it into a beautiful silver ice bucket to remain chilled.

I couldn't help but peek at the label. It was a French wine, a white burgundy, which I had never heard of. The label said Le Montrachet - Grand Cru, 1977. I had an inkling it was something quite special.

CHOCOLATE

Mr. Morelli lifted his delicate glass in his strong firm hand. I brought my own glass to his, and as the rims touched slightly he said, "I hope it's your year."

My year? My year? Heck, I buy what's on sale and the year had never come into question. But I was not about to tell him that.

I glanced at the bottle again, just to check the year. Oh my God. 1977. It really was my year. I couldn't believe destiny had served me a glass of the most fabulous white wine I had ever tasted; from a bottle labeled with the year I was born. I was beside myself trying to interpret this additional sign of good fortune.

After taking a sip of the smooth and delicate wine, I smiled and said, "This is definitely my year."

We both enjoyed another sip of the marvelous vintage together.

"How was the ride over?" he asked after a moment.

"The ride over was wonderful. I mean, this whole day has been one of the greatest days of my life."

I had to ask one thing, though. "Excuse me, Mr. Morelli, I have a question I must ask. There is one thing I need to know."

"What is it, Chocolate?"

"Well, it's about that check you gave me earlier today."

"What about it?"

"Well, if I don't accept the contract, you won't do a stop-payment on it, will you?"

That provoked an unexpected reaction, and he started laughing out loud.

"Did I say something funny?" I asked.

"Yes, you did, Chocolate. But seriously, business first. I would never do a stop-payment on a check that I've given you. Why are you asking such a silly question?"

Perhaps it was all the alcohol, or so many surprises in one weekend, but I didn't think the question was all that silly.

He could see I felt a bit slighted and changed the conversation. "The view is magnificent, isn't it? I was hoping you'd like it. It's quite a grand place for a special occasion such as this."

I knew before long we had to get down to real business. And the time had come for us to discuss the real reason I was dining in the legendary Top of the Mark.

"Chocolate, do you prefer dealing with business before or after we eat?"

"It really doesn't matter to me. How is it usually done, Mr. Morelli?"

"Please, I prefer being called Vince. I'm not an old man and I happen to like my name. So from now on, please call me Vince. No more Mr. Morelli. Deal?" I nodded.

"Now back to what I was saying… I don't really like dealing with business on an empty stomach, so let's eat first, okay?"

"Let's do," and dinner was served shortly.

The meal was divine, but what was to follow was better than anything I could have possibly ordered.

"Here are some numbers I hope will satisfy you, Chocolate," he said as he handed me a contract. I started to look through the papers as he continued to speak.

"We are prepared to start you off at five thousand dollars a day."

"Five thousand dollars a day!" I blurted out. "Are you serious? Stop playing." I had lost it. My mind just went blank. As I sat in disbelief, he was seemingly unaware of why I was so blown away.

"What's wrong, Chocolate? Are the numbers okay? If not, I can easily have my people look over them again."

The whole notion put me in tears. "Mr. Morelli, I mean Vince. You don't understand why I am crying," but I couldn't explain.

He looked disappointed and asked, "What's wrong, Chocolate? I thought all this would have made you happy."

"What's wrong you ask?" I wasn't quite sure myself and it was more of a statement than a question. "Nothing is wrong, really, Vince. I'm not unhappy at all. In fact, I have never been so happy in my whole life. It's all just happening so fast… that's all."

"You don't have to sign anything tonight, Chocolate," he reassured me. "Take your time. Look over the contract with someone you trust and then get back with me when you've thought it over."

He went on to explain some of the general conditions for me. "Of course you won't be working everyday, but when you are, we will be shooting at least five hours a day, at a thousand dollars an hour. There is some fine print you'll want to look at carefully, so take your time. We are in no hurry. It's important to us that you are comfortable with the way everything is structured."

I could not possibly think of any clause or fine print that could stand in the way of my making that kind of money, but for the record I had to clarify a few things.

"What exactly are some of the things you think I might be worried about?"

"Well, for instance, while in the first two years of your contract, we ask that you don't have any children."

I nodded as if that was fine with me. I really couldn't foresee having children in the near or distant future.

"Okay, I can handle that. Having children is the last thing on my mind at this point in my life. What else?"

"There is always the issue of weight," he said matter-of-factly.

"Oh, I see. Of course there must be guidelines."

"Indeed, and the contract states that a model's weight can not fluctuate by any more than three to five pounds. That is to protect our interests as well as yours." He stopped to assess my reaction. "Any problems so far?"

My weight had been fairly stable since I started college. A few extra pounds were easily shed. Besides, I was back to the money. For the amount of money in the contract I was sure I could frequent a gym to stay fit.

"No, no problems. Everything sounds great. Where do I sign?"

"Oh, one last detail. If you sign tonight, Dramatic-Impressions is prepared to offer you a one-hundred-thousand dollar signing bonus."

Before he finished enunciating the numbers of the full amount, I had already started signing my name. Just for the hell of it I threw in a smart-ass comment.

"What? All that money and no car? Come on now, Vince, you can do better than that now can't you?" I asked sweetly. I really was half-joking and half-drunk.

When I realized what I had said, I decided to let it play out. I was careful not to allow him to intimidate me. I had been taught that a closed mouth won't ever get fed, and I didn't want that statement to apply to me. I wasn't about to miss out on any money by taking the shy route. So I opened up my mouth again.

"Well?" I asked simply.

"You really drive a hard bargain, Chocolate. But, okay. Just sign here, and we'll see what we can do."

I took the pen and willingly signed away the next five years of my life.

Vince was a very handsome man; I couldn't deny that fact. His money made him even more attractive. He had gorgeous dark brown eyes and to-die-for jet-black curly hair. And I had never seen a man with such perfectly straight white teeth before.

We rode together in the limousine and held hands all the way home. When the car finally stopped in front of my apartment, he leaned over closer to me. I closed my eyes and tilted my head to accept a kiss. Instead of feeling the anticipated pleasure on my lips, he leaned further down and gently kissed my hand. I attempted to lift my face up off the floor to recover from what had to have been one of my most embarrassing moments. I started blinking my right eye acting as if I had something in one of my contacts. He was such a gentleman; he pretended I was really having an issue. I knew he saw me getting my lips ready, but he allowed me to save face.

I tried to disguise my discomfort, and managed to pipe up with, "So tell me, Vince, when do I start earning my money?"

"Three weeks from today. We'll expect you next month, right after you graduate. That Monday at nine. So read over the do's and don't's this week and enjoy yourself until then. Perhaps we'll see each other in the meantime."

I thought, perhaps indeed.

"Goodnight, Chocolate," he said gently.

"Goodnight, Vince."

I climbed out of the car one hundred thousand dollars richer. My face might have looked a little dull from one of my most embarrassing moments, but my bank account was getting ready to shine.

I was both exhausted and excited, and in desperate need of someone to talk to. It was too late to call my father, and neither Tina nor Mia would answer their phones at one o'clock in the morning. They were both too damn afraid of receiving booty-calls. So there I was, stuck in the middle of a long dream, just dying for someone to crawl inside and join me.

I poured myself another glass of wine, from who knows what vintage, crawled into bed and watched TV until I fell off to sleep. But not before thanking God for everything.

The next morning I got up to look for the glass slipper. I still couldn't believe it had all really happened. I do remember placing both checks underneath my pillow and clutching them tightly all through the night. Much to my surprise, they were still there when I looked that morning. I was so relieved and still so sleepy, that I climbed back into bed and fell back to sleep.

At about noon I awoke to a knock on the door. It was a familiar face; our neighborhood postman with a certified letter.

"Claudia, that sure is a nice car you have parked out there," he said.

At first I didn't pay him much mind. Then I shook the cobwebs from my head and peered over the railing. Could it be? Was I on the roll of my life? I left the postman standing with the door wide open, ran to my room and put on my glass slippers, I mean my flip-flops of course, and raced back to the door.

I didn't want to look too stupid, so I slowed down and waited for the postman to join me. He gave me a suspicious look as he followed me down to my parking space. He watched me approach the car from the rear as I peered in the windows. He finally made his delivery, gave me the letter and a wink, and went on his way. It suddenly dawned on me that the certified letter and the car were connected. I didn't bother to wonder where my other car was.

As I admired the new car, I noticed there was a note underneath the driver's side windshield-wiper. And I felt I had every right to read it, seeing that the car was parked in front of my apartment, in my space.

It read simply, "Chocolate, I hope that you like black, because it was the only color available on short notice, and it sure looks good on you."

The car was magnificent - a black on black convertible Jaguar, and it was all mine. Chocolate had gone and hit the jackpot, and the gold was real, and like Cinderella, the shoe fit.

Graduation Day

Graduation day was quite memorable. Everyone I loved was there. Everyone except Sweets, and my mother of course. But I could feel my mother's spirit smiling proudly down from heaven.

My father and his girlfriend, Nicole, and several friends were there for me. My Uncle Jimmy couldn't be there, but Aunt Jackie showed up with her new husband, who just happened to be the pastor of his own church.

Tisha Morgan, from high school, was there, and I couldn't believe Bruce Emerson showed up with his wife, Sabrina, and their daughter!

I had kept a secret from everyone, but it was to be revealed that day. Partially because of my cumulative 4.0 g.p.a., I was honored by being named valedictorian of my graduating class. I could see my father just bursting with pride at the seams.

Tisha couldn't wait to come over and whisper in my ear after she saw Bruce and his family.

"Now, that's more like it, girl. Graduating from Cal as valedictorian. Look over there, Chocolate," and she pointed to Bruce and his wife. Two gorillas and their little gorilita. Girl, just think. That could have been you. I just thank God, it was only a kiss."

I didn't pay her any attention. She was such a fool at times and just doing what she does best. I couldn't imagine how Bruce got married and cranked out a kid in four short years, though.

Tisha took Mia's potential job prospects we joked. She had become a stand-up comedian by that time and was headlining at all the Bay Area clubs making people laugh. She had found her niche and was working the crowd there at graduation. I saw her whisper asides to people in every direction every time one of the deans spoke. Politeness and decorum forced people to keep from breaking out in full-blown laughter I could tell.

I spotted the rest of my fan club from my vantage point on stage. Tina and Mia were side-by-side in their caps and gowns, looking lovely and proud. Amy, my freshman roommate, also graduated and showed up with her boyfriend, Tyrone. She was smiling like she had just invented the cure for racism. The brother was one shade away from being as dark as the end of a bat cave. I also noticed both Veda and Felicia had made it through.

My graduation meant the world to my father. I lived what he taught, and finished what I started. He insisted I never allow a job to go undone. I recalled his noble words, "When we as individuals hurdle the limits imposed by others, we will reach our goals and our capabilities will become endless. When we allow our adversaries to limit our hopes, we indirectly empower ourselves with their limited vision."

As I finished my valedictorian speech with cheers to his words, I felt a gentle breeze graze my neck. The tassel on my cap brushed against my cheek, and I knew it was my mother congratulating me with a kiss from heaven.

She knew that I would never limit myself by society's standards. She saw me reach another milestone in life and we both knew I was far from finished. I knew that God was in control, and as long as I placed Him first in everything I did, I believed He would empower me with enough insight to reach my objectives.

In Mama's honor my father placed a picture of her in the empty seat to his left. Nicole was seated on his right, and she welcomed the memento. She knew how fitting it was for the occasion and even helped my father place flowers around the chair before the ceremony.

When I received my diploma, I glanced down at the front row and caught my father's eye. He stood up to take a picture of me as I walked across the stage. Even as designated family photographer, the focus wasn't enough to keep his emotions in check. The reality of his only child obtaining a college degree, suddenly overwhelmed him, and his emotions got the best of him.

Through his tears, I could see his bright smile. His front row seat, his height, and darkman complexion made him stand out to others as well. I was determined not to cry even though I saw him lose his composure. I held on until he leaned down for something. He picked up the picture of my mother and held it up over his head towards me as I passed by. I turned my head to see her lovely face and I literally felt her spirit as our eyes touched through the photograph.

"That's my baby! That's my baby!" my father yelled.

"I love you, Daddy!"

When Nicole saw that my father was crying, she began to cry as well. The ceremony was beautiful, but seeing my father loved by someone who so genuinely cared for him touched me deeply. Nicole had reached me at a moment in life when I felt unreachable. Her love for my father was evident and her spirit moved me.

After the ceremony, we all met back at my father's house. It was obvious Nicole and her mother, Mama Lawson, had taken their shoes off in the kitchen the night before, and had been dancing around in the pots all through the night.

Mama Lawson had a profound look that was soothing to the soul. She was closer to seventy than she was to sixty, but you couldn't tell, even though her hair was pure white like fresh sea salt. She had bright rings around the darkest part of her eyes, which gave her a distinct look. When she smiled, all forms of confusion cleared.

Her voice was soft yet firm. She was a woman of few words, but the words she spoke had the ability to heal the woes of the common man. Although I had only seen her twice, her personality was unforgettable.

Nicole talked about her mother's cooking all the time, but that wasn't unusual. Everyone I had ever come in contact with felt that his or her own mother was the best cook in the world.

No sooner had we walked into my father's house did we smell a sumptuous feast. I could discern candied yams, greens, neck-bones, turkey, ham, and both beef and pork ribs. There were bowls of this and platters of that all through the house. Mama Lawson was indeed a bona fide old-school cook. The greens were screaming, and the ham was so tender that you could cut it with a fork.

All the food was great, but adhering to my modeling contract I couldn't really eat like I wanted to. I had to be satisfied with tasting small portions, listening to the oohs, aahs and mmm-mmms, and savoring the mouth-watering aromas.

Mama Lawson gave me a hug and said, "Child, you better get you something to eat and stop walking around here just smelling this food. There's something of everything. Here,

here's a plate. Now go over there and help yourself," and she turned me in the direction of the buffet.

"I know, I see everything. It all looks and smells absolutely wonderful, but I have to show up for work in a couple of days. Unfortunately, if I eat like I want to, I won't be able to fit into anything."

"Fit into anything? Child, look at you. I don't know how you get around on those small legs of yours! If it wasn't for your butt, you'd be built straight up and down."

I held my hand over my mouth feigning shock. "Mama Lawson, that's mean."

"No, starving yourself is mean, child. What I'm telling you is the truth. Back when I was a child, we didn't have models."

"So, what did you have then? I'm sure there was somebody prancing around town thinking they were cute?"

"Oh, is that what you want to call a model? Now if that's the case, child, *I* was a model. I was always prancing around, and I didn't need no camera in my face to strike whatever that is they tell y'all to do."

"That's strike a pose, Mama Lawson," I said with a smile.

"Well, child, I just don't think it's healthy not to eat. And it just doesn't make sense to starve yourself for a job," she said, and put her hands on her hips and nodded her head once for emphasis.

"Baby, back when I was coming up, we worked hard for the few things we got, and being able to eat was a blessing. I never thought I'd live to see people starving themselves to keep a job."

She picked up a small bowl of greens and said, "Baby, do what you have to, but take a few bites of these greens while you're starving yourself to stay employed. Nicole told me there's a lot of money involved so who am I to stand in your way? Child, don't listen to me."

She had earned another hug.

I left her to mingle with all my guests. I spoke to everyone at least twice. Tina and I had stayed up late the night before and I was getting delirious by the second round. But everything worked out for the best. As soon the older folks were full, they got sleepy and were ready to leave.

Coming Out of
My Shell

By six o'clock that night nearly every one had gone home and it was time for Mia and me to head towards San Francisco for some real celebrating. Nicole offered us her car for the night so we didn't have to drive the Jaguar to an unknown area. Some of the graduates had planned to meet up at a new club called 'Doin' It' and we were supposed to meet Vince there.

By the time we got to the club, the line was out the door and down the street.

"Damn, girl, are you sure we're supposed to meet Vince here?"

"Yes, I made sure. I had him write the directions down when I dropped by his office yesterday. This is the right place. Just wait right here and hold our spot, I'll check with the bouncer."

Rowdy party-goers who had been in line for a while jeered as I moved towards the door. "Hey, who in the hell do you think you are? If we have to wait in line, then so do you."

I paid no attention and walked as fast as I could towards the front of the line.

"Hey, lady, the line is back there," the bouncer indicated with a jerk of his thumb.

"Yes, but I'm with a party inside. Maybe you know him. His name is Vince from..."

"Do you mean Vince Morelli, the owner?" he asked. I could tell he was impressed, and I was happy to be a name-dropper. Vince had neglected to mention he was also the owner of the club. He was so evasive, and so full of surprises. I should have known.

"Yes, we're talking about the same person, Mr. Vince Morelli."

"Well, that's all you had to say. Is anyone else with you?" he inquired politely.

"Yes, thank you. Let me go find her."

I turned and waved for Mia to come to the front of the line. She saw my hand and was on her way.

When we entered the club, there were people everywhere. I thought it would be hard to find Vince in this crowd, but much to my surprise, he found us. As soon as we made it to the other side of the dance floor the night truly began.

My eyes were temporarily blinded by a strobe light as I attempted to find Vince's voice. I knew I heard it over the din. He had walked into the DJ booth and taken over the microphone. He had the music turned down when the crowd didn't respond at first.

"Ladies and gentlemen," he repeated, "It is my honor to present to some, and to reintroduce to others, a young lady who will become one of the world's most familiar faces over night. Today she is one of UC Berkeley's most celebrated graduates and valedictorian of her senior class. I ask that you help me celebrate this occasion by welcoming her and having the best time of your life doin' it here at my newest club."

It was hard to hear every word over the roar of the crowd as we were jostled closer to the dance floor.

"Ladies and gents, the next round of drinks is on the house as I introduce... the lovely, Chocolate!"

The crowd cheered as he announced my name, and I felt someone push me to the middle of the dance floor. The spotlight found me as Vince said, "That's right! Your next drink is on me! Thank you all for being here tonight, and remember to tell everybody you know that we're talking about 'Doin' It.'"

I had automatically assumed a pose, and began nodding to admirers as some people even took out their cameras. Mia was by my side just eating it up. After his surprise speech, Vince joined us on the dance floor and planted a great big kiss on my cheek.

"What do you think about the surprise?" he asked, obviously quite full of himself.

I was too happy to speak, and just stood there having my photo snapped. I saw Mia nudge Vince's arm, and knew something was up. I figured it out in another instant. Of course she was aware of the surprise.

"How could you not tell me about this party?" I demanded.

She smiled and said, "Girl? And mess up this surprise? How could I have done that? What I want to know is why didn't you tell me how fine he was?"

"Girl, he's all right," I said sheepishly.

"No, Claudia, that man is bringin' it. Look at him. He's even got a nice butt, for a white man. And besides, he's totally cute as hell."

A drink magically appeared in my hand and I took a sip of my wine. Mia was staring at me with her head tilted to one side.

"What is wrong with you, Mia? Why are you looking at me like that now?"

"You know why I'm looking at you. I'm looking at you like this because I want to know..." and she left me to fill in the blanks.

I was not going to make it easy on her. "Know what?" I feigned naïveté, but she wasn't buying it.

"Come on, Claudia. I want to know if you guys have ever..."

I stopped her before she could spell it out. "Nnoooo," I sang, "we haven't, thank you. It's strictly a working relationship, and that's all there is to say!"

"Do you know what I think you said?"

"No, but I'm sure you're going to tell me."

"Well, you just said he doesn't like you that way, but you never said *you* didn't like him that way, now did you?"

"That's beside the point. I'm not about to go running after a man. Any man."

"A man. Hmm. Child that's not just any man, that's a million dollar man. That is a fine piece of work right there."

I gave her an 'ask me if I care' look, but she wasn't having it.

"Girl, don't look at me like that. He's strong where you need him to be... don't look at me like that. He's a strong-where-you-need-him-to-be kind of man. Most woman have run after far less, believe me. So, you better go home and put your running shoes on and at least start jogging towards him. Hells bells, I would. Just think, you could make it part of your workout."

I started laughing. Mia was such a fool, in a fun kind of way. She always knew what to say. She had a comeback for everything, but I guess she was right. Who was I fooling? It's true, I was digging Vince, and from what I could tell he was digging me.

I had just turned twenty-two years old and had never had a sexual relationship with a man. I was following my personal mantra and saving myself for the right person, but who could be more right than Vince? He was nice to me in every way imaginable, and a part of me wanted to give myself to him as a token of my appreciation.

Vince really seemed to care about me. Maybe it was time for me to make my move; after all I had just purchased a brand new pair of running shoes that week.

The fact that he treated me like I was someone was what did it for me. We had spent some time together in the past few weeks, and I had become so relaxed around him, at times I felt like putty. It was more than safe to say that I had gotten weak over a short period of time.

I felt vulnerable and longed to be touched by him. I had a strong desire to be held in his arms. The more I was around him, the more fragile I became. I had spent an extraordinary amount of time dealing with controversy and I was ready to try joy.

Life had taken so many twists and turns, and now my soul was begging to be touched by ecstasy. Vince was as close as I had come to sensing ecstasy and his unique style had somehow unlocked the doors of doubt.

He was the man I wished to invite into my special place. He had indirectly won that right by directly demonstrating his knowledge and disapproval of those things that are wrong. He knew what I needed and he had been able to give it to me so far.

That night Vince was dressed in black again. His ensemble, an extremely beautiful black silk shirt with wide leg pants to match, fit him well as it unleashed my sexual cravings. He was wearing a medium weight silver necklace, with a matching chain link bracelet. His understated platinum Rolex accented his beautiful olive skin, and when he stared at me, I felt like a schoolgirl getting a note passed to her by the most popular boy. I decided right then and there, if Vince asked me to be with him that night, I would check yes a million times.

The mere thought of him touching me stimulated every inch of my being. For the past few weeks I would close my eyes and imagine him as my first lover. I was his coffee and he was my cream. Together we were pure stimulation, smooth to the tongue, like the sweetest candy in a warm mouth.

When the world wasn't looking, I closed my eyes and touched myself, pretending that my hands were his. I hoped that one day his physical affection would embrace my own, causing my spine to tingle as our bodies mingled. I attempted to commit to memory his last words, his first hello, and my unwillingness to say good-bye.

His charm had disrobed my fears and my barest love for him knew no disgrace. I had fallen in love with a man who had never touched me, and I longed to feel his breath blowing against my neck. I had never believed my emotional limitations were so evident, but around him, my lack of control was obvious. Though I was well versed in the English language, I craved his guidance through the uncharted waters of my anatomy.

My shame was removed by timeless hours of emptiness, which had now been filled with hopeful moments of passion. I wanted Vince like I wanted nothing else. There was no time to waste. I had to create a plan of action. I took Mia by the hand and pulled her into the ladies' room.

But she stood at the door looking back over her shoulder. "Girl, did you see him?" she said looking at a guy at the edge of the dance floor.

"He is fine. Have you ever seen him before? I think he has a friend with him, too. So what do you think?"

"He's cute and all, but I have something to tell you."

"What is it? Tell me, I'm listening."

I knew she wanted to listen, but she really wanted to know if the cute brother she had just seen was still around.

"Will you close the door and listen to me? This is serious."

"Okay, okay, I know. But his butt was too."

"Mia, I have something to tell you."

"I'm listennning. Go ahead."

She gave me her attention that time, as she ran the length of the bathroom checking each stall to make sure we had privacy.

"You know what you said about me running after Vince... Well, you're right. I do need to be more aggressive. I mean, I really care about him."

"Girl, come here and look at me." She proceeded to peer closely at my face.

"What is that in your eyes? I see something. Ahh... I see the love light," she teased. I tsked heavily, as I was reminded of Tisha checking my eyes after my first kiss.

"Are you in love with him, Claudia? Girl, I never thought I'd live to see the day when you'd care about anything other than school. I don't believe what I'm seeing. Somebody pinch me. Chocolate, really, I'm so happy for you."

"So, what am I going to do about it, Mia? I've never felt this way about anyone before."

"The best thing I can tell you is to be more spontaneous when you're around him. Wait a minute; we forgot the most important part. Does he feel the same about you?" she asked seriously.

"I really don't know. We haven't talked along these lines at all. I mean, he sends me flowers almost everyday, and he's taken me shopping several times. We've held hands and said innocent sweet nothings. He's even told me that he cared about me. Perhaps it's all just wooing for the job. I don't know.

"But no, he hasn't said anything I could interpret as serious, not in so many words."

"Not in so many words. Humph. What does that mean, not in so many words? Has he asked you to be his girl?"

"NO! Nothing like that. But he tells me that I'm beautiful everyday I see him, and he is always so sweet and generous..."

"Yeah, yeah, yeah. I've seen the car, and I've seen the money, but has he ever kissed you or even tried to get the honey?"

"No, that's what I'm saying. He's not like that. He tells me that I'm special and that all of that can wait. He's just not like that."

"Not like what? He's a man isn't he? Now, we have discussed this before, Chocolate - the difference between a dog and a man - and I understand that there *is* a difference between a dog and a man, but even an obedient yard dog likes to come in the house every once in a while, if you know what I mean."

"Girl, you're crazy. You're never going to change," I said, but I was smiling at her, shaking my head back and forth.

"Why do I need to?" she asked defensively.

"You don't. No, you don't. I love you just the way you are. I don't ever want you to change. But Mia, what should I do?"

"Does Vince even act like he might want you to be his girl?" she asked.

"He tells me all the time that I'm the one for him, and that he would like for me to meet his mother one day. I'm sure of it, just not in the conventional way. I mean he's never actually verbalized it or anything like that," I said.

I was adding confusion to my own mess.

"For example, there was this one time he came over after work to bring me some company papers. It was late and we were just sitting on the sofa reaching for conversation. Out of nowhere he said, 'Chocolate, don't you think we look great together?' I smiled and said, 'Sure we do, Vince, 'cause here we are together. We're all of that...' But that's as far as it's ever gone," I told Mia.

"Have you ever wanted him to make love to you?"

"Mia, I'm not like that either. I mean I don't really think of that."

That really felt like a downright lie.

"I mean sure, I have needs, but I haven't ever been touched that way."

"Are you saying what I think you're saying?"

I didn't respond.

"Are you saying you've never had sex?"

"Yes, I have never had sex."

She just glared at me.

I added reluctantly, "Okay, sure, I've thought about what it might be like to make love to him, but Mia, I've only kissed one person in my entire life."

"Girl, do you mean they still make girls like you? I thought all this time you were playing."

"Why would I play about a thing like that?"

"That's it. You've got that look in your eyes," Mia said.

"And what look might that be?"

Mia obviously found all of what I had just said amazing. She threw both of her hands up in the air and said, "Can I call Tina? I have got to fill her in? It's got to be some kind of record. I mean, this is like finding a dinosaur on the freeway."

"I don't feel special because I haven't had sex, I feel right."

"Girl, believe me, ain't nothing normal about what you just told me."

A sly smile began to appear on her face.

"Wait just a minute! Let's verify your meaning of sex. You know, President Clinton had that same problem defining specific words."

I grimaced.

"Now, have you ever had sexual contact of any kind?" she began as if I was facing a congressional panel.

"No, not ever," I answered truthfully. "And just in case you are going to ask, the answer is no, I've never done anything to warrant inhaling."

That didn't even get a laugh out of her.

When she asked her next question, she pointed down between my legs, "Girl, not even a kiss... down there?"

"No... not one kiss 'down there' from anyone. Ever. Vince has pecked me on the cheek a couple of times, but never anything serious."

"Okay, okay. Let's just go back out there and wait on him to come over again. Remember to be spontaneous if you can, but maintain your composure. Does that make any sense to you?"

I nodded.

Mia leaned in closer to the mirror to powder her nose. She turned to me and said, "Okay then, spontaneous yet in control. Hey, let's go be beautiful."

She took my hand and we wandered back out into the crowd. She said that I'd know when it was time, and when the opportunity presented itself I wasn't to hesitate; I was to make my move.

We were smiling at each other as we rejoined the crowd. By the time we were midway through the club, there was a break in the crowd. We took advantage of the room and didn't stop for the lies and the causal murmur of deceit.

CHOCOLATE

We weren't out there five minutes before thoughts of the man I was attracted to began pulling away at my emotions. I could feel him walking towards me, yet he was nowhere in sight. My hands begin to sweat as my feet suddenly froze; much like the infatuation festering inside of me. I could smell the distinct aroma of his cologne the closer he got, and its fragrance was driving me crazy. When I finally spotted him my feet thawed and I was able to move. I reached out and touched his beautiful face and kissed him on the cheek.

"I hope that introduction didn't embarrass you," he said.

"No, you did that weeks ago, Vince. I'm almost used to it now."

"Well, I took this opportunity to let the world know you were special. They will all meet you on the newsstands tomorrow. One of your 'day-one' swimsuit shots was picked up and is being used for the cover of this month's *Elle* magazine. Congratulations, Chocolate."

I melted. It wasn't what he said, it was the way he said it. No one had ever pronounced 'Chocolate' the way he did. The sound of his voice filled my mind with obsessive thoughts. I could hardly process the news about the *Elle* cover.

He continued to speak as he held my hand. "Chocolate, can I have the first dance?"

I wanted to say, 'Yes, you can have the first, the last and the rest of them, you sexy fool,' but I kept my composure and said, "Sure, if you'd like."

As we danced close to each other to *Tonight I Celebrate My Love*, I could feel one strong hand touching my waist and the other pressing against my upper back. I closed my eyes in an attempt to capture the moment. My body craved his as we rhythmically intertwined. I was captivated as we moved together for what seemed like forever. But the song ended all too soon. I wanted to take my shoe off and throw it at the DJ booth.

Vince brushed that thought from my mind as he turned to me and whispered, "I want to show you to your seat, then I have to go in the back and check on some things. There is plenty of food and lots to drink. Enjoy yourself, Chocolate. I will be back soon."

I was trying to show him with my eyes that it was time to take me in his arms and have his way. I was ready to unveil a spirit of unyielding passion. But he had something more important to tend to. Something more vital, more exciting than the Chocolate I was ready to feed him.

He walked me over to the reserved section of the club and made sure I was comfortable. A bottle of chilled Veuve Clicquot champagne was waiting for me. The DJ smiled down at me from his booth, as if to welcome me to the seat of honor. I rolled my eyes and gave him the meanest look I could conjure up. I felt like pulling back three of my fingers to show him how displeased I was with his last selection. His smile turned to a frown faster than Mike Tyson knocked out Michael Spinks.

He held up his hands in surrender and silently mouthed, "What did I do?"

"You destroyed the moment," I said loud enough for him to hear me over the Plexiglas barrier.

A guy running for DJ of the Year interrupted my first attempt at spontaneity.

When Mia saw Vince leave me at the table she strolled over and sat down with me. She saw my frustration as I took another sip of champagne.

"Claudia, what is wrong? Why aren't you smiling? Shit, I would be if I were you. Girl, where did his fine ass go?"

She was craning her neck and tipping from one butt cheek to the other as she scanned the club.

"Better yet… does he have any brothers? You know, a brother with some money. Now before you say anything, I know that my standards have been a little high of late, but in this case, I'll take a short one, a skinny one, ball senile… just any one brother he has with some money."

Mia was funny, but I was not ready to laugh. All I could do was point up at the DJ. She mistook the pointing and quickly knocked my hand down.

"Him? Girl, that's a damn DJ. We can't be settling for no damn DJ when we've got Donald Trump in the house. No, no, and hell no. Get your mind back on the millionaire."

She turned and pointed in the opposite direction. "He went that-a-way," she said.

"Mia, I was pointing at the DJ because I am so mad at him for stopping a song when Vince and I were dancing."

"Oh, now that's my girl. I more than understand your frustration with dancitis interruptus. Now, if it was me, I would be getting put out of this club by now."

"Vince and I were having a great time. That is until Sir-Play-a-Lot went on a roll."

She giggled on my behalf, but asked seriously, "So where is he now?"

"Well, he said he had to go and take care of some business in the back."

"Some business? What in the world could possibly be more pressing than all that Chocolate you're carrying around back there?" she said as she pointed towards my behind.

"He told me he had to take care of some business is all. And that's what he's doing, I guess."

"What kind of business is more important than taking care of you? Girl, I just don't know. Something ain't right. I smell a rat and his ass is close," said Mia.

"What do you mean?"

"If I knew, I would tell you. Here, have some more champagne," and she refilled my glass then continued, "but something just doesn't feel right, Chocolate. You're a beautiful woman and you've been knowing each other for how long? Okay, maybe only three or four weeks, but for him not to have never even tried to smell the coochie, something is wrong. Come on, he's a white man... and admit it, all white men dream of tasting a black coochie at least once."

I stared at her in mild shock hoping no one could overhear us. If she had been drinking her comments might be more understandable. And I'm sure I only had mild shock because I was drinking.

"Believe me, I know these things," she nodded confidently to support her own opinion. "And, I'm not going to tell you what I'm *really* thinking, but I'll say one thing again, something doesn't smell right."

When Mia was right about something she got a crazy look on her face. I saw the look in her eyes then, but I hoped that this time she would be wrong.

We decided to dance until Vince returned. And we had a ball. We got more attention than anyone else grooving to the DJ's tunes. After about thirty minutes, Mia gave me a nod and we sat down for a rest. She pointed out that Vince still hadn't returned.

"So, Claudia, is this normal behavior for him?"

"Is what normal behavior?"

"Okay, so we're playing stupid now, right?" She had to make a list. "Stranding you, leaving us here, abandoning you with no good-byes..."

"I haven't experienced this exact situation, but this doesn't seem normal for Vince. But I don't see what the big deal is. I mean, it's not like he's my boyfriend or anything. He does have a life, you know. Besides, he is coming back."

"Hmm. We'll see. He could have had the common decency to make every effort to stay here with you on your special night. I mean it is graduation day, and he invited you here, Chocolate. And now where is he going?"

"He's in the back handling some business," I said.

"Oh, is he then? That's what you said before."

"What are you saying, Mia?"

"I'm saying that I haven't seen Vince for a while, but if you say he's here then I have to believe that you know something I don't. I mean, maybe there are two of them. Does he have a twin brother? Because if not, lover-boy's out of here."

"When? Where? How long ago?"

"Oh, while we were out on the dance floor, about ten or fifteen minutes ago now. I don't really know, Claudia. Who knows? Maybe it wasn't him anyway…"

I felt irritation with her games, yet looked to her with a hopeful plea.

"No, girl. It was him. He was wearing his all black and everything."

"Why didn't you say anything when you saw him leave?"

She sighed heavily and I could tell she was exasperated with me.

"Well, he isn't your boyfriend, is he. I mean, one minute you want to play Little Miss Innocent, and then the 'he's not my boyfriend' shit, and now you want me to keep tabs on him. Come on now, Claudia, make it plain. Better yet, let's just get the hell out of here. I'm really sleepy, and it's a long enough drive home. I think I need a cup of coffee before we get on the road."

She saw how hurt I was and tried to soften the blows.

"There's an all-night spot around the corner, just walking distance from here, come on I'll show you," and she lovingly took my arm as we got our coats and quit 'Doin' It' for the night.

We had our late night lattes and walked back to the car arm in arm, head to head. Just as we were getting ready to jump on the Bay Bridge, Mia noticed the man driving the car next to us.

"Hey, Chocolate," she said and nudged my arm. "Don't look now, but doesn't that look like Vince?"

I did a double take as I looked across her in the direction she was pointing. It was so dark I couldn't clearly make out who it was in the car.

"Are you sure it's Vince?" I asked.

"Look, names are really not that important to me, but faces are. I've always made it my business to remember faces. It's Vince all right, and he has someone in the car with him. It looks like it might be a blonde."

"What are you doing?" I asked as she changed lanes and sped up.

"I'm going to follow them," she said loudly.

"No, you can't do that!" I was mortified.

"Sure I can. I'm driving, and you're not. Besides, I told you that you needed to be more spontaneous, and what could be more spontaneous than this?"

"Mia, what are we going to say if he sees us following him?"

"I don't know, but maybe it's something like, 'Hey, since you ditched us at the club, is it all right if we come in for coffee with you and your friend?'

"Don't worry, Chocolate, besides he doesn't know this car, it's Nicole's remember? Besides, I am the designated driver and I say we're getting coffee at Vince's house."

"Mia, you're crazy, but that's why I love you."

It turned out Vince lived in a gated community in the Oakland hills. When the guard at the gate recognized Vince's car he just waved him in.

"Mia, let's just turn around and go home. This is crazy," I said. "We'll never get in there."

"What? And miss all the fun? Girl, sit back and watch Mia work her magic."

Mia was taking this too far, and just when I was about to insist she turn around, she pulled up to the gate. She placed the car in park and before the guard acknowledged us she raised up her dress and took off her panties as fast as she could.

When he approached the car, she said, "We're with Vince Morelli. I won't be needing these sweetheart, keep them for me, will you? I'll be right back."

The guard caught her panties in mid-air with one hand and a big smile, while he pressed the 'gate open' button with the other. Mia was more than spontaneous, she was a damn fool, and I was growing more envious of her by the second.

"Girl, you are crazy! I mean reeeal crazy."

"Did I get us in here, or what?"

I just shook my head in disbelief.

It wasn't hard to find Vince's house at two o'clock in the morning. There were only a few houses that still had their lights on. When I spotted his car in the driveway a part of me wanted to leave, but the truth is sometimes easier to see with the eyes, than it is to hold in your heart. My heart was racing and I was too anxious to see the woman he had chosen instead of me.

"Well, that sorry piece of crap," Mia stated before we had any proof. "How could he have chosen her over you? That man is crazy as hell. I'm going to let him know that when you mess with Chocolate, you've got to mess with Mia, and baby, it can get bitter."

We walked around the right side of the house, but the windows were higher up than most and we couldn't see anything from the ground.

"I can't see anything," whispered Mia. "Here, lift me up."

I followed instructions and placed both of my hands together for a step up. I lifted Mia high enough for her to peer into the living room window.

I held her up there for almost a minute, and she didn't say anything the whole time. Something was wrong.

"Well, what do you see?" I said.

"Nothing. There's nothing to see. Put me down, and let's get out of here," she said flatly.

I could tell she was lying. "Lift me up so I can see that same nothing that you just saw."

"It's time to go home, Chocolate. It's just time to let go."

"Come on, Mia. I can take it. What does she look like? I need to know what she looks like. Lift me up," I insisted.

Now that I look back on it all, it would have been better if I had kept my feet on the ground.

"It's not worth it, Chocolate, believe me."

I could tell that whatever she saw hurt her deeply, and she knew that it would hurt me if I saw it too. But I had to see for myself. Mia relented and made a step for me. She boosted me up underneath the window so that I could see.

Vince was making love to a blond all right, but it wasn't a woman, it was a man. His bare back was to me as they kissed passionately and pressed their bodies against one another. There they were, two strong, beautiful men caressing each other wildly, as Vince held him in his arms, much like I had held Vince in my dreams.

His mate was as handsome as I was beautiful, and as strong as I was meek. He ran his fingers through Vince's hair as I had done so many times in my mind.

They were naked down to their souls. As he turned Vince towards the window in a motion to set up for penetration no doubt, Vince's eyes were closed, and I could tell he moaned with pleasure.

His eyes opened up ever so slightly, perhaps to gaze up at the stars while being served thrusts of insanity. By the time he focused, his eyes met mine. They never stopped making love nor did Vince take his eyes off of me. But we both released tears at the thought of what that moment meant to us both.

I climbed down from the window and headed back towards the car.

Vince opened the front door and yelled out, "Chocolate! Please don't leave like this. I didn't know how to tell you. We were getting so close."

"Not close enough to be honest, I see."

"I wanted to care about you, but I couldn't let go of my past. I've been fighting this for some time now, and I've made my choice. I love you, Chocolate, the only way I can. I can't love you like a man loves a woman, but I can love you like a friend loves a friend."

Mia walked over to Vince and asked, "Why did you lead her on like that? You, you...faggot!"

Vince brushed off the insult and looked directly at me.

"I know I have been very selfish and I've treated you unfairly. The first time I laid eyes on you, Chocolate, I felt that you were the only woman who could possibly turn me away from this life. Members of my own family have always told me I just hadn't ever met the right girl. When I saw you, Chocolate, I tried to go straight. But no matter what happened I just couldn't break away. My weakness for men is greater than my desires to please my family. I fell in love with you, Chocolate, but I couldn't let go of my love for men. Your touch was soothing, but it wasn't strong enough to calm my need to be held by the strong hands of a man."

Vince fell to his knees and began sobbing like a baby with both of his hands pressing down on the back of his neck.

"I love them, Chocolate. I love the way they make me feel."

With the last bit of self-pity I had left inside, I asked myself, 'Why? Why me?' A part of me hated every word he spoke, but I couldn't walk away just yet, not while he was pouring out his soul. I felt compelled to listen to the empty sound of his sorrow. A spirit of compassion came over me, allowing me to open up doors of consideration.

"Please, please, don't go," he begged me.

Assuming the role of a victim was not very attractive or healthy. I managed to cast all that aside and I stretched out my arms to embrace him. He was reeking from intense sweat conjured up by unveiling his reality. As we embraced, I could feel his confusion. I started to cry as our souls somehow reached a mutual understanding. I needed to hear why he couldn't love a woman, just as bad as he needed to explain it.

My tears were compassionate. No longer thinking of myself, I began cuddling his pains as if they were my very own. After a few minutes I walked over to Mia, who was sitting in the car waiting on me.

"Mia, Vince is going to bring me home. We need to talk, and it's going to take a while."

"Girl, are you sure? I really don't know what you two could possibly have to say to each other at this point. What Vince needs is a good old fashion beat-down."

With that she pulled some bobby pins out of her purse and attempted to pin her hair up. The whole motion only took a few seconds, and then she started taking off her earrings.

"Oh, no, Mia," I said, quick to interrupt her momentum. "It's not time to fight, it's time to listen."

"Listen to what? Haven't you heard enough already? Didn't I hear his gay ass in there moaning? Didn't you hear that? Hell, if you can't get mad, let me get mad for you," Mia said.

"Beating him down won't solve anything."

"Yeah, girl, you're right. But it sure as hell would make me feel a whole lot better. He just hurt my Chocolate and I'm mad as hell."

"Mia, we've been taught that cooler heads must prevail, right?"

It took her several moments before she reluctantly agreed. "Okay, I'll go home, but only if his friend leaves. Only a daughter of Marvin L. Williams could stay here and have a conversation with someone who has just broken her heart. Call me if you need me, I'll keep my phone on."

Before Mia drove off, Vince's friend came running out of the house. "What's wrong, Vince? Are you okay? Who is *she*?" Lance pointed and indicated me as if I was a threat.

"Sure, I'm fine, Lance. Why don't you get your things and leave for now."

"Leave? You know my car is at the club."

"Then call a cab. I'll pay for it. I need to talk to a friend."

The blond lover was just standing there with a paranoid expression, apparently emotionally unable to move. That was until Mia got out of the car and started walking towards him.

Vince saw Mia walking towards his lover and yelled out to them both, "Pleeeeease, leave us alone so that we can talk."

He was pitiful to say the least, and he wasn't ready for one of Mia's episodes. He made a subtle gesture and Lance quickly turned around and walked back into the house.

"I'm not leaving, until *it* leaves," she said.

Within ten minutes a cab arrived and took Lance away. He came out of the house flaming like a forest fire, rolling his eyes widely as he strutted past us in disgust.

When he opened the cab door he screamed out, "I hope he tells you the truth, honey, because he apparently hasn't told me the truth.

"He told me that he didn't like fish, but I guess everything that comes out of his mouth is a lie."

Mia had her shoe off in a split second and was ready to throw it as she yelled, "You better get your sweet ass in the car before I brand the side of your head with this shoe!"

Mia was back at it, but this time it was short-lived as Lance got in the cab for cover. She was somewhat under control when the cab pulled off, and she walked back to her own car and waved good-bye.

Vince and I were alone and went quietly back into his house. The living room was very beautiful; elegant, and tastefully filled with Italian furnishings. We sat down on the leather sofa and stared at each other in silence.

"Would you like something to drink?" he offered after an awkward moment.

"Sure, Vince."

He walked across the room to the marble topped bar and poured me a glass of wine. As he handed it to me my questions began.

"So, Vince, why me? Why might I have been the one?"

His response frustrated me and the thought of calling a second cab was now on my mind.

"I picked you, Chocolate, because you are the most beautiful woman I had ever seen."

"So is that what this is all about? Did you invite me into your world because I'm beautiful?"

He was dumbfounded, and I could tell he didn't enjoy my line of questioning. I wasn't about to ease up on him though. I wanted him to feel the warm burning effects of heartbreak.

I took his head and pressed it against my chest, so that he could listen to the beating sounds of dejection. I closed my eyes and placed my hand on the side of his face.

"Listen to my heart, Vince," I instructed.

"Listen… as it struggles to regain its cadence. Do you know how a heart sounds when it is hurting? Well, this is how one sounds. Vince, can you hear the distress that I'm feeling? All of my life, the ignorant souls of this world have taught me that only a black man could make me feel this way. But are you black, Vince?" I asked rhetorically.

"No, Chocolate, of course not," was all he could say.

"Well, I guess that destroys that myth then, doesn't it? You know what I've learned from all of this, Vince? I've learned that any color is capable of being a fool. All that's really necessary is that one possesses the callous selfishness of a coward. Vince, a woman's beauty alone could never derail your basic desire for men. Only one form of beauty has the power to untangle the lustful webs of deceit, and that is the beauty of God's grace.

"Vince, my father taught me that egotistical cravings that embody our surroundings taint the beauty that is spun in the midst of a man's eyes. I am not a spider, and I do not know, nor will I ever possess the power you seek. I am allergic to deceit, Vince. And that has nothing to do with your sexual preference. What I have to give is greater than the lust that fills the mind of any man. The next time you get that crazy notion in your head, do something for me, will you?"

"What is that?" he asked.

"Get down on your knees and pray for God's grace to remove lustful desires from your heart and mind. Supply yourself with facts and denounce the premise of the perverted spirit that now plagues your soul. Choose a partner that fills other needs, more important needs."

He absorbed what I had to say, then reached out to grab my hands. "I know you're right, and I am wrong, Chocolate. Can you ever forgive me?"

I didn't need time to think about forgiveness. I smiled at him and said, "Yes, Vince. Of course. I was brought up with a spirit of forgiveness, and my convictions leave me no choice.

"I stayed here with you tonight for three reasons and three reasons only. First of all, I needed you to know that I am hurting. Secondly, I stayed to hear the confessions of a fool. And lastly, I stayed because I love you and I care about you.

"No one has a right to play with another person's heart. No matter how much money we have obtained, we will never gain the authority to tear away at the emotions of another human being. It is inhumane to tamper with the essence of a fragile soul.

"Please, don't ever do this again, Vince, to any woman or any man. At this moment, I cringe at the thought that I wanted to make love with you. Your life, as you must live it, has important rules and the consequences could be deadly. It frightens me that you could have been my first lover. But, Mia was right. I needed to be spontaneous tonight; I needed to be here with you."

"Chocolate, you're treating me like I am dirty."

"No, my friend. On the contrary. I want you to honor yourself with your choices. Think about what you're saying, and be careful where you aim your blame. People are not lab rats that you can do your little experiments on. I'm a human being. Vince, these are real tears that I'm crying, and they flow because of the lies you brought into my life.

"I didn't come into your world, you came into mine. I want you to know that my beauty is deeper than the skin you're able to see. I'll be all right, though. You see that I come from good stock and, good stock is hard to find."

He just sat there as I rambled on, knowing that I had every right to get it off of my chest.

"Vince, I'm not mad at you for being gay, I just feel that you should have used some of that gay pride and told the truth. My father taught me that I must respect a man's life-style for what it is. We are driven by our choices. I, too, have a choice, and right now I choose to believe that this is all happening for a reason. I have to believe that something good is going to come out of this and that in time I will learn to trust again. I hope your course of life fulfills you. I pray that life never stops giving you its best, and that one day you'll find it in yourself to warn your next victim. Better yet, that you will choose not to have a victim."

"I believe, Vince, that physical beauty is still the most overrated facet of life. This world must somehow establish another method by which truth is measured. It has to be something deeper than flesh. There has to be another way to institute a deep coherence within society."

We talked through the night and occasionally held each other close as we unveiled the infected spirits of sexual secrecy. I finally fell asleep in Vince's arms, with both my body and mind fully clothed.

There were some jagged edges when it came to where I stood on the artistry of lying. I believed that I helped to smooth them that night. I was more than pleased with the efforts we both made in our attempt to make right our wrongs by unveiling our deepest fears. I was ready to get on with my life.

Vince got up and cooked breakfast early the next morning.

"I don't mean to be rude, Chocolate, and believe me, I've listened to everything you've had to say… but I've always been curious about something."

"Curious? Curious about what, Vince?"

"Maybe this isn't the time."

"After everything we've talked about, there's nothing off limits at this point," I reassured him.

"Okay, then. Why do they call you Chocolate?"

I smiled at the innocence of his curiosity.

"Since as far back as I can remember, I have been called Chocolate. It's a combination of the dark brown color of my skin and a little chocolate mischief I was in as a toddler. My parents just got lucky and gave me a nickname that suits me." I smiled more with the recollection of that sweet memory.

"Why? Is there something wrong with the name Chocolate?" I asked.

He looked over at me as my temporary joy produced tears of sadness. Suddenly I felt dejected.

"What's wrong?" he asked sincerely.

"I don't just want to be just a pretty woman, Vince. I am a woman of substance and value. So tell me, am I still soothing to your eyes, Vince, after all that I've said?"

He couldn't respond to my last question, and he just hung his head in silence. Something told me that he had had enough and it was time for me to go. After breakfast he drove me home and on the way, we reassured each other we would still be able work together despite all that had happened.

That day, I came out of my shell and I would never turn back. I refused to stay the same. I became who I am because I was able to come face to face with the consequences and shoulder some blame. The tears I cried that night were valid, but the anger could not be justified.

CHOCOLATE

Anger gives way to bitterness, and a bitter man will never be able to taste the true essence of a joyous fruit. I had a right to be angry, but the annoying spirit of anger shall never nullify my ability to feel the pains of hurt. I was taught never to harbor the irritating attributes of madness in my heart, for a heart that is filled with madness is empty.

I ask no one to ever cry for me, but as they go through their own trials, they should prepare themselves for the coming miles. We will never reach our desired destination without having to endure the pains of provocation.

Hold who you will, and kiss who you must. But never ever forget, that it's yourself, who you must trust. In the hour of truth we must be willing to stand taller than our highest fears. Yes, trouble may come, but it will not last. We must learn to brace ourselves as the winds of trouble blow, and like an oak tree, we must be able to weather the storms. We must stand tall on the legs of hope as troubling storms try to uproot our ambitions.

Then we can truly face our realities and come out of our shells.

Love is Black and White

Dramatic-Impressions welcomed me the week after graduation. Vince and I were able to get right down to business, and within six months I was on the cover of three more magazines. I was what the industry called 'an overnight success.'

The few months after Vince's coming out episode were still personally difficult, however. In that time, the prevailing winds were strong but they were only able to bend me emotionally, not break me. It took days to refocus, but I was finally able to see that segment of my life for what it was, and then all was well, once again, in the sweet land of Chocolate.

There were no melancholy, got-to-get-down-on-my-knees-and-cry-for-sympathy blues. The lingering efforts of sorrow vacated my heart and an unforeseen joy had taken its place. I was loving life again, and life was loving me back.

I wanted to live the American Dream, without dreaming. So I stopped sleeping and started working hard to make my dreams come true. I immersed myself in my modeling career and started to develop an international identity.

With my father's and Vince's advice, I made a few good business investments using my six-figure modeling income. I had decided to invest in my future.

I moved out of the Berkeley apartment my father had been renting for me since my junior year to become a homeowner. I bought a beautiful four-bedroom home just before Dramatic-Impressions went on tour that summer. The house had a mid-size swimming pool in the back yard, and a cozy little Jacuzzi hot tub next to it. Everything was plush, from the front door to the back gate.

My father said I was living high on the hog. My only response was, "If hogs live this high up, there wouldn't be any mud for them to wallow in."

I purposely moved closer to my father, so that we could take better care of each other. I lived in the small town of Fremont, and my new home wasn't but twenty minutes away from his comfortable place in the nearby city of Sunnyvale, back in the South Bay where I was raised.

It was early November, when life took its next big turn. I was on top of the world and just like a star in the sky, I was shining brightly. I had finished doing several important photo shoots in New York, London, Oslo, Milan, and Rome by the end of September. By early November the company was in the Caribbean, at a variety of island locales, for yet more work, when I found out I was gong to be featured on TV.

Several of our shows had been filmed and edited over the last six months, and one of the producers had told me in passing that a feature to promote local models was being compiled. After an especially exhausting day, I was told that the piece would be aired in two days. I was excited and couldn't wait to call home to let everybody know the schedule.

I wanted them to see their Chocolate on TV. Even with all the photo shoots, runway shows, and magazine covers, it never occurred to me that I would be featured on TV after six short months.

As soon as I got back to my dressing room I called home. The phone seemed to ring forever, but finally my father picked up.

"Hello," he answered in his monotone.

"Daddy, guess what?"

"Chocolate! Hello there. Where are you calling from? What is it, baby?"

"I'M GONNA BE ON TV!" I shouted.

"What? When? Chocolate – how exciting! Hey, Nic, my baby's going to be on TV!" I heard him yell to Nicole.

"So, when is it, Chocolate? Tell me when you're going to be on TV so that I can tell everybody!"

"It's this coming Friday at seven, your time on NBC."

"Baby, you don't mean NBC, the largest network in television?"

"Daddy, what are you saying? That I'm not good enough to be on NBC?"

"No, baby, I'm not saying that at all. I just wanted to make sure we've got our channels straight. If you tell me it's NBC, then that's the channel I'm going to be tuned into."

I was right to call my father first. When he heard the news, he called up everyone we knew and asked them to come over and join him as he watched his beautiful daughter model on TV.

On the night the show was aired, my father and I spoke briefly on the phone prior to the telecast.

"Well, I hope seeing me on TV makes you proud, Daddy."

"Baby, I've been proud of you all of your life. You being on TV will just give me a chance to brag that much more about how proud I am. Everyone's going to be here at the house around six or so."

"Everyone? Everyone like who?"

"You know, Nicole of course, your Aunt Jackie and her husband, Mama Lawson, Mr. Bobby from across the street, and the rest of the family."

"So what are you guys making to eat?"

"Food is it? Is that the first thing on your mind? Oh, I never know anymore. Nicole and Mama Lawson are always cooking up something fabulous around here."

"Okay, Dad, I have to go now. I'll call you after the show airs."

My father had a real nice time pointing at the TV they told me. Every time he saw me on the runway, he'd point at the screen saying, "That's my baby! Just look at her, isn't she beautiful?"

A certain long, white fitted dress was just loose enough for his approval. At least one clothing change suited him. After the show, they said he was strutting around with his chest busting out of his shirt, like the proudest peacock.

Shortly after ten I called home and spoke with my father. He still had a house full of people there. Everyone was screaming out my name in the background. I was feeling good inside just knowing they were proud of me.

When the spotlights focused on me, I was indeed happy. I was happy because I could control the moment. I felt like I could make the world stand still. When I was out there on the runway, I even amazed myself. I had what Vince called, 'it.' And I worked 'it' to the best of my ability.

"Baby, you were beautiful and everyone told me to tell you, 'hello.'"

"Thanks, Dad. I could hear them rooting for me. Where is Nicole?"

"Oh, she's in there somewhere serving drinks and having a good time."

"That's great. You really seem to care a lot about her. Daddy, you and Nicole really have been spending and awful lot of time together. Are things getting more serious between the two of you?"

I could feel him grinning through the phone.

"Baby, I wanted to wait until you came home, but since we've already shared your great news, I feel that it's only right that I share mine."

"What great news is that, Daddy? Are you talking about what I think you're talking about?"

"I don't know, let's see. Wait just a minute."

I was on pins and needles, trying hard as hell not to speculate about what my father was about to say.

"Nicole, baby, pick up the phone," I heard him say as he held the mouthpiece into his chest.

Within seconds she did just that.

"Hello, Chocolate," she said in her beautiful soft voice.

"Baby," he said to Nicole, "now I know we promised not to tell her until she came back, but this moment feels good, and I can't hold it in any longer."

I couldn't take the suspense anymore, so I yelled out, "What is it? Tell me, Dad."

"Baby, Nicole and I got married last weekend in Lake Tahoe."

I paused for a gulp of much-needed air and plopped down in my dressing room chair.

"You mean, you two are married, as in husband and wife?"

"Yes, silly girl. What other type is there?"

My old spirit of selfishness began to take over, but I fought it off and said in my most cheerful voice, "I'm so happy for you both. You two really look great together. Tell me about the ceremony."

My father was sounding more content by the second.

"Oh, it was just like any other, short and sweet."

"Well, the most important thing is that you are happy, right?"

"Right!" they both chimed in together.

"Well, baby," Nicole said, "I hope you're not working too hard and that everything's going well. By the looks of the show, it seems like things couldn't be better. I have to go now, though, Mr. Bobby from across the street has just spilled his drink on the carpet and you know how your father feels about his floors. I'll talk with you later, okay? Congratulations, Chocolate."

After she hung up her extension, I said, "So, Dad, what do I call her?"

"Call her Nicole, that's her name. She didn't marry me so that you could treat her any different. She understands her role in my life and she knows she can never replace your mother. Give her a little credit, Chocolate. Just know that I am happy and be happy for me, okay?"

"Sure, Dad. I am happy for you; it's just that it caught me off guard. I like Nicole, and she seems to really love you. That's really all that matters to me."

"Well, baby, I am happy, and just so you know, Nicole makes me feel whole again."

"I can't tell you how pleased I am with your selection, Pops. You take care of each other, and I'll call you back in a couple of days." I may not have sounded too convincing.

I thought I was outgrowing my selfish attitude, but it reared its ugly head once more. I really hoped that my father hadn't seen through my superficial conversation. I was nervous that my self-centeredness had made its way across the ocean and through the phone lines. Hopefully their joy overshadowed my annoyance. More than that, I found I was really shaken by the news of their circumstances, and overwhelmed by the possible ramifications.

The basic fact was that my father was married to another woman. I mean, legally married with the ring, the vows and everything, as short and sweet as he insisted it all was. I probably would have to return my father's house keys!

I couldn't express what I was feeling to just anyone. I mean this was the nitty-gritty, the low-down bottom of the barrel truth. I had to discuss it with someone. Where was my Sweets when I needed her?

My childish reactions had me yearning for my mother too. I was definitely feeling like a child inside. I wanted to speak on her behalf, but I knew I had no right to. I should have trusted that my father was doing the right thing. After all, he was a good man, who had never invited negativity into our home.

A voice consoled me as I sulked. There she was by my side.

"He wasn't trying to replace me," I heard my mother whisper, "he was simply filling the void in his life. For the better part of your life, Chocolate, he has remained noble in his approach to regain a sense of self, and now the emptiness that has been with him for years is finally gone. I can see that easily, and soon, you will too. He has my blessing, and is waiting for yours."

It is true; in my eyes my father was always a man of honor, self-respect and pride. Who was I to pass judgment on his choices, seeing that I was the product of his first choice, and I turned out just fine. I had to remember that I was his child, he was not mine.

I tried to call Tina later that night, but her phone had been disconnected. That worried me a bit, but I just figured she had had one too many hang-up calls and finally changed her number. I tried her cell but she wasn't answering that either. I still felt no reason to be alarmed. Whenever she received the news, she'd be happy for Nicole and my father and give them a call.

We were nearing the end of a four-month tour and I had to stay focused. I was the featured girl in the company show, which meant I had to look glamorous every night. The tour was getting the best of me, though, and it seemed like the runways were growing longer and longer. With less than two weeks to go, I threw myself into work-mode and concentrated as hard as I could, as I inched deliriously towards the finish line.

I had lost weight on the tour and at times I felt almost too weak to smile. My stamina was depleted and only God knew just how many more steps my feet could take.

We were scheduled for three shows in five nights on our last few locations, and fatigue was my friend. It seemed like every time I got comfortable enough to sleep, I would hear those famous words, 'Girls, it's show time.'

No matter how tired we felt, the show must go on. People had paid good money to see us be beautiful, as Vince put it, so we couldn't let them down.

Once, while on tour, I just happened to be in a monthly way, and cramping badly for a few days. The thought of strutting down the runway was the last thing on my mind. I really wasn't feeling well and my tired body was reaching for sleep.

I stayed in the dressing area as long as I could with a heating pad on my stomach, waiting for my cue. When I heard Eve call for me, my competitive spirit pulled at my tired body as my feet reluctantly planted themselves back on the floor and in the direction of the stage. I relived those times when I used to fake my period to avoid verbal confrontations with my father, but I couldn't avoid the stage. It had become my drug of choice and I needed its light to ease the pain.

Eduardo was our stage manager, and the girls all called him Eve. He was a beautifully built older gentleman with perfectly groomed salt and pepper hair. Eve was in his mid-fifties, about the age of my own father, and loved men more than most women did. He was as gay as they came, and had a special thing for black men.

He was a taskmaster more than anything, and his sing-song, high-pitched voice carried well when he let us know it was two minutes to show time. He was cranky and moody if we didn't jump through hoops for him, and at certain times of the month you would think he was on his period. Some of the girls would tease him and ask if he needed a pad or a Midol.

By the time he gave me the signal that night, my body ached too much to move. But Eve had his persuasive ways, and before I knew it, I was moving towards the stage. I could feel the lights lingering around the corner waiting just for me, and the anticipation never ceased to fill me with excitement.

Like any other star, and because I really did love and respect Eve, I closed my eyes and reached inside myself and gave them everything I had left. Modeling had become my life and being pampered, adored, and looking beautiful was fun. I owed it all to Vince.

He and I became the best of friends. After our life-altering experience, we were like two giddy girls. We were always chatting about something or someone. My circle of friends had been limited to females before Vince, but I embraced the change. I had never had a male sidekick.

Consummating our working relationship had been easy. Unlike many employer-employee relationships, Vince and I shared our deepest thoughts and revealed our base-line issues to each other. We had an up on where the other stood, and had developed complete trust in one another.

He gave me another perspective of life from his own male/female point of view. He may have had feminine insight, but he was stronger than most men. He was one of the wisest men I came to know, aside from my father. That may have been what kept me attracted to him.

Our working relationship wasn't tarnished one bit by what had transpired in our recent past. I loved the direction he was taking me in and I was willing to ride with him until the wheels fell off.

I was also attached to the incentives that came with becoming successful, and the plan that Vince had orchestrated for me was astonishing.

When we were on the road, Vince saw to it that we were like one big family. If there was friction in the air, Vince knew. Not only was he our boss, he was our girlfriend, and girlfriends can sense friction. We all came to accept that Vince Morelli was gay, but more importantly we found out that he was a genius. Dramatic-Impressions was on the top.

He ran the cleanest show on the tour, but some of our girls did have drug habits. Vince knew of those who were battling with drugs and he was prepared to yank them out of the show if their addictions became too obsessive to manage.

There were a few stuck-up people in our modeling group, especially Marianna. She was a two-faced hussy from Norway who had been signed by Dramatic-Impressions when we did our Olso show. She was great in passing, but annoying as hell to actually talk to. She was five-eleven and weighed about two and a half pounds more than your average long-term crack head. She had a lovely smile and the best set of breasts money could buy. Her sassy hairstyle was accented with shimmering blonde streaks.

We call her two-faced because one minute she was laughing in our faces, seemingly with us, and the next minute she was stabbing us in our backs. She had a thing for telling Vince what went on while he wasn't around. I knew, because he told me everything. But Marianna didn't know that. And I kept that my little secret.

Another secret Vince and I shared was that he came from old money. Rumor had it that he was the grandson of the late Arturo Vincenzo "The Eye" Morelli, a well-known Italian crime boss. Apparently he had lost his right eye as a child in Italy. An expose on Court TV named him as one of the last first generation Italian Mafia members at the time of his death over three decades ago.

Vince had never revealed details of his wealth to anyone, like the smart little rich girl he was. I never pressed him for any more information than he was comfortable imparting. Besides, I knew he had done well enough on his own to deserve everything he had.

One night after a late summer show in New York, Vince and I went out for drinks. Our third stop was in the neighborhood of Little Italy. We parked around back of a family neighborhood Italian restaurant called *Vincenzo's*, just off Mott Street. Vince said that his family had owned it for three generations, and as if I needed proof, most of the older family members greeted him with raised glasses and loud embraces as soon as we stepped in.

"*Vincenzo! Vincenzo! Ciao! Ciao!* Why you don't see us for so long?" they wondered. "We wait for you beautiful face, *ti bello faccia,* every day. Still you no come back home."

Vince smiled at their warm greeting and indicated to me that they said the same thing every time he came by to visit.

I gathered that the name of the restaurant held great personal significance for him, and was going to ask about its history when I heard some commotion in the far corner. Vince stiffened slightly.

I had noticed that a few of the younger patrons held back when we arrived. There was an instant air of disgust, which clouded the initial welcome. The farther in we walked, the more evident it became. In the eyes of some present generation family members, Vince was an outcast and a disgrace to the family. They saw him as a weak excuse for a man. He was known to be the sole heir of his father's business, and he was an embarrassment to the so-called young men in his family. They did not want *Vincenzo's* being run by a gay Vince from California.

One family member had no problem saying what was on his mind. He was Vince's first cousin, Mario. He was a cocky, late twenty-something Italian, a bit shorter than Vince at about five-eleven, but he displayed other family genes, and was splendidly built. He had dark curly hair and a distinct scar on the left side of his face. When he walked, I noticed he favored his right leg a bit. He dressed well, like most Italians I'd met so far, and gave the impression he was still associated with the Mafia.

He approached Vince and gave him a strong whack on the arm. "Long time no see, Vince."

"Likewise, Mario."

"That's a real pretty girl you've got there," he said as he gestured towards me.

"Another *bella faccia*, we've got a pair of 'em right here."

"Just in case you haven't noticed, Mario, she's a lady. But you're not familiar with real ladies, now are you?"

I could feel the long-worn animosity between those two crazy Italian cousins, mad at each other for only God knows what. Nervous and unsure about where this was all going, I attempted to cut the tension.

"This is a real nice place your family has here. The décor is so traditional and inviting. How long have you been in business in this location?"

"So the moolie speaks as well, how clever she must be."

A man who seemed crazy enough to end my life without blinking an eye had just called me a nigga. He obviously lived off insulting other people, and seemed happy begging for a reason to kill another nigga, regardless of gender. I began shaking like a leaf, and stood there feeling helpless.

"There is a way to speak, and a way not to speak when in the presence of a woman. And I believe an apology is due to the lady, Mario," Vince said calmly defending my honor.

I really did appreciate him for coming to my defense, but that was not the appropriate time to be brave, I thought to myself.

"Why should the thoughts of some homo cause me to alter my way of speaking?"

"Because this homo's going to make you, if you don't."

The older folks were stunned at Vince's revelation. But some of them nodded in support.

"Oh, is that right?" Mario challenged. "Va all'inferno!"

Before Vince let him utter his last word, he struck Mario on the side of his face, and the fight was on.

There were several rapid-fire blows thrown, but Vince was getting the best of him. Seeing him in such a macho light was somewhat of a turn-on, although the fighting seemed so unnecessary. As they rolled across the floor I tried to position myself, in case Vince needed any assistance.

The rest of the family just stood around and watched as though the fight was a normal occurrence. From across the room, I jumped up and down, taking mid-air swings as I wishfully administered blows to Mario's head.

There were a few older gentlemen taking bets over near the bar as Vince and Mario continued to fight on. Vince, for the moment, was an animal, a real live barbarian stud. By the way he was carrying on, one might never think that he had embraced men the way I knew he had. Regardless, the fact still remained, he was gay, and now the whole family knew it.

Before too long they both began to shout back and forth at one another.

"*Sci pazzo, Vincenzo*? Are you crazy? Why are you fighting me over this moolie?" Mario wondered.

"She's my friend, and she's not a moolie!"

"She's blacker than anyone woman I've ever seen, so she has to be a moolie. Vince, have you forgotten how often we both said nigga while we were growing up?"

"No, I'll admit to that juvenile stupidity. But since then, I've learned that we are no better than the lies we were told, and the lies we went on to tell."

Vince had to lean over with both hands on his knees to catch his breath.

"We all have a right to be respected, Mario, so apologize to the lady and let's be done with it."

Mario turned to me with his face bloodied and both of his eyes beginning to swell.

"Okay, okay, I'm sorry," he said perfunctorily.

Turning to Vince he said, "There. I told her. Now stop it already."

Instead, Vince grabbed Mario's head and banged it downwards into a table nearly knocking him out. He lifted him up by a fistful of hair and asked, "Now, Mario, what color do you see?"

He held Mario's head up as blood dripped from both his eyes.

"I can't see no color, Vince. My eyes are just about swollen shut. And I think you broke my nose."

"Good, then remember this for me."

"Remember what?"

"Just as you were given no choice of the color you wear, neither was she given a choice of the color she was to be at birth, you shallow piece of shit."

Vince let go of Mario's head but it fell back onto the table with a thud. *"Ti sta bene,"* he said to Mario.

"That serves him right," he said to me, and he grabbed my hand and started walking towards the front door. As he moved, I moved.

On our way out of *Vincenzo's,* Vince never looked back. He was still breathing like a wild animal. His soft black curls were angry locks scattered in a tousled mess, but I was proud to be with him. No man had ever taken up for me that way. I was honored to be his friend, apparently just as he was to be mine.

Still trying to catch his breath, Vince spoke his first words when we arrived back at the car.

"No one's ever going to disrespect you again, at least not while I'm around. Do you hear me, Chocolate? I won't ever allow you to be hurt again."

"Yes, Vince, I hear you. Just try to forget about it, okay."

He felt compelled to offer an explanation.

"All my life, Mario and I have been fighting about something. Tonight it was you, and tomorrow it's going to be something else."

"Is he really your cousin?"

"Yes, he's my first cousin on my father's side," he admitted.

But that's all he was willing to reveal.

"Could you please pass me that bottle of wine in the back seat? Will you?" he asked.

Reluctantly I reached back and grabbed the wine. Vince took the bottle and swallowed the wine in gulps. The more he drank, the faster he drove. I wasn't really worried at first, but eventually we were headed across the Brooklyn Bridge away from Manhattan. We had left the luxury and safety of our hotel far behind. I grew quieter as we drove farther into the night. I was hoping that my silence would cause Vince to speak, and that he might be inclined to tell me where we were headed.

Vince kept tossing the bottle straight up, throwing his head straight back until he polished off the whole thing. He was scaring me. I had never seen him this way. He was out of control, and there I was stuck right in the middle of his personal madness. The drive was beyond unpleasant and I wanted out. I wanted a glass of wine too, but accompanied by some girlish conversation in a swank hotel room, not out for the Mad Hatter's joy ride through New York City.

The only saving grace was that we were gallivanting in the wee hours and traffic was beginning to lighten up.

After driving in what seemed like circles for more than thirty minutes, Vince finally turned off on a road that appeared vaguely familiar to him. It was dark and as the car slowed I was finally able to speak.

"Where are we going, Vince?"

"Oh, so you're still awake? Chocolate, I thought that you had fallen asleep."

"How could I sleep through all of this? Vince, it's getting late, and I am really tired."

He jerked the wheel and pulled the car over to the side of the road.

"Why are we stopping here?" I asked.

"I've never taken anyone here before. I come here by myself sometimes when I'm in town."

I had been drinking myself earlier that night and was a little light-headed when we first left Vince's family place, but by the time we parked I was completely sober. The only thing I saw was a cemetery up ahead and a few dim streetlights. He pulled forward and through the cemetery gates.

"Okay, now just in case you haven't been told, this isn't the most appropriate place to take a young lady in the middle of the night."

He turned to me and smiled, but he could tell that I was not amused.

"Why are we here, Vince, of all places?"

He gripped the steering wheel and stared straight ahead into the darkness.

"I need to visit a relative."

"Vince, at three o'clock in the morning? I mean, I'm not trying to be insensitive or anything but couldn't this have waited until tomorrow? You know, like when the sun was up."

"Come on, we won't be here long, I promise."

He opened the door and got out and stumbled towards the gravesites. I had no keys, no flashlight and my only help, should something happen, was disappearing into the night.

The deliberating was over in an instant. I jumped out of the car and caught up with Vince. We walked for about five minutes until he suddenly released my hand. I didn't know what to expect, but I sure as hell wasn't going to leave his side. Before I knew it, he started to relieve himself on one of the graves.

"What are you doing, Vince? Let the man rest in peace," I implored him.

As he zipped his pants he said, "He never let me rest in peace."

I didn't know what to think.

"This is Mario's father, my dad's beloved brother, the late Uncle Oscar. My father paid him to watch over me as a child. I practically lived with Mario and his family. Over the years his death has ignited the hatred between me and Mario."

"What did he do to you?" I asked.

"By day, he was the perfect uncle, by night he was one of the world's most notorious perverts," he said with obvious detest. Spittle shot from the corners of his mouth as he began to recount his story.

"My father was always away on business, or back in Italy, and I was conveniently sent to Uncle Oscar's home while he was gone. My mother had died when I was born, and I had so many surrogate parents, it became just one big happy family.

"My Aunt Elena, bless her heart, had a mental illness which progressed in her late thirties and, after time, was unappealing to her husband, I guess. She was also incapacitated in the evening hours, so Uncle Oscar would come into my room to check on me regularly at night.

"Mario was barely three years old when my uncle first started in on me. At first I thought that it was normal, even though I was uncomfortable. I was too young too know that what he had me do was improper, but I was eager to be a good boy. He taught me to touch him and told me that all young boys did it to show their appreciation. It became a game that in time got out of hand.

"One memorable night when everyone was asleep, he came into my room and violated me as usual. He always instructed me to get down on my knees, so that I could please him down there. But that night things changed. Everything got out of hand, and what he did hurt me bad. I bled for hours after he finished. I hadn't even seen my seventh birthday before he had bedded me down seven times. Eventually I got used to the way he penetrated me and I even missed his nightly visits. The older I got the less frequent the visits became, though. But by the time I knew that what I was doing was wrong, it was too late to dare tell. Besides I thought I was too in need of his physical attention.

"Just after I turned thirteen my uncle was killed. When I heard of his death I cried for days. In my own perverted way, I could say that he was the first man I loved. For years I reached for him through the night. I needed him to pacify my wants and to appease my weakness.

"I know I have always been gay, but if Mario ever found out that it was his own father who baptized me into this way of life, it would kill him."

By then it was almost four o'clock, and I was standing in a cemetery listening to a man heal himself as he stood at the gravesite of his perverted ex-lover. He acknowledged the fact that he was too weak to stand alone, so I stood there as his friend. I allowed him to draw the necessary strength from my already tired, nearly depleted soul, as he unveiled his darkest secret.

"Chocolate, I loved this man, even though I know what he did was wrong. After his passing, I stood beside my father at this very gravesite as he praised Oscar, his only brother, for being one of the greatest men he knew."

"Are you telling me that nobody ever knew what he did to you?"

"No. No one."

I could see that he was hesitating.

"Well there was one person, who may have known. My Aunt Elena. There she is in the grave beside him," and he pointed sadly to her resting place.

"One night she went looking for him and saw that my bedroom door was open. When she peered in to check on me, she caught my uncle on top of me, just having his way."

I was aghast. "What did she say, Vince? Surely she intervened."

"She was the wife of a mobster. What could she say? She simply closed the door and went back to sleep. If she had confronted my uncle or told anyone else, she would have been killed. I'm sure she feared for her life on a daily basis."

We held hands again and stared at the headstones in silence.

"Come on, Chocolate. Let's get out of here and get some sleep."

Back in the car I was too speechless to utter a word, so I placed my head against Vince's shoulder and fell asleep as we drove back into the city.

Neither one of us ever talked about what was said in the cemetery that night again. My ears were his and I will take his secret to my grave.

Real Love

I was thinking about enjoying the company of a man after being with the girls for so many months, but I had still not allowed anyone to get close enough to me to develop a relationship that would have warranted or justified intimacy.

A real man was harder to find than a cure for cancer it seemed. There was always something in their past that prevented them from feeling the true essence of a woman. They wanted to feel what it was to be like to be inside of me, rather than to walk beside be.

Being under the tutelage of Marvin L. Williams for as long as I was kept me in check. He taught me that choosing a man was like ordering a meal. He said that the owner of a restaurant, just like a man, will dress up a menu to lure the diners. "Know what you like, and never allow yourself to indulge because of enticing pictures on the menus; for the dishes are never quite what they seem," he said.

When it came to men, I knew exactly what I wanted and I was never willing to settle for the soup of the day. I was always looking for something more appetizing and (ful)filling.

I had already done my part. My schooling was complete and my finances were in order. My morals were in check and my life had no room for neglect. I was a self-made woman in search of nothing but the very best. I felt that if I could afford the top shelf beverages, then I deserved a top shelf man by my side.

If I could acquire my own personal necessities in life, then he could acquire the aptitude necessary to meet my needs. Though I have always known life wasn't prefect, applying these beliefs on a daily basis felt good, and that was all that really mattered.

So much had changed over the course of a year. Touring the world was fine but it had taken its toll on me. Though society could say I had been well compensated, I was still drained. My eyes burned from lack of sleep. My body was exhausted from the constant physical demands. The hourly runway strut had done a number on my legs, and I was more than tired of pretending to smile.

There was no misconception as far as I was concerned about the financial rewards, but I grew tired of watching people around me move roughly like mummies. A few of the other girls were often too strung out to even know what city we were in.

I lost count of how many girls I had to soothe after they had awakened from a drug induced stupor. I became an enabler and found myself with something or other in my purse to comfort the next victim of the night. Some girl was always too high, too helpless, too something to stand up on her own. And when I saw that someone was too far gone to care, I cared for her. When I saw one about to disrespect another, I intervened.

But I wasn't being paid to babysit, or counsel. I was being paid to model and to make people desire the clothes that I wore on stage. I despised the way the dirty old men gawked at my semi-clothed body, but I never once believed that getting high would change what others felt about me.

I told myself in the beginning that if I ever became ashamed of what I was doing, I'd walk off of the runway.

Now, after only six months, I was just plain tired. I needed to lie in my own bed, and curl up in some fresh sheets. I needed to feel my naked body against familiar warm fabric and inhale the dreamy aroma of scented candles throughout my new home.

I arrived back in the Bay Area a few months after the New York stint, and just days after we wrapped up in the Caribbean. I had been away on tour for almost six months, and within that time I had learned my best boyfriend's traumatic lifelong secret, my father had re-married, my best girlfriend had gone astray, and it seemed as if my life was in disarray once again. My shining star had faded.

The holidays were just around the corner and I so badly needed to feel the spirit surrounded by family. I missed home-cooked meals and the simple everyday pressures of life. I missed my father and I just wanted to be near him. It was three days before Thanksgiving and there was a festive feeling in the air.

The first thing I did was race over to my father's house. I needed to see it for myself. My father remarried. What was this world coming to?

Within two hours after landing at San Francisco International Airport I was knocking on his front door. Nicole greeted me with a glorious smile.

"Chocolate, my dear. When did you get back?"

"My plane just landed a few hours ago, and I raced over here to get my first look at the newlyweds," I replied happily. She took my hand and led me into the living room.

"Your father is in the shower. He's been out there in the garage working on something or other all day. You know him, he's always tinkering with something, child."

"Yeah, that's my dad," I agreed. "Mmm, what is that I smell?"

"Oh, of course you must be hungry. I cooked some roast beef, mashed potatoes and mixed vegetables. Let me fix you a plate."

I placed my purse on the kitchen counter and walked as fast as I could towards the bathroom to wash my hands. Nicole walked into the kitchen grinning from ear to ear. She seemed overjoyed to fix me a plate of food.

As I headed back to the kitchen, the lights were on in the hallway and I couldn't help but notice that the portrait of my mother had been removed. I tasted instant betrayal, but took a deep breath and moved towards the kitchen with a childish pout.

My mother was in heaven probably preparing dinner for God and no doubt shaking her index finger down at me.

"Child, get in there and sit down at that table," I heard her scold. "Stop acting silly. Nicole's a very nice woman and besides the food is getting cold. Straighten your face up and act like you've got some sense."

Before I could reach the kitchen the swirling aroma had destroyed my selfish spirit. I was more than prepared to replace the bad taste in my mouth with some of Nicole's to-die-for roast beef. As I neared the table I could see steam rising from the plate. The smell alone caused me to smile.

"What would you like to drink?" Nicole asked.

"I hope that it's not asking too much, but do you have some of that strawberry lemonade Dad always had around? Always my very favorite."

"Yes, how could you even ask such a question? Learning how to make strawberry lemonade was one of your father's criteria when we first met. Child, the only excuse that would be good enough for there to not be any lemonade made in this house, would be that the refrigerator wasn't working properly. And if that were the case, your father would have those tools out trying to fix it in a hurry. You know that, now don't you?"

With that she turned to the refrigerator and poured me the tallest, coldest, sweetest glass of strawberry lemonade I had ever tasted. Nicole had also warmed up some homemade bread that almost looked better than the roast beef.

She stood over me while I was eating and said, "Baby, slow down. You're going to bite one of your fingers off!"

"You might be right, and if I get any more of this gravy on them, there's a chance that I might be missing a few fingers by the time I'm finished."

"Is that my baby sitting at that table?" I heard my father ask from the hallway.

I was really excited to see him, but I had just taken a bite of Nicole's homemade bread and for the life of me I couldn't move from the table. My father walked over to me and kissed me on my cheek.

"So, how does it feel, Daddy?" I asked with my mouth half full.

"How does what feel?" he replied.

"Come on, Dad, stop playing. You're a married man now. How does it feel to be somebody's husband again?"

He walked over to Nicole and gave her a great big kiss.

"Marriage gets sweeter every time we kiss. She's the friend I've always wanted in my life. We are so good together and I love her for staying alive long enough to touch my life."

Nicole was smiling as he continued to stroke her ego with every genuine word he spoke. They were obviously in love, like two people should be. Destiny had them meet on the brink of despair, and unlike so many who conspire to get married, they were ready.

They were so in tune with each other that it was almost laughable. I could feel the love in the air when they glanced at each other simultaneously, as all dreamers of love hope to when and if love was right. What they had at that very moment needed to be bottled up and sold to those who dared to ever dream of obtaining such an inseparable love.

I had never seen my father kiss another woman before, but it felt good. Their joy signified that hope for love in my future was real. Their warmth was encouraging. Watching them need each other took away my appetite for homemade bread, and replaced it with an inner yearning that only true love could satisfy.

Nicole opened doors inside my father's heart that had been barricaded for years. Only the power of love could tear down the practiced defenses of loneliness. Nicole possessed such a love. She was that necessary someone who helped cultivate love's reality. My father smiled at her as she softly stroked the side of his face and placed her head upon his shoulder.

"Look at you two, in love like two little school kids. I've got to go home and unpack. I haven't seen my house in months."

"I've been going by your place twice a week, Chocolate. Making sure no newspapers were cluttering up the yard and that the water sprinklers were working properly."

"Thanks, Dad, I really appreciate you. You're the best dad in the world."

"Well, the most beautiful model in the world should have the best dad in the world. I mean, it's only right, isn't it?"

"You always know just what to say, Pops. I'm going to get out of here and let you two love birds get back to what you obviously do best."

I drove home that night feeling relieved. Witnessing real love right there back at home had displaced my selfish thoughts. I was not only relieved that my father had finally found someone to hold through the night, but most importantly, that the someone was right.

The Butcher

There was a supermarket a couple of blocks from where I lived. I needed to stop by and pick up a few things that Friday after Thanksgiving. I hadn't made off with many leftovers from our family feast.

As I walked over towards the deli I saw the most beautiful man I had ever laid eyes on. While reaching for a package of mixed vegetables, I clumsily dropped one on the floor.

When I reached down to pick it up, there was an enormously strong hand attached to the package.

"Let me get that for you, miss," the man said.

"Th-thanks, that's s-so nice of you," I replied with the faintest stutter.

"It was just the right thing to do. If I was really being nice, I would be cooking them for you. Allow me to introduce myself. My name is Omar; I am the butcher.

"My name is..."

But before I could get it out he said, "Chocolate, right?"

"Right you are. Well, I guess I'll be going now. It was nice meeting you, Omar. Thanks again for the hand," I said.

I had been awaiting the usual flurry of compliments, which never came. But when my eyes met his, they were engulfed with pleasure. Omar The Butcher had a calmness about him that was quite alluring. Not saying anything about who I was showed me a level of uncommon genuineness, which was long overdue. His down to earth approach and the fact that he was unaffected by my star status somehow humbled me.

I could gauge anyone's height based on the heels I wore at any given time. Omar had to be about six-one, because we were almost eye-to-eye with the particular shoes I was wearing that day.

His hair was natural, like wild grass, and he wore it short and un-combed. He had high cheekbones and adorable dimples that punctuated his face. At first glance his skin appeared rough, like slightly burnt butter, but it was actually quite smooth. His brown eyes were mesmerizing and his noticeable strength instantly unleashed a craving inside of me. Though his build was finely assembled, it was his bulging veins that ran up and down his arms, which aroused me the most.

His strength pulled at me and made me feel helpless. His willingness to walk away from me made me want him even more.

As I turned to walk towards the cashier his mere presence begin to envelop my senses. It seemed like the more steps I took, the closer he felt. I was almost out of the aisle when my need to know got the best of me. I paused nonchalantly and looked back to see how close he really was. To my surprise he was nowhere in sight. I was dumbfounded. I purposely walked as slowly as I could, hoping he'd come back and talk to me. I didn't know this person from Adam, but boy did I want to.

In line at the checkout counter I felt quite silly, and flashed on the last time I had met a man in a grocery store. I rolled my eyes at myself.

I willed the clerk to move at a faster pace, so I could pay for my things and elude any unforeseen embarrassment brought on by the schoolgirl crush I had just obtained.

While waiting my turn, one of the other checkers called back to the meat department for a price check. Omar was on his way.

I felt my knees grow weak and my hands begin to perspire. I had walked in front of large crowds of people with ease, but for some reason I had grown nervous making my way through the checkout stand.

The elderly lady in front of me was searching around in her purse for the correct change. When I noticed her futile efforts, I automatically reached inside my own purse and offered, "Here, how much do you need?"

"Thanks so much, child. I would have been all day trying to locate that thirty-seven cents."

"No problem at all. I saw you searching and I'm glad I could help."

My own bill wasn't more than fourteen dollars, but I threw a twenty on the counter and said, "Keep the change. Buy yourself lunch tomorrow. I'm in a big hurry, so just place these things in a bag for me, please."

I thanked God that the cashier wasn't one of those employees-of-the-month types, who did everything by the book. She was cool, and just smiled at me as she bagged my things as fast as she could.

She looked back over her right shoulder towards the meat department and smiled as if she understood my need to rush.

"Omar, right? Girl, I understand. If I didn't need the money, I'd be running out of here too, he is so fine. You better go now before he makes it to check stand number three. He's on his way."

I smiled and nodded as she handed me my groceries. I walked out of the store mildly embarrassed, but relieved for a bit of understanding from the local gal.

On my way home I relived the frozen vegetable incident and I could feel Omar's presence, just as if he was right there kneeling down next to me. Just thinking about him made me smile.

Hours after I had settled into my home, I searched for any and every excuse to justify going back up to the store. Omar had done a job on me without even knowing it.

Yes, he was only a butcher, but the vibes I got made me believe that he was so much more. The fact that he got on with his life after saying good-bye to me made him a candidate to win my heart. I needed a man who wasn't threatened by my financial status. Unlike so many guys before him, when he spoke, his eyes were focused on me and me alone.

The next day I awoke before my alarm, and waited for what seemed like forever to start my day. Father Time was holding back on the passage of each second, and it seemed like minutes were taking hours to pass. I was fidgety and just couldn't wait a second longer.

I finally rushed over and grabbed my purse and ran out of the door as fast as I could. I drove like I was an employee at the supermarket myself; rushing off to the store like I was late for work. I moved so fast it was all a blur, and before I knew it I was in aisle two. I didn't even remember parking my car.

Out of desperation, I walked up to the butcher's counter and tried to look interested in the red meat selection, knowing good and well that I didn't eat anything but fish and chicken.

"Can I help you?"

I heard someone speak to me but his voice didn't sound familiar. So, I ignored it and kept staring into the glass display. It was apparent that Omar didn't work the same shift everyday.

"Hello, miss. Can I help you?" he repeated.

I read his tag and saw that the man's name was Jim. I glanced up to notice he was a short, broadly built Caucasian gentleman who looked nothing like Omar. There was absolutely nothing he could do for me.

"No thanks," I said with a smile, but I was thinking, 'if you were Omar on the other hand, now that would be a different story.'

"Is Omar working today?" I asked casually.

Jim was loading the display trays when I asked, and by the look on his face, he obviously found my question slightly amusing.

"No, he doesn't work on weekends. He'll be back on Monday. But maybe I can help you out with something?"

He held up what appeared to be a Polish sausage, and had a knowing smirk on his face and a slightly lustful look in his eyes. I thought to myself, 'you dirty old man, you ought to be ashamed of yourself.'

He continued waving that Polish sausage as if the two of them really had something in common. He was making a complete fool of himself, all five-foot four of him. Smiling like I was a brand new Christmas toy and he was an only child.

"No," I replied. "But, thanks anyway."

As I turned to walk away, I could feel Jim's perverted eyes running up my backside. However, all was not lost. I left the store that Saturday morning with the butcher's schedule. As thoughts of being held by Omar ran through my head, I wanted to kick myself for not allowing him to 'really be nice,' as he had offered yesterday.

But once again, I reminded myself that Marvin L. Williams didn't raise me to be easy and I couldn't go out like that. Omar being a butcher wasn't an issue, but I wondered if my being well known hurt our chances of getting to know each other.

My Mandingo Warrior

For the rest of the weekend I was in search of the perfect outfit. Would it be black or blue, purple or pink? Would I wear a multi-colored sundress or some tight fitting jeans? I must have changed my clothes more than a dozen times, and I felt like I was working a show. I just wanted to be pretty for Omar. Not runway-model-stunning, just one-of-a-kind pretty.

The company was on hiatus for the winter, and I wasn't scheduled to go back to work again for three months, which would allow more than enough time for me to get acquainted with The Butcher.

Early Sunday morning, glimpses of the immature sun reached inside my bedroom window and gently touched my shoulders. Like a child on the first day of school, I had become too excited to sleep in. So for the better part of darkness, I simply tossed and turned with anticipation of seeing Omar again. Replacing sleep was the easy part, waiting to caress his image: that was hard.

My body was running on pure adrenaline with the excitement of seeing a man I barely knew. I had never really cared to befriend the spirit of anticipation, because it seemed severely overrated. So, as I lay on my back I eagerly reached for an explanation, something to hang a hat of logic on.

Though we all would much rather play the game of life by our own rules, I've learned that every race has its appointed starting time and only God knew its outcome.

My father once told me that if we have faith in what we are told, we must succumb to the realization that our destiny has already been written. If that is true, then the thought of pressing forward towards the unknown is frightening at best.

I had never been so sure yet so afraid about what I was feeling. But I knew I had to continue pressing forward towards the finish line of truth, no matter the outcome. Who knew what God had planned for me?

I had remained steadfast in almost everything in my life up to that point, and this time would be no different. Was Omar heaven sent? Probably not, but how was I going to know unless I gave him a chance?

He was a man I had barely met, who somehow had aroused something fresh inside of me. As I closed my eyes, I could feel my soul dance to the beat of a butcher's drum. I could feel his strong hands caress my neck as my eyes closed from the pleasure of his touch. The fact that he had shown no interest in me was a total turn on.

My mind had taken snap shots of the ridges of his strong firm lips as they formed my name. And part of me was ready to participate in the game of emotional warfare; a part of me that for years had been too scared to even dare partake in the tedious conflicts that dating brings.

My father, and more recently Vince, had prepared me for all the smooth things a man could possibly say, yet they told me nothing that would quell the level of emotional intoxication I was experiencing. I wanted a man who appeared not to want me, and I was ready to pass any test necessary to gain his attention.

Did my father teach me all that I needed to know? Did Vince fill in enough gaps? Those were the questions I was ready to let life answer.

When the sun finally broke through I got up and took a shower. Afterwards I flopped into the kitchen and made myself a great big bowl of cereal. Eve, the stage manager, wasn't around to count my calories, and after a couple of spoons full, I was out of control and liking it.

I had thrown my diet out of the window and gorging was the plan for the day. Once again it was time for me to relax and let my hair down and God, was it flowing.

I felt a sudden burst of energy, so I ran into the dining area and turned on the radio as loud as the speakers would tolerate. I began to dance, and kept on dancing intensely for hours. After a while I had a glass of wine to keep me company.

I was listening to the local 'Oldies But Goodies' station, and the more I danced the more familiar the songs became. I listened to classic Motown resurrected, some Ray Charles and Lionel Ritchie. The DJ even referred to Smoky Robinson as the 'one-man hit factory' of his time.

He also played music from the eighties and I found myself reminiscing about the good old days, back when time virtually stood still. Back when hip first met hop, and it was still cool to go dancing fully clothed.

When we were kids, my father would always call Sweets and I into the room where the grown-ups were. They set us up for a few minutes of fame. Sweets was a better dancer than I was, so she'd always steal the show. Her dad, my Uncle Jimmy, and I would always pair up and do the bump. Sweets did every dance that came to mind, which were too many for me to remember.

As I danced around the room with my eyes closed I could see Sweets moving gracefully, dancing along with me. She had the ability to see a dance on TV and within a matter of minutes create her own choreography to match. I was never jealous of her, but I must admit there were times that I wished I had it like that.

Reminiscing about the good old times was therapeutic. I was listening to one song after the next, having the time of my life as the music evoked memories that had shaped me. In between the station breaks I poured myself another glass of wine. I was half-naked, but without a care in the world. I mentally ran my fingers through the hair of my symbolic past and anxiously awaited brushing with care what lay ahead. I closed my eyes and smiled, as the songs just kept playing.

For the life of me, I could not ever remember being so in tune with music like I was at that very moment. I closed my eyes and remembered my Aunt Jackie showing my mother how to do the funky chicken.

When *ABC*, a favorite Jackson 5 song came on, I almost lost it. It was a song my father once danced his version of the robot to. Such nerve! He looked a mess then. He had a few too many sips of red wine that night and decided he'd display his gross motor skills. It didn't take long for me to discover which one of my parents I had gotten my moves from. Even though he was rhythmically challenged, I loved watching Pops make seriously intense facial expressions while flaunting his horrifying, yet comical moves.

His soul hugged each lyric as tightly as it could, but his feet just would not cooperate. He couldn't wait for his chance to strut down the Soul Train line. When he got to moving, he always stole the show.

When he started in, house guest spectators would begin chanting, "Go Marvin, Go Marvin, Go Marvin..."

CHOCOLATE

Mama and I weren't quite humiliated, and we loved to see him reach deep down inside and work his groove-thang.

In middle school it was embarrassing as hell to have my father stand up and make a fool out of himself, and sometimes my mother, may her soul rest in peace, would search for somewhere to hide. But in time it grew on me. Something told me that he was dancing to something other than the beat. And now just watching him groove soothes my heart.

None of our laughter ever seemed to bother him. He would simply block us out by closing his eyes tightly and moving his head from side to side. When Marvin L. Williams was in tune with his inner-drum, to him that's all that mattered.

The bottle of wine I had been drinking was empty and I was too tired to stand, yet too excited still to close my eyes. The feeling I had was better than anything I had ever experienced. I was emotionally on top of the world and that's all there was to it. I had danced up a storm and reflected back so far that I had almost touched three generations.

I was having fun but the matter at hand had to be dealt with. I loved myself enough to give this so-called love thing a try. Though my eyes and ears had filtered deception many times, my heart was finally willing to reach out for the one thing that had always eluded me: a real man.

Was I ready to enter the gambling casino of love and play Russian roulette with my emotions? That was a question that needed to be answered. I lay down on my bed to rest my body, but my imagination got the best of me and a whole gamut of emotions began to travel through my mind.

I saw love moving towards the corner of Pain and Disappointment Avenue. As I clutched my pillow I could almost smell the aroma of distress hovering over me and I made a sharp turn onto Fifth and Frustration. The streets were long and seemed to run forever. They reeked of anxiety and hopelessness. I began to perspire from the confusion of it all.

I didn't know what to do, as my soul started making its way up and down the streets inside my head.

Whether consciously or not, something was happening to me, and I couldn't disconnect myself from this emotional ride. The spirit of doubt had crept into my soul and was trying to derail me from my quest to find love's affection, as it had done so many times before.

It was true that I had driven up Compassion Lane several times only to run into the dead-end street of Dishonesty. And although I had already traveled down the winding road of Discontent, and made many left turns onto Despair, I was still prepared to go on. I was too far gone to turn around, and too ready to let go.

And I needed to get out of this car!

It had been some time since I had felt the need for another human to ignite my internal flame. Though I had barely allowed feelings for another person to sway my emotions, I was more willing than ever. I had gathered enough strength to suffocate my concerns, and held them at bay long enough to listen to the cadence of my heart.

My wants had power enough to relinquish the awful taste of bitterness I had for years held on to. I found a sense of peace in swallowing my supplemental vitamins of truth. In order to possess love, I had to allow my fears to dissipate. I needed to establish the level of hope necessary to urge love into my soul. For only the soul has the power to unlock doors that have been bound by fear.

Just remembering that I had a relationship with the Creator, the founder and distributor of love, was enough to make me believe that I too could caress the affection that comes through possessing love.

Courage to conquer my fears welled up inside me and I leapt up off of the bed. My soul cried out for love's company all the more, as my body craved its refuge. Though my heart had never sent out an invitation to love, much to my surprise, I was ready to invite Omar into my world.

I got down on my knees and began speaking from my soul, in an effort to escape the cruelties of life. My father had taught me that my soul was connected to the voice that speaks from heaven; the voice which supplies my needs. Remembering his words helped me destroy carriers of deceit, which often plucked away at my self-esteem and dismantled many hopes. To sustain my mental stability I needed to remain encouraged, not only by the ways of society, but also by those things that are pure and natural, and love was no exception.

How clever would it be to go through life without ever engaging in such a relationship? The subject is timidly broached, for many people find it very hard to express their inner thoughts. I was willing to give it a go.

O'Lord, there are times when I find it hard to communicate,
 but I know that this form of expression
 has the power to bring confusion and sorrow
 to an end.
I have been taught that there is much to be learned
 in our hour of loneliness.
 But nothing can be acquired
 when the soul is not in question.
Father, allow me to use this level of compassion
 as a compass of hope
 for brighter tomorrows.
When it is your will,
 create a hunger in me that surpasses
 all understanding.
When my feet refuse to move toward the
 spirit of repentance
 for the wrongful deeds I have committed,
 force them to lift up and down
 as I move in the direction of remorse.

As I expose my weaknesses,
        know that I do so in an attempt to one
        day become strong.
If I haven't told You lately,
        I love You from the bottom of my heart.
All that I am is because of You,
        and all that I am to become shall be no different.
When this world gets dark,
        I shall reach for the light that stems
        from your garments,
        in an attempt to be led by your mercy.
I've been told that your light is never dormant.
        Allow my behavior to guide an earthly
        love light my way.
Ready my tongue in a humble way,
        so that it might be able to receive love's promises
        in the hour of its conception.
When there is no support from those who
        claim to love me,
        it is then that your words ring true.
For I know, Oh Lord,
        that the answer always lies in you.

Amen

By praying that night my soul was fed by the truth and, in return, I was able to dine at the table of reality. I prayed to God that He might somehow wash my soul in the waters of reasoning. And by doing so, I prayed that the water might penetrate my mind and elevate my level of understanding. I prayed that my dreams of one day finding love would not be dismantled, not as long as I was able to breathe.

That whole weekend I had searched within myself for the will to carry on, refusing to live in this world without a love to call my own. I had acquired many things in life, but the love of a man wasn't one of them.

I had dated, for lack of a better word, a few brothers, but neither one of them were emotionally stimulating enough to warrant taking off my clothes. Vince didn't count here.

I deserved more than a physical relationship. I was not willing to open up and allow anyone to enter my body, or my world, until God gave his emotional stamp of approval.

I was tired of being a dreamer. I wasn't about to sleep through this part of life. I wanted to get to know someone intimately. Discussing the necessary do's and don't's seemed like the real stuff that mattered most.

My friends often chastised me for being so overly cautious, but if being cautious was going to reduce the heartaches, I was okay with waiting for Mr. Right! That way I wouldn't have to be wrong twenty times before I found him. Continual worry about all the what if's and the maybe's had become too consuming. And since the margin of emotional perfection was minimal at best, I just decided to let my hormones rest.

My peers wanted the maleness. I on the other hand was in need of a man. I was allergic to B.S. and wasn't about to settle for a fly-by-night nigga. I needed some stability, so to hell with passion, I needed some promise. Passion would come second.

I watched my peers' relationships come and go, but none of them had an ounce of 'I-want-do-right' in them. They all seemed to find over-sexed, irresponsible, insubordinate males with the IQ of a bean sprout, and the neglectful tendencies of a crack head on payday.

I wasn't about to let anyone pee on my head and call it rain, and I damn sure wasn't about to endure anymore self-inflected strain. I was woman enough to deal with my own anxieties. Just because my name was Chocolate, didn't mean that I had to invite a nut into my life.

If I was willing to stand in line for as long as I had, at least I could order the kind of man I desired. I wasn't looking for some stray dog or miss-matched puppy, I wanted myself a soul mate.

I wanted someone to care enough to be bothered with my concerns. I wanted it so badly that at times I could feel the anticipation warming me up inside. Finding someone who possessed the type of substance my heart required was surely going to take time, but I had never been in a hurry.

I could feel my nipples begin to harden, as thoughts of Omar's strong hands gently brushed against my needs. I understood the need to be touched, but my need to be respected would always take precedence. I needed what few women ever demanded before furnishing their goods to their temporary mates.

Though my self-imposed biological clock had me tripping at times, I never allowed the stressful clouds of emptiness to spur me. If the tension of the incessant ticking happened to persist, my morals would never disengage nor would they collapse under the pressure of man's irrational reasoning.

I was getting tired of spending my nights alone, but the thought of lying next to a warm body with a cold soul was a great deterrent. Many nights I felt darkness creep into my bedroom and sympathetically rock me to sleep. I often lay there half-naked wondering what it might feel like to roll over and give myself to the man I had emotionally committed myself to.

I always knew that I was not meant to be alone; that my single status was only temporary. I knew my needs better than anyone else, yet over time, my body had matured past the satisfaction of self-touch. No matter how hard I tried to go it alone, no matter how many times I tried to please myself, there was always something left unfinished, always a feeling of emptiness. My hands were neither wide enough nor strong enough to convince me that I didn't need him, whoever he was.

I wasn't born to heighten my own erotic appetite, and experimenting the way I did showed me that. At least I was able to discern what I was, from who I was; and a man I wasn't. The verdict was in, and although I had repeatedly tried to state my case; I had done so to no avail. I came to understand my limitations, and I was okay with not having a penis.

There I was again trying to juggle reality in one hand as I balanced pride in the other. I had come too damn far for that routine though. I was ready for more and I had more than a clue where to get it.

Monday morning, after bathing myself in the warmest, sweetest water I could create, I walked over to my closet and selected something warm and sweet to entice the Mandingo warrior of my dreams. I held my head up and set out to get myself a man. It was a quarter past something, but I was in too big a hurry to focus on the hour hand.

I only knew two things just then: it was Monday, and the supermarket was open. Just as I found my keys the phone rang, and I reluctantly stumbled towards the phone.

"Hello, Chocolate. This is Vince."

"Oh, Vince. I can't talk right now. I do have something to tell you, but I was on my way out the door. I'll call you later and tell you all about it, okay?"

"Okay, sure. I can't wait to hear what you have to say. Is everything all right?" he asked.

"Sure, everything's great. It's nothing to be alarmed about," I reassured him.

"It's a man, isn't it?"

"N-nooo, it isn't," I lied, but badly.

"Yes, it is, Chocolate. I can tell. It's a man isn't it? Come on now, Chocolate, at least tell me his name."

We had been around each other long enough to know if one of us wasn't telling the truth.

"Come on, and tell me who this lucky man is, missy. I'm not ever gonna give it up, girl."

"Okay, okay, you're right. It is a man. Now are you satisfied?"

"Well, no, because that's not the question. The question should be, do you think that he can satisfy you? Don't forget you're the self-proclaimed Miss 'ain't-no-man-good-enough-for-me' Williams."

I discovered Vince was funny as hell after I got to know him. He had an innocent soul with a giving heart, a deadly combination for heartbreak. He cared about me like a brother cared for his sister, but in our case, like a sister cared for… Well, I'll leave that unsaid. Anyway we were always there for each other and that was all that mattered.

"Vince, I really do have to go now," I pleaded.

"You know that you're wrong to leave me hanging like this, don't you?"

"Girl, I got you. Just give me a day and I'll fill you in on everything."

"Call me as soon as you get in, okay, Chocolate?"

After I hung up the phone, I moved as fast as I could through the kitchen towards the garage door. I started the car and backed out and was startled to hear someone call out my name.

"Chocolate! Baby, I didn't know you were up. I would have knocked on the front door. I was just trying to be considerate and let you get your beauty rest."

I turned at the voice of the only man in this world I couldn't say no to, my father. I didn't see him at first. He was kneeling down near the shrubbery that ran along the front of the house. He was content taking care of my garden, but I hoped this would be the last time he had to tend it for the season.

As he stood up I peered over my shoulder. "Hi, Pops. I haven't really been able to sleep in much since I've been back home."

"Why is that?"

"Maybe I still have a little jet lag, but it will get better eventually." Again I was lying.

When I lied to my father as a child, he said I always touched my left ear with my left thumb, and no sooner had this lie emerged from my mouth was I staying true to form. I couldn't lie to him and he knew it, but now wasn't the time for a question and answer session.

I had gone through the garage hoping to avoid any sort of neighborly contact, but to no avail. Marvin L. Williams was going to get down to the bottom of things and that's all there was to it. I was driving the same black jaguar Vince had given me for my signing bonus and the convertible top was already down, even though it was November. I turned off the car and braced myself as my father attempted to once again reveal my current deepest secret.

"Daddy, it's really nothing," I said as I unconsciously stroked my left ear.

"Oh no? Then why are you about to rub your ear off?"

I hated the fact that he knew me so well, but I loved him for being so in tune with my emotions.

"So where did you acquire such a wonderful morning glow?"

My father was the greatest interrogator that ever lived. I didn't want to tell him my glow was premature but I had to say something or we would be there all day.

"So, Daddy, why do you think I'm smiling?"

"Chocolate, how much time do *you* have to waste? Baby, in case you've forgotten, I'm retired. I've got all day to be lied to. I don't have nothing but time, so make it easy on yourself."

"Oh, really, Daddy. Okay then. I met a man, okay? Yes, I'm interested in him and I was heading off to see him."

"Oh, so you're going to meet him for lunch? That's great. What restaurant?"

"Well, we're not really meeting for lunch."

"You're not? Then where are you meeting him?"

I was feeling as silly as I no doubt looked. How was I going to tell my father, of all people, that I had a crush a man I had only seen for a few seconds? As I reached for something to say, my father stepped closer to me. I prepared to converse with him on a subject I knew nothing about.

"Daddy, he's just this guy I met. I mean, someone I saw the other day while I was running some errands."

"Does the young man have a name?"

"Sure, his name is Omar."

"Omar? Do you mean Omar, as in Omar The Butcher?"

Now my expression was as completely blank as the one a game show contestant wears when the curtain is pulled back and there's nothing behind it. Was nothing private? I couldn't believe my father might know Omar, and I was desperate to fend off any open-ended questions.

"Well, I don't actually know where he works, Pops. I just met him."

"Chocolate, girl, you better release your ear before you rub your earlobe off."

My father was standing only about three feet away from me wearing an old pair of blue overalls. He was laughing at me as he reached inside his pocket for a lighter to stoke his pipe, which was dangling from the corner of his mouth. I was smiling at him like Daddy's little girl, so in search of sympathy. But this time, there wasn't any in sight.

"Why, is it so hard for you to admit that you've got a thang for The Butcher?"

"I really have only seen him once and I don't know if I have a thang…"

"Come on, baby, now I don't mean to interrupt you, but this is your dad. Not some stranger you just met. I know you like the back of my hand. I'm not ashamed to tell you that the first time I saw your mother I knew I had to have her. It was a feeling that still to this day I can't describe. What were you about to do just now? Go into the store and hope that this time you'll make a better impression on him?"

His ability to ferret out any ruse was uncanny. I was caught red-handed. "Yes, I guess I was, Pops," I admitted, albeit reluctantly.

"You have a lot going for yourself, Chocolate. If you like him, just tell him."

"Just tell him? Now come on, Daddy. There has to be a better way, some other way for me to let him know."

"Chocolate, it would help if you'd just stop trying to reinvent the wheel. Just let him know how you feel."

Never in a million years would I have thought I would hear this advice from my own father. I slunk deep into the driver's seat as he performed his world famous turn to walk away from me. Grinning from ear to ear, he slowly placed his lighter back into his pocket and walked back to his gardening.

"I'm sure that Omar would be more than flattered, I mean, I would be if I had a world famous model crazy about me," he called over his shoulder.

"So, how should I let him know?" I yelled.

My father had a way of making a point, by challenging me to be creative.

"Take a step back, Chocolate, from all of the excitement. Then take a deep breath and do what comes natural."

My father's words began to curb my uncertainties. I backed out of the driveway and headed towards my prey as originally planned. It took less than five minutes to reach the store and twenty more for me to open my car door.

Sitting in the parking lot, I threw in my favorite CD and allowed Sade's song, *Please Send Me Someone to Love,* to calm my nerves. I pulled down my sun visor and opened up the mirror to check my lips. I was ready. I had chosen to wear my sundress, the one that Eve called 'killa.' As I opened my door, I placed my first foot out of the car onto the runway of reality. I caught a glimpse of myself in the store window, and did a double take. I swore I was looking at my mother wearing her sundress the day she died.

I shook my head and moved forward.

Each step closer to the store raised a new question: Was I who I needed to be on this day? Was I tall enough? Was I strong enough? Was I Chocolate enough to interest this man? I answered them all with the smug smile I had just selfishly borrowed from my father and two simple words: 'Sure am!'

I had gained the confidence necessary to take on my new quest for love, just as the doors to the store opened. I stepped in ready to claim my man. The automatic doors opened up for me, just as the curtains on stage had done so many times before. That proffered me the much-needed rush to continue. I still didn't have a plan, but I knew that I wasn't going to leave without an answer from The Butcher.

As I made it to the middle of the store, I took that one last deep breath as my father had instructed. I reached inside myself for the next move. It came to me like a windfall of free groceries. 'That's it...' I thought to myself. I knew what to do.

I made my way over to the frozen food aisle and grabbed a nice size bag of frozen vegetables. I let the glass door slam and headed back towards the meat department. I could see Omar from a distance, so I poured it on. I was in a zone and loving it. I was feeling pretty from the top of my head, right down to the bottom of my soles. I had come to make The Butcher a proposition that he could not refuse. I was Marvin L. Williams' baby girl, and I came bearing some much-anticipated news and with it, all of my other prospects would get the blues.

A gentleman waiting for his meat order, that he had no doubt planned to take home for his evening meal, made some remarks that seemed to seal the deal for me.

"Damn, Omar, look at this fine ass woman coming here."

Omar was placing the man's order up on the scale and turned around to see what all of the commotion was about. His dark brown eyes took in an image that simultaneously weakened both his arms and legs. Before he could recover he dropped the man's meat on the floor.

I stepped in front of the gentleman and handed Omar the bag of mixed vegetables, before he could regain his composure and pick up the customer's meat. With it was a small piece of paper with my phone number on it. He accepted it with his strong hands.

"Damn, dog! You are a lucky man. What I wouldn't give to be you. Maann! You da shit, Omar. That's got to be one of the finest pieces of candy I've ever seen. Wait, wait just a minute, aren't you that mod...?"

Before he finished I said, "No, I'm not. And can you excuse me for a second?"

"Well, sure. Anything for you, my sweet."

I wasn't trying to be rude; I just didn't want Omar to get uncomfortable with the whole superstar modeling thang.

After he took the frozen vegetables, I executed a Marvin L. Williams turn, and walked away.

I had taken a few steps towards the front door when Omar yelled out, "What am I supposed to do with this?"

I stopped as only Chocolate could, and looked back over my right shoulder. "You're a big boy... you'll figure it out."

This time I walked and never looked back, hoping like hell he'd follow me, of course. No matter what I heard, I promised myself, I wouldn't dare turn around. When I felt sure I was out of his sight, I reached into my purse and pulled out my sunglasses. As I placed them on with a certain flair, the cashier from the other night seemed to remember me.

She yelled out, "Damn, girl. Work that dress, work it."

I walked through her empty line as fast as I could, pausing just briefly enough for us to give each other a high-five. She twisted up one side of her mouth into a smile. She shook her head from side to side, and said, "You go, girl... work it."

I never looked back. I kept on stepping, but I could feel someone gaining ground on me. By the time I made it to my car and reached for the door, a gentle breeze stopped all movement. The now familiar hands reached ahead of mine and opened my door.

"So, is that how it's done? You just come into the store and cause me to make a mess... and just leave?"

I turned around to come face to face with Omar. His manly strength instantly weakened my own knees. But I held my own and managed to reply, "I've seen you pick up things, and I know you're more than enough of a man to handle it."

"What's up with the bag of vegetables?"

"The other night when I was here, I dropped a bag similar to that, and you picked it up for me. And I thanked you. I told you how nice it was of you. It was your response that prompted me to come back here today."

"What did I say?" he asked innocently.

"Well, you said, 'no, the nice thing to do would be for you to cook them for me.' Well, Omar, here I am. I'm ready for vegetables when you are."

My father would have been proud of the way I had just handled myself. I left Omar standing there with the same blank expression I had worn in front of my father just an hour earlier. I just didn't know whether my spontaneous plan was going to work.

Stepping back and taking that deep breath was the key. Thank you, Daddy. When I allowed myself a chance to step back from the situation, I was able to see things more clearly. By doing so my approach to ratifying the deal became more obvious.

By the time I arrived home, I was exhausted. The endless hours of anticipation had taken its toll on me and my body was now ready for slumber. Though my heart then beat to the rhythm of love's irresistible delight, at that moment I was only interested in one thing; rest.

I secured the house alarm as usual and started to undress. My shoes were the first to go. I kicked one off after the other as I walked down the hallway towards my room. By the time I reached the foot of my bed, I was as naked as the day I was born.

I was just one leap away from falling into the arms of a deep sleep, and I could feel Omar reaching out for me. So I reached down inside myself and released my tether to soar into his arms. The welcome darkness pressed against my eyelids, and my mind and body transcended into an ethereal state of relaxation.

I didn't know how long I had slept. I had crawled into bed at three o'clock the previous day, and now my clock read 1:00 PM. It couldn't be.

The first thing that came to mind was that the electricity had gone out, because no one had called either. I was usually a light sleeper and the slightest sound could awaken me. I hopped out of bed to investigate and retraced my steps back down the hall. I stepped around the maze of scattered clothes and turned on a light switch. There went my electrical blackout theory.

I gathered up my clothes and put them away.

I wasn't expecting Omar to call; it was too soon. I had been told that it goes against a man's codebook to phone a woman before the seventy-two hour mark, and I wouldn't want him to lose his cool points.

I walked into the living room and turned on the TV. Something told me to check and make sure that the telephone wasn't off the hook, which would explain no calls. I reached down beside the sofa and picked up the receiver. Much to my dismay, the phone had a dial tone, which indicated it was working. Had I missed calls after all? Suddenly the additional beeps indicating I had messages registered in my ear.

I saw there were five messages, but there was no doubt in my mind that they were from my father, and either Tina or Vince. I was tired of speculating, so I called to retrieve my messages from voice-mail.

The first one was, of course, from Pops.

"Hey, Chocolate. This is your dad. I just called to see how things went with you and The Butcher."

The second call said, "Hello, Chocolate. If you're there pick up the phone. Now you know that you're wrong for not calling me back. I need to know the details, and I will stay up as long as I have to just to get them. Just in case you've got another friend who sounds like me, this is your best friend, Vince. Now call me back, girl, so we can talk."

I was in the midst of a good laugh when the third call came in. "Hello, Chocolate. I think I've got something that belongs to you. It's wrapped in a medium size bag and needs to be steamed up. I was thinking that maybe I could come over and..."

Damn. He hung up before he finished. I wondered what I had missed as I tried desperately to replay the message. As I fumbled with the buttons, I convinced myself the machine had malfunctioned. After several attempts at retrieving message number three, message number four started to play.

"Hey, Chocolate, this is Omar again. I don't know what happened on the last call, but I got cut off. Let me be brief this time. I would like for us to meet somewhere, if that's okay. My number is 510-555-67…"

Oh no, I lost him again. He was leaving his number and the damn phone cut him off.

There was only one message left and I was feeling lucky, but I braced myself before checking the last one.

"Okay, I was just playing. Here's the rest of it. 21."

...21, 21, what was 21? It dawned on me before I felt too dense. He had left the last two digits of his phone number on his third message.

After replaying the last two messages I wrote his number down completely. I tore off the surrounding paper bit by bit to frame his phone number into one small square. There he was, just ten tiny digits away. I wanted to run and even jump for joy but not before I heard that sexy voice of his.

With phone in hand, I ran from the living room to the kitchen and back again, in an attempt to calm my nerves. I walked over to the sofa and placed a few throw pillows under my head as I reclined. I was in search of that special somewhere to have a meaningful conversation with that special someone. I had to be in the proper position. It had to feel right. There was a mood, which needed to be set, and I was going to find it.

My mind was racing a mile a minute and the anticipation was killing me. I wanted it all to go well. I was queasy with excitement. My heart was laughing and my soul just couldn't stop smiling. If I blew it, at least I would fail trying. I jumped off the sofa and ran back into my bedroom. I turned off all the lights and cuddled up underneath my warm covers. I decided to do a practice run lying in bed.

'Hello, may I please speak to Omar? Oh? This is he? Well, it's Claudia, you know the young lady who came into your store yesterday and handed you the bag of frozen vegetables? Yeah, that's me. Oh, nothing, I was just sitting around the house bored, and checked my messages and decided I'd give you a call back.'

After the mock call, I decided I was ready to do the real thing. I was ready to do it for real. I mean, for real. Who was Omar anyway? He was only a butcher, and after all, *I* was a super model.

My thoughts longingly turned to Sweets. What would she do? Where would she go to talk to that special someone in a time like this? Suddenly it hit me. Why didn't I think of it sooner? It was finally making sense to me, and like the wind, I was on my way. But not without my favorite pillow.

In an instant I situated myself in my closet, lying on my back. I gave my eyes time to adjust, but the instant I was able to see the numbers on the phone, I attempted to call Omar The Butcher, my self-proclaimed Mandingo warrior.

I placed the receiver against my ear and waited for him to answer. The phone rang only four times, but let me tell it; it rang forever. Just when I was about to hang up he answered.

"Hello."

"Is this Omar?" I asked.

"Yes it is, and who may I ask is calling?"

"Well, this is Claudia," I replied trying to keep to my rehearsed script.

"Who?" he asked with skepticism.

"It's me, Claudia."

"I'm sorry, you must have the wrong number. I don't know a Claudia. Have a nice day."

It slipped my mind he didn't know my real name and he obviously wasn't the type of man to play games.

"NO! No, wait a minute! This is Chocolate," I managed to slip in before he hung up the phone. This wasn't going at all like I had planned.

"Oh, I'm so sorry. Is Claudia your real name?"

"Yes, it really is my real name. But since you already know me as Chocolate, if you'd like you can call me Chocolate."

"I would like to call you by the name you're most comfortable with," he offered.

Such a gentleman.

"Okay, well, thank you, Omar. You can call me Claudia. That would be just fine."

The closet thing was working well for me. But after I agreed to have him call me Claudia, a most uncomfortable minute passed and neither one of us spoke a word.

Then, thankfully, Omar broke the silence.

"That was kinda neat what you did yesterday. I felt it, and I was moved by your creativity."

I was feeling quite silly reaching for words which seemed too far away to touch, and too near to remember. I tried to suppress the butterflies that were soaring inside me.

Omar's voice was strong, yet soothing, and I visualized the way he had formed his lips to say my name. It sent waves of calmness through the airwaves.

"Are you still there?" he asked.

Like a juvenile struggling to find the words, I left Omar The Butcher waiting for me to speak.

"Sure, I'm here. I was just trying to think of something to say is all."

"So what's next, Claudia? Where do we go from here?"

"I was just thinking the same thing. I don't know, though. I've never really done this whole mixed vegetable thing before. I did think you were cute and that it would be nice to get to know you."

Wow! I couldn't believe I had just put myself out there like that. But I did think he was so cute, and it felt great to say so.

"I would love to get to know you too. So please tell me when and where? I know that it's too early for us to see each other at our respective places. So why don't we do something simple, like go and get some ice cream? Or if you don't like ice cream, maybe we could get some…"

I interrupted him and said, "Sure I would love to get some ice cream. I haven't had any ice cream in such a long time. Ice cream is fine then. I really like ice cream, and it would be great to have some ice cream. In fact, I haven't had any ice cream since…"

He interrupted me now. "Great. I can tell you like ice cream. Then ice cream it is. Why don't we meet later on this evening… if that's okay with you."

"Sure, yes of course."

"There is a new ice cream parlor that just opened in the same shopping center where I work."

"Oh, yes. I noticed it last Friday. They must have opened while I was away. Isn't it crazy how fast businesses are opening these days? I can't believe how many new shops are in the area…" I started to ramble again.

Omar was enjoying a quiet giggle.

I slowed myself down and simply said, "Okay, then I'll meet you there... at seven?"

"Okay, I'll see you then," he agreed.

I was so relieved to finish the call. My silly ice cream ramblings were two scoops too many I was afraid. But we did hang up with a meeting place and time. I had less than three hours until we were going to have our first date.

Since Mama's sundress style worked for me once, I was not about to change the way I was bringing it. I walked over to my closet and pulled out the heavy-hitter. It was a beautiful sleeveless blue sundress that I promised myself I wouldn't wear until that very special time called for it. Well, this was that moment. I tossed it across my bed and walked to the bathroom to run a bubble bath. I poured myself a glass of wine, and turned on KBLS, my favorite soul radio station. I broke into my stash of European oils and grooved as I soaked for over an hour.

Time was ticking and the long hand indicated I had less than thirty minutes to make the appointed rendezvous. I left in time to be a few minutes early.

The ride over to meet The Butcher was short and sweet and before I knew it I was parked in front of the ice cream parlor. I tried to park my car where I could see Omar pull into the parking lot from any direction.

I was eager for my next glimpse of one of God's greatest creations. No sooner had I placed my car in park, did the man of my dreams appear out of nowhere. I was quite startled when I felt a thump on the trunk of the Jaguar.

It was Omar. For whatever reason he was standing next to a bicycle. I must admit that I was caught off guard, but the bike thang worked for me when I noticed his sexy shorts. They were basic black and basically tight as hell. He was standing close enough to touch, and God was I glad that I was wearing my shades. The top was down on the car for the second late November day in a row, and his crotch was at eye level. I could not take my eyes off of...

"I didn't know you'd be riding your bike," I said, hoping he didn't notice I wasn't even looking at his face.

"I didn't mention how I'd be traveling. Does it matter?"

I did look up then, and from the look on his face, it seemed as if I had offended him.

I tried to back pedal. "Oh, no, of course not. In fact, it's great biking weather. You can see I have the top down on the car too. I just wasn't expecting you to be on a bike, that's all. It really doesn't matter how you got here... what matters most is that you are here."

"Okay, so we're both here. Let's go inside and get some ice cream."

While we surveyed our options and ordered, he held my hand as if it was his own. There I was, standing in an ice cream parlor feeling complete for the first time in years. I was living and breathing inside a dream I didn't ever want to end.

"What are you having, lovely lady?"

At least I was decisive when it came to ice cream. "I'll have a double scoop of you... uh, I mean, cookies and cream," I said with a blush and a sheepish grin.

"That was funny." He smiled and winked as if he would be happy to oblige. He turned to the clerk and said, "Excuse me, she'll have a double scoop of cookies and cream, and I'll have those same two scoops in chocolate."

That was not fair, I thought. There wasn't a chocolate flavor anywhere on the menu board, but I was dying to lick me some as soon as I saw his fine butt ride up on that beautiful blue bike of his.

"Where would you like to sit?"

"You're the man, you lead the way."

"Well, I was thinking it was such a nice day out, that maybe we could sit outside and talk while we lick."

'A man with vision; now that's what I'm talking about,' I panted to myself. I loved a brother who knew when to take charge.

When we were served I noticed there obviously was chocolate ice cream to be had, and I had obviously taken the double entendres way too far.

Omar held his two scoops of chocolate ice cream in his right hand, and walked proudly as he held the hand of the most precious piece of chocolate God had ever created in the other. We actually took a long walk through a nearby park, and who was I to turn that down? Besides I had just thrown down a double scoop of cookies and cream and a little exercise was definitely in order.

Omar was a perfect gentleman all night. When he wasn't complementing me he was allowing me to lead off the conversation. He was unlike so many other brothers who spend the majority of the date giving you a big spill about themselves.

He was far from the norm. Rather than go on and on about himself he seemed to really care about me and took the time to get to know me.

In turn, I learned that he was an avid moviegoer and he didn't mind opening the door for a woman. I thought I could allow that. He appreciated nature and preferred the natural look. I gave myself points there. He liked the simple things in life and that was intriguing. We bonded with every step we took, as we strolled through the park conveying our likes and dislikes.

After an hour, we stopped and sat down on a park bench. There we were just as my father and I had been; talking over ice cream after Sweets left me almost seven years ago. I hoped beyond hope that wasn't a sign of things to come.

"You're nothing like I thought you'd be, but everything I've ever hoped for in a woman," Omar murmured as he moved in for his first kiss.

My heart started racing as he tugged my hand and pulled me close. The anticipation of our lips touching was almost too much to bear. The gentle breeze did nothing to cool me off. I could feel my nipples press firmly against my dress, and I tried to move inconspicuously as I adjusted it.

"Do you mind this?" he asked.

"No… no, I don't mind at all."

When he leaned over to kiss me, much to both our surprise, I became the aggressor. The moment his lips touched mine, I reached up and placed the palm of my hand gently against the side of his neck. I wanted him to know, without a doubt, that I was definitely feeling him. I didn't want to leave any room for speculation.

Our first kiss was instantly addictive. After our lips parted that night, I knew they would never be the same and neither would our hearts.

I finally got home around ten o'clock, but I must have floated, or maybe I flew. I didn't even remember walking back to my car or know how I made it home. One thing I did know, however is that I was convinced that Omar The Butcher was my guy; my Mandingo warrior.

Big Mama

For the next three months Omar and I saw each other almost every day. He either rode his bike, if the mild winter weather allowed, or caught a cab, and I thought it quite odd for a grown man not to have a car. I waited for a 'right time' to ask about it, but until that opportunity presented itself, I wasn't about to say anything.

I would not have minded picking him up or dropping him off, but he was a man with a great deal of pride. Whenever I offered he'd always say, "Claudia, now you know that's not the way I do things."

Other than that, things were going well. Whatever his reason for not having a car was his business. I was just there to make him happy.

The more I talked to him, the more I was convinced I had made the right choice. Omar was one of the most positive men I had ever known, second only to my father of course.

It became apparent that he was sort of a homebody, and to put it more plainly, he was a Mama's boy. Underneath all of that muscle he was a softy; a real keeper.

Omar was my Mr. Right-now, and I was his Mrs. Right-on-time. Wherever we planned to meet, I was there like clockwork, and every day we did something different and fun. Before we knew it the holidays had passed us by, and we were well into the new year.

We were poetically drawn together, like the smooth crisp sounds of harmony that embodies the song of a lark, or the last breath of air that was needed to live.

Three weeks before I was due to go back on the road with Dramatic-Impressions, Omar and I had planned to meet at a soul food restaurant called Big Mama's then go out to a movie.

As strong as he was on the outside, he had a remarkable affinity for dramas. In fact, he was an aficionado of dramas with romance. In fact, his favorite movie was *Love Jones*. I too had an appetite for movies steaming with affection.

We had planned to eat soul food then head to the local cinema and take our chances on what was playing.

I arrived at Big Mama's a little before seven and went inside to meet Omar, who also prided himself on always being on time. When I walked inside, I spotted him sitting at a quiet corner table with a menu in his hand. He didn't seem to notice me at first.

A young lady greeted me at the door, "Good evening, Miss. Will you be alone this evening, or will someone be joining you?"

Before I could reply, Omar looked up and motioned me to join him at the table.

The hostess saw him and said to me as an aside.

"Damn, is he with you? If you were alone, I was going to tell you about the catch of the day, but I can see that you've already caught it. And excuse me for saying this… I mean, I ain't gay or nothing like that, but, sista you're beautiful as well."

She had gotten out what she wanted to say when Big Mama herself walked over to us.

"Nora, will you please leave that child alone and let her set down?"

She turned to me and apologized, "Please excuse her. She new here and is as nosey as they git. I woulda fired her already but she work so cheap, that I'm forced to keep her. How are you doin', Miss? I is Big Mama, and this is my place. Welcome, child, and enjoy yourself."

By then Nora was greeting the next diners and Big Mama knowingly walked me over to Omar's table.

"Omar, I didn't know you had it in you. But she a beautiful young lady, just as you said."

Omar was blushing so hard his forehead was throbbing. I could tell that being there was a little awkward for him. From what I could see, Omar and Big Mama had some history and before the evening was over I learned all I needed to know.

"Do you know how long I known Omar?" Big Mama asked.

"No, ma'am, I don't. How long have you known him?" I was eager to learn all I could.

Omar excused himself politely when she started her recollections. When he left, presumably for the restroom, Big Mama sat down at the table with me and started back in.

"I known Omar longer than he know hisself. He's a good man, and he need a good woman in his corner. Omar been through a lot and sometime he feel the whole world aginst him. He told you about what happen?"

"No, tell me, please. What is it that happened?" She had my undivided attention.

"Well, child, maybe it ain't for me to tell. Why don't I just let him tell you, after all it is his life. I is just his Godmother... someone who always love him and shall always care. I knew him before he ever uttered his first sounds, and I held him in my arms long before he take his first steps."

Omar returned just as she was finishing her introduction. He obviously overheard Big Mama talking.

"That's just like Big Mama... always reminiscing about the good old days. What has she told you, Claudia? Did she tell you about the time she caught me stealing some of her banana pudding? She's always telling that story."

"Omar, go out back and bring some things in for me," Big Mama ordered. "They settin' by the door out there. I just set here and keep her company."

I knew Big Mama had something more to say and if Omar was going to pretend to be gullible enough to leave me there, I was going to remain intrigued enough to listen.

As soon as he turned the corner Big Mama started back in. "Baby, has he told you why he don't drive?"

"No, he hasn't, Big Mama. And perhaps I don't want to know."

"Okay, girl, now I is not stupid. Who do you think you foolin'? I is Big Mama, and when I begin talkin', the whole world turn to a sponge and absorb every word I speak. What I is about to tell you will help you better understand my Omar. Don't you want to know why he don't drive?"

Of course I wanted to know why he didn't have a car, and since Big Mama had known him all his life, who better to tell me? I sat there ready to listen to the words of a stranger. I would let her tell me about a man I wanted desperately to fall in love with. I nodded as if to give her permission to continue.

"Well, about two, or is it three years ago now, Omar and both his mama and daddy and his sister went on vacation up the Oregon Coast. On the way back home they drive the Redwood Highway, back down 101 through the big forest. A lady was stuck on the side of the road with her two children, and she just ran right out into that road when they drove by.

CHOCOLATE

She was tryin' to flag their car down out a desperation. She claimed that one of her children was severely sick and need emergency attention.

"Omar was drivin' at the time. Both his parents were asleep and his sister, Brianna, was feelin' restless. She kep' insistin' that Omar put in a tape she brought along on their trip. She was settin' in the back seat on the passenger side next to their mama, when she reach over the seat to hand him the tape. Omar look back over his shoulder for only a second, but a second was all it took.

"When he turn around to fix his eyes back on the road, he see the lady wavin' her arms all wild in the air and jumpin' up and down. Without much time to think, he turned the steering wheel hard to his right to avoid hittin' the woman. Within seconds he collided onto a large redwood tree. Omar was the only survivor.

"To this day he still blame hisself for what happen. He tells me there are times when he can still hear his sister screamin'. He miss them all and he go to visit their gravesite as often as he can."

I was silent for a moment; my heart filled with sadness and compassion. "How does Omar deal with it all?" I asked quietly.

"Child, Omar has a strong soul and he'd be all right. With you in his life he be just fine."

I could tell she had some inside information. I could also tell that Big Mama must have loved them all deeply by the way she described the tragedy to me.

Her smile was so bright it outshone any I had ever seen. At that very moment I understood just how precious her love was for Omar.

"How far does Omar live from here?" I asked.

"Oh, girl… he ain't told you," and she heaved a big sigh. "Omar live here. He probly in his room right now as we speak."

"But I thought you sent him out back to get some things for you."

"I did… but you know how you children are. When did you start doin' everything you were told?"

She continued before I could reply.

"I is his Godmother and I couldn't see him livin' in that big house all by hisself. So I convince him to sale the house and move in here with me. We built an extra room around back… large enough for him to have his space, and he love bein' here."

"Can I ask you a question, Big Mama?"

"Sure, baby. Go right ahead."

"When was the last time you saw Omar drive a car?"

"Omar ain't drive a car since the night of the accident. And with the exception of catchin' a cab every now and then, I don't think he ever really been in a car with anyone for over two, three years."

I was overwhelmed with grief for Omar. After hearing about his personal tragedy, losing his family the way he did, I knew how devastated he must feel. The whole thing was mind-boggling. I couldn't believe he had the strength to go on each day. He obviously blamed himself for what had happened to his family, and over the years he had become distant. I was hurting for him but not nearly as bad as he was hurting himself.

In life we all have our challenges, and with them we must defy the premise of despair. I had seen throughout my years that our characters are molded by our trials. Omar had taken the worst the world had to offer and was still standing.

Right now, Omar needed me, and I needed him. Knowing how I felt about my parents, and losing my own mother, I was filled with empathy.

Though I was humbled at the thought of Big Mama confiding in me, more than anything I was eager to help ease the sorrow that my man had endured.

I was lost in thought when Big Mama said, "I heard many stories about you, baby. In fact, I is the one who ask him to bring you here. He know I is talkin' to you, but he don't know that I's tellin' you this. So please don't let him find out I told you about his tragedy."

"I promise, Big Mama. I won't ever let him know that you told me."

"Young lady, this is not about us, this is about Omar."

I nodded in agreement.

"Sometime we have to carry the burdens of our loved ones in their hour of weakness. Until they have the strength to carry them for themselves. I can look into your eyes and tell that you really care about my Omar. Besides, I know what you do for a livin'."

"You do?" I asked.

"Of course I do. Yes, indeed. I picked up a magazine or two in my day. I know that you care about Omar, seeing that he is just a butcher."

"Why do you say that? He's not just a butcher to me."

"Child, stop sounding naïve. Let's just say that ain't no Billy Dee Williams ever come around here lookin' for Big Mama, the soul food cook. And back in the day, when I was your age, believe me, I was a looker. But ain't nobody with lots of money every paid me no damn attention. So that's why I say what I do. Omar is a butcher. Period. And even though he a hard worker and all, he ain't got no whole lot a money."

She kept eyeing me for a reaction, but I sat silent and motionless.

"But you somehow look pass all a that and saw the good in him. And that's how I know."

I smiled gratefully in acknowledgment of her compliment for my character.

"Big Mama, has he gotten any better? Since the accident, I mean."

"Child, yes. But I is thinkin' he ain't never gonna be whole again. Death has a way of scarin' us that not even time can fully heal. No one totally recover from somethin' like that. They just learn to deal with the lost, in their own way. Omar been through a lot, but I guess you could say that he on this side of pain. It surprise me to learn about you, but believe me... it was a pleasant one. You is the first young lady that he allowed into his life since the accident."

"No." I was incredulous.

"I know, I know, girl. He a lot to look at. But he been hurtin' too much to care for anyone else. Then you walk in his store. You was different. I ain't hear him talk about a young lady since he came home with a magazine with... who? Oh, that old Holly Berry girl on it."

I giggled at the thought of Omar admiring Halle Berry, because she was one of my own idols.

"I know about you long before the little frozen vegetable thang you did down at the store, and I must admit, that was better than anything I done ever conjure up. I thought I done it all, but, little girl, that takes the cake."

Big Mama wore a great big beautiful smile as she acknowledged my ingenuity. I began to smile myself.

Big Mama was in her early seventies. I could tell that back in her day, she had it going on. She was almost as dark as I was. Her hair was worn short and natural; nappy and as white as Georgia cotton. She was a large woman, and when she walked, it seemed like her hips just never stopped coming. There was an aura of affection that beamed from her big brown eyes, and I noticed that a bright gray ring shimmered, surrounding the deep brown pools.

CHOCOLATE

I was sitting across the table from a southern legend, and listening to the voice of a soul that had endured the mighty struggles of yesterday. Her spirit was gentle, yet her words were bold and courageous. She naturally conveyed a sense of how people should be treated, and she dismantled my fears completely.

She knew that I would help Omar through his internal suffering. She said what she had to in the short time allowed. She sold me a reality that I had no other choice but to embrace.

"So what do I do now, Big Mama?" I asked. I felt like I was asking advice from my own mama.

"When the time is right to speak on this, you will know. And I know you hear this before," and she closed her eyes and proceeded to speak a timeless song of true love.

"When a man love a woman, he trade the world for the good thing he found... in his eyes, she can do no wrong."

She gave Percy Sledge a run for his money with her paraphrase.

"When she speaks, he will listen... And when you know that he love you, without a doubt... all of your question shall be answered," she added on her own.

Tears came to my eyes as my heart sang with words that were never truer.

Big Mama opened her eyes and continued with her priceless guidance. "If you will, please remember this for me, child. Never caress his pains, instead try your best to diminish his hardships with compassion. It be okay to never know sorrow, but it be suicidal to caress despair. You being there is enough. You ain't never had to climb on top a mountain to prove to the world where you stand. Just 'stand by your man,'" she said with a wink, "and the rest will be easy."

"Big Mama, have you been bad again?" Omar's sudden appearance startled us both.

"No, child. I'm too old to be bad. I'm better."

"Better than what, Big Mama?"

"Better than anything your young eyes has ever seen. That be for sure." With that, Big Mama took her leave, and went to tend to her restaurant.

"So, Omar, why haven't you ever told me about Big Mama?"

"Haven't you seen by now? Big Mama has her own voice and nobody can tell you about her better than she can. Don't get me wrong, Claudia, I would have told you about her but I couldn't have done her justice. Talking about her would not have been enough. Can't you tell? You had to come and see her for yourself. People are always so ready to speak about their loved ones, but not me. I brought you here so that she could sell herself."

I found myself doing a lot of nodding.

"She is my Godmother. My reason for living, and my hope for brighter days. I love Big Mama for teaching me the things she has, and for always keeping it real. I don't even want to guess what she's told you, but I can say that she's never lied to me."

I appraised those two and all I felt was genuine love.

"So, Omar. This is where you stay?"

"I live here on earth, but in my mind, I live alone," he answered in a riddle.

"What are you saying exactly? What is the difference between living here, and, as you put it, 'living alone?'"

"I will tell you everything you need to know about me, Claudia. But now is neither the time nor the place."

I gave him my most seductive look and said, "Sure, Omar. Whatever you say, baby. I've got the rest of your life to hear about you."

His blush spread from ear to ear faster than a forest fire over dried sagebrush. And he pretended to ignore what he just heard.

CHOCOLATE

"I thought we were going to see a movie," he said, "and we haven't even eaten dinner."

"Well, we missed dinner, and we'll miss the movie if we don't go now. But Omar, it's cold outside tonight and I can't have you following along side my car on your bike. If you won't let me drive you, I'm going home."

Big Mama had been hovering, none too inconspicuously, and easily overheard my last statement. She maneuvered her big wonderful self behind Omar, winked at me and gave me a thumbs up.

She gently jabbed Omar's shoulder and ordered, "Go get your jacket and take a ride with the young lady. And stop lookin' at me like I's crazy before you make me walk back in the kitchen and grab one of them frying pans and do what Big Mama do best."

I looked at her to force an explanation.

"Omar know. That child know I don't play. When I tell him to jump, he know it's time to start leapin'."

Omar sat as still as a scolded tot.

To me she said, "Child, I know this boy since they bring him home from the hospital, and he know when it come to pots and pans... I ain't playin'."

Her face wore a great big smirk as she looked down at Omar.

"Ain't that right, Omar?" I saw another shoulder jab.

"Yes, Ma'am. You're right, Big Mama."

Omar felt it necessary to punctuate her remarks by divulging another family incident.

"One night I was staying over at Big Mama's house and was feeling a little older than I actually was. Big Mama was calling me to come inside the house, but I wanted to stay outside a little longer just to hang out with the fellows. I was talking to one of my friends and forgot who was calling me.

When she said, 'Ooooo-mar,' without thinking I said, 'Whaaatt!?'

"The next thing I knew, Big Mama was walking down the sidewalk towards me with a great big frying pan in her hands."

Involuntarily, my eyebrows exclaimed surprise.

"What happened next?" I asked trying to keep my reaction out of my voice.

"You should have seen everybody in the street. There had to have been at least six or seven guys out there, but as soon as they saw what was in Big Mama's hand, they all went their separate ways as fast as they could."

Omar suddenly stopped his story just as I was getting into it. I wanted to know more.

"So? Soooo, what happened?"

He shrugged as Big Mama walked over and gave me a big hug. She answered for him.

"You'll see what happened… if you ever hurt my baby." I took that as a serious warning.

"Now, it's getting late. If you two are gonna check out a movie, you best leave now. Come back another night and I have the best dinner waitin' for you."

The Cinema

When we got to the car I couldn't help but notice that Omar was tentative. But he opened my door, then went around and got in. I was overly cautious as I drove to the theater, trying so hard not to make Omar nervous.

"I've never been in a Jaguar before," he said. "It's a real nice car, Claudia."

"It's not that different from any other car; it needs gas and oil just like the rest of them."

"Sure, you say that now... but I bet when you first got it you were excited."

"Not as excited as I was the first time I saw you," I said with all sincerity.

"Oh, just stop it, Claudia. I bet you say that to all of the Omars you know."

"That's right! Every single one of them. And guess what? The one and only one I know just happens to be a butcher."

He smiled contentedly to himself as he looked out the window. "Where are you going, Claudia? I've never gone to the theater this way before."

"Relax. You're in good hands. I'm sure that we both can learn a thing or two from each other," I said as I turned into my driveway.

"Well? Are you going to come inside, or are you going to just sit in the car all night?"

"Man, Claudia. Who lives here? This place is real nice."

"I do, silly. Now come on in. Let's go watch that movie we talked about."

When we entered the house, I said, "Make yourself comfortable, Omar. There is some wine in the fridge, but if you want something stronger the bar is in there, through those doors." I pointed him in the direction of the living room.

"Look around if you'd like… I'll be right back."

I left him alone for about ten minutes; long enough for Omar to make himself a drink and find a place to sit. I walked into the living room feeling edible and looking delicious.

If Omar's mouth hadn't been attached to his face, it would have fallen to the floor. I obviously had the desired effect in my ticket-girl teddy. It was a short purple and black lace see-through number. It was tastefully made to best represent the curtains at the movie theater. The word *Chocolate* was stitched on one side of the bra, while *Matinee* was on the other. I was also wearing g-string panties with the words *Special Feature* stitched on the tiny triangle.

When he saw what I had on, he knew what was on my mind. I walked into the middle of the room to model my tailor-made teddy, and turned around in a circle to model for my man.

I held both of my hands in the air and said, "So what do you think?"

"I think I'm as close to heaven as I am ever going to be. You're beautiful, Claudia..." I stopped him from saying more by pressing my finger to his lips.

"Omar, come with me," I whispered. "I have a surprise for you. Close your eyes and don't open them until I tell you to."

I reached for Omar's hand and led him down the hallway.

Earlier that week, I had purchased a 72-inch big-screen TV and turned one of the bedrooms into a screening room. It was a little extravagant but the look on Omar's face made it well worth it.

We passed through the doorway and I turned on the light.

"Surprise!"

When he opened his eyes he couldn't believe where he was. The room had been transformed into a private cinema.

"This is great," he said almost ready to cry.

"Just go over there and have a seat on the adjustable couch."

I turned the lights off and sat down next to him, and handed him the remote.

"Now this is my kind of theater," he said.

"Baby, push play," I urged.

He pointed the remote towards the screen and asked about the movie. Again, I placed my hand over his mouth, so that he wouldn't ruin my surprise.

As soon as he realized what the movie was he yelled out, "No... no, you didn't. You better stop before I hurt myself. This is the best surprise I've ever had! What could be better?"

I took that as my cue and encouraged him to follow my gaze down between my legs.

"Well, what would a theater be without a 'special feature?'" I asked coyly.

Love Jones might have been Omar's favorite movie, but he wasn't a fool. He knew he had plenty of loving to do... on me.

He was the man.

He turned off the TV, and asked about music.

I walked over to get a second remote and handed it back to Omar.

"What's this button here for?"

"Oh, that button adjusts the couch."

"Get out of here... This couch reclines?"

"Sure, baby. Hold the small button back on the left."

Omar followed instructions and within seconds it was on. After the couch turned into a bed, he reached for my hand and pulled me towards him.

"Baby, are you sure you're ready to do this?" he asked.

"Yes, Omar. I've never been so sure about anything in my whole life."

"Do you have any condoms?" he asked.

I smiled at myself because I had thought of everything.

"Listen, do you think I would have had this teddy made especially for this moment without stopping at the drug store and picking up some condoms?"

Omar smiled back.

"Baby, I'm sorry. I was just making sure. We don't want any little illegitimate chocolate drops walking around here, now do we?"

I reached inside my bra and handed him a condom.

"Claudia, are you seducing me?"

I looked into his eyes as deeply as I could and answered, "Hmm... That was my intention. Is it working?"

"Baby, I was yours the second you dropped that first bag of vegetables. Just tell me what you need and I'll do it."

"Just act like we're at the car wash and give me the works," I responded, paraphrasing an old line from a forgotten movie.

When Omar took off his shirt my mouth started watering. He sat down on the edge of the couch/bed with his back towards me. He leaned over and took his shoes off, then he stood up again. When he unfastened his belt I felt like a fisherman who had just cast his hook knowing there was a big catch waiting in the water. I was praying for the biggest fish I could get.

The first thing I saw was his magnificent butt, and then he turned around. My mouth flew open into the 'wow' position. I crossed my legs and wondered how we… Just how were we going to get all of that… in me?

I felt like a child being told that I had bitten off more than I could chew. Tina and Mia had always told me if I just got enough to feel, that would be a successful first. But Omar, being a butcher, brought over enough beef to cut up and put in my freezer for a couple of days.

He crawled towards me dangling from side to side, smiling his beautiful smile. The closer he got, the more afraid I became. I needed to relax, and fast. My confidence in my sexy introduction was quickly coming to a halt.

"What's wrong?"

I could tell he sensed my tension.

"There is something, Omar. Something I forgot to tell you. Something that's very important."

He had reached me, every inch of him, and started nibbling on my neck.

"What is it, Claudia?"

For a second or two, I lost my train of thought. What he was doing turned me on and made me feel so warm inside. His kisses were filling a void; a hollowness that had existed far too long. I knew I had to tell him that I was a virgin, but since

I had waited that long, I reasoned a few more minutes wouldn't hurt.

"Could you nibble a little on the other side for me? I like that," I purred.

"Oh, you do?"

I felt like putty in his hands and I was ready to be molded. He cared enough about me to take his time, and I appreciated him for that. He tilted my head by holding both sides of my face in his hands.

He looked me straight in the eyes and said, "I know."

"You know what?" I asked.

"I know this is your first time."

"You do? How can you tell?"

"Let's just say that I'm into you, and we'll leave it like that."

Omar's clairvoyant spirit embraced my heart. He was the right man at the right time in my life. That was hard to find.

With the tips of his fingers, and without saying a word, he spoke to me in such a way that I knew he could interpret my desires. He gently stroked my body and my fears disappeared. He ran his fingers through my hair causing my toes to spread, and worked his way down to give me oral pleasure.

I had heard about this aspect of sex and was dying to experience it for myself. I was weak with anticipation, and wasn't about to stop this revelation. I let him push my legs wide, not knowing that in a matter of seconds I would be reaching the apex of physical satisfaction.

Seconds passed, then minutes. This was not what I had heard about. For some reason Omar was moving so darn slow. A part of me wanted to assist him by pushing his shoulders down towards the warmest part of my love. I didn't know what to do. He was taking his time and I was in a rush.

He was pleasing me by teasing me, and I didn't know it. Though I didn't have anything to compare it to, I knew it was time for intermission to be over.

With every kiss, my skin tingled. I wanted to feel his beautiful lips pressing against mine, but I was perfectly satisfied with kisses elsewhere. As he moved lower, I stretched out both of my hands and gripped the sides of the bed. Instinctively I knew I should brace myself for what was about to come.

I thought I could participate a bit, and attempted to lift myself enough for him to remove my panties. Omar ignored the opportunity and did the unthinkable. He kissed them instead.

I didn't know who I was happier for, my panties or me, but there was one thing for sure, we were both very wet. After kissing my 'special feature' over and over for what seemed like forever, he lifted up the lower portion of my body himself, pulled my panties off, and positioned my legs above his head. For the next eight or ten minutes I left this world as I knew it.

I felt as helpless as a baby, with my legs dangling in mid-air. Every now and then I peeked down at Omar as he devoured my passion. My body was shaking out of control as I tried to hold on to the last bit of it. It was all too good to be true.

Was it all a dream? If so, then I was not about to open my eyes ever again. If this was indeed a dream, I was determined to remain asleep for life.

At that moment Omar blew on my love. My grip on the couch intensified, and my eyes saw faint explosions of white light in the lovely darkness. He just continued handling his business, but I couldn't take it anymore. I was finally convinced that it wasn't a dream, and I had to open my eyes. I needed him to stop.

I practically screamed out, "Omar! Please, I can't take it anymore! Please!"

While tasting the warmest part of my love, he raised up and said, "Relax, Claudia. I've got you. Just let it go."

He was a man of men dedicated to making me reach a sexual height that could never be duplicated.

"No, really Omar. No. I can't take it anymore."

Omar rose up and reached for the condom. I was feeling too good by that time to even worry about what he was doing. Within seconds I could feel him gently penetrating the outer walls of my love. Though it was a bit painful, I longed for the rest of him to enter me.

"Yes, Omar. Yes. I want you to give it to me."

"But baby... it's going to hurt..."

"Don't worry. I'm fine. Just put it in slow... I'll be fine," I said almost pleading with him.

He didn't want to hurt me, but I didn't want him to wait for me any longer. We were both anxious, so I took all he had to give. I closed my eyes and buried my face against his chest. I hung onto his strong arms as he submerged his needs inside my wants.

I didn't want to just lay there lifeless, so I moved in unison with the man of my dreams. I broke down and gave myself to him. The pain subsided as I continued to spread my legs and receive his passion, stroke after stroke.

His composure was out of reach and I knew it wouldn't be long before he had to submit to the power of orgasmic pressure. He changed his rhythm and gave himself to me as fast as he could. His facial expressions told me that my love was pleasing him. I stared into his eyes as I received each thrust that led to his pleasure.

I started rubbing the arms of my Mandingo warrior as the climax of our version of *Love Jones* was about to occur. I could feel him stroking faster as he moaned.

"It's all yours," I offered.

I held on for dear life as he went temporarily insane and gave it to me with conviction. Omar looked into my eyes and said, "Hold me, baby, hold me."

Within seconds he released his neurotic ecstasy inside of me.

"Damn, what a movie," he said, and we fell asleep wrapped in each other's arms.

I woke up in the middle of the night still cuddled up in Omar's strong arms. Lying there next to the reason I had given in to lust, I still sensed a need to reach for closure; closure which had for years eluded me. A conclusion of some sort was in order.

Sweets had now become the sole beneficiary of my thoughts. I missed her more than ever at that very moment. My selfishness towards her had become a bottleneck in my thirst for joy. I knew I had to ratify the wrongs I had committed before it was too late. I was determined to do something about the neglected relationship with Sweets.

Long before I came to know who I really was, there she was. Pamela Renee Montgomery, my earthly soul sister. I knew that I couldn't sleep on this forever. So in one of my most fragile moments thoughts of Sweets resurfaced and they were too strong to shake.

I still had unfinished business to take care of. I needed to see my best friend. I wanted her to know that I was doing fine and that time had taught me how to see past myself, into the needs and wants of others.

It was about four o'clock in the morning when Omar noticed I wasn't able to sleep. I had rolled onto my back and pulled his arm from around my waist. I made an attempt to reach out for my soul sister's face. I was staring into dark space when Omar rolled over and saw that not only was I unable to sleep, but I was also crying.

Omar cared without uttering a word. He made me feel safe by remaining silently strong. But he had acquired a sudden weakness that gave him a breathtaking appeal; he couldn't stand to see me hurting.

"Claudia, what's wrong? What is it, baby?"

I knew that it was a bad time to be thinking about Sweets, but I just couldn't help myself.

"Nothing is wrong, Omar. I just can't sleep. I've got some unfinished business to attend to, that's all."

"Things like what?" he wanted to know.

I didn't ever want to lie or hide anything from him, so I took a deep breath and I told him about Sweets.

"I have a friend that I've never told you about. Her name is Sweets. She is actually my cousin and I did something years ago that I shouldn't have done."

"What did you do, Claudia? Tell me."

"I turned my back on her. When her father came and moved her away, I turned my back on my Sweets. I thought I wouldn't have to deal with the pain of her absence that way, but I was wrong. I've missed her dearly ever since she left."

"Has she ever called you?"

"Sure, she has. She's called several times, but I always avoided her. Again, I thought that if I disconnected myself I wouldn't have to miss her as much."

"Do you know how to get in touch with her?"

"Well, she calls my father at least once a month, so I'm sure he knows how to get in touch with her. I never listened to the updates he had and he always made excuses for me."

"Do you know what I'm thinking right now? Right at this very moment?" Omar asked.

I gave him the opening he needed.

"I need to know your Sweets. I really know nothing about the situation and it's unfair of me, or anyone else, to pass judgment on something I know nothing about. So, why don't you tell me about her. First of all, tell me what she means to you."

"She is not just my cousin, she was like my own sister. She was one of my reasons for living and at times she has been my earthly comfort. I love her with every fiber of my being. Together we were unstoppable. She was my right now, when the world had left me for tomorrow. When I'm on the road, I think of her morning, noon and night. When I get lonely, she is the first person that comes to mind."

"So what hurts the most about not having her in your life?" he asked.

"Do you really want to know what hurts me? What hurts me the most is that *I* drew this wedge between us. I've been so selfish and blamed her for leaving me. But I couldn't see past myself long enough to see that her feelings might have mattered.

"I want to be able to pick up the phone and call her and tell her that I've just lost my virginity," I said and buried my head in my pillow.

"Why are you being so hard on yourself, Claudia?" he asked as he rubbed my shoulders and turned me around. "I'm sure you didn't think you were being selfish at the time, did you?"

"No... not really. The problem was that I didn't think at all. Not once did I try to see past my own needs, though. So, today I have myself to blame. Today when I think about where I am, I am saddened because I don't know were Sweets is. I let go of her hand so I would be free."

"Free from what?" Omar asked.

"Free is all. Free from the pain that loneliness brings, free from the hurt of it all. But I am tired of trying to fool myself. I miss my friend, now more than ever."

"Where is she, Claudia?"

"She's somewhere in Europe having the time of her life. My father tries to keep me updated on her whereabouts, but I would be lying if I told you I knew exactly where she was. As far as I am concerned she is a million miles away. Sometimes at night, I cry myself to sleep. I cry because it tears me apart to think of us not being there for each other."

"Why don't you call her and tell her you're sorry. I'm sure she would accept your apology."

"I think she would. But I have often wondered if I would accept an apology if the shoe was on the other foot. Don't get me wrong, I love her, I do. But at the time, love had nothing to do with what I did. It was my inability to love. I see that now."

Omar reached over and pulled me close to him. As our naked bodies united once again, he comforted me in my hour of grief. I placed my head in his chest and felt at ease as he ran his fingers through my hair.

There in Omar's arms, my eyes closed as the windows that once enclosed my biggest fears were opened wide. I was amazed I was able to verbalize my past, to unleash my shame and suffering simply by acknowledging my shameful actions.

With a long overdue confession off my chest, Omar wrapped me in his loving arms again, and I slept like a baby for the rest of the night.

When we woke up the next morning Omar and I were a couple. Were we in love. But what comforted me the most… was that we were.

I had indeed found the man of my dreams and it was true that he had filled a tremendous void in my life. But my broken heart still longed to be reconnected with Pamela Sweets Montgomery. She had been my confidante long ago, when comfort seemed light-years away.

"I don't think calling Sweets is a good idea."

I sat straight up in bed as I decisively said, "I have to go and find her. When I apologize to her I want to be standing in front of her. When I can see her face to face, the guilt will melt away and I will have no need for foolish pride."

Omar was listening and nodding.

"I have to go and find her, while the spirit of reconnection is tugging at my heart," I said.

"Yes, Claudia. And when you make that right, remember, I will be here waiting for you."

I Love Paris
in the Springtime

The next day, and just three weeks before I was to go back on the road, I called my father and told him I needed to talk. He was the liaison for Sweets and me. Every chance he'd get, he mentioned that she had either called or written, but I had always cut him short.

That day we decided to have lunch at an old sandwich shop not far from where we both lived, and talked about life, as we knew it. When our orders came up we sat down at a table near the window. We overlooked a beautiful view of the trees and mountains to the east. The view didn't hide anything, and my father could tell that something was up.

I had seen the better side of most things by the time I was eighteen, and just about everything else four years later by the time I graduated from college. Pops knew that I was just waiting for the most opportune time to express myself.

After opening up to Omar, I was finally ready to speak on a subject that I had avoided for years. My father didn't enjoy silence and I knew if I didn't say something right off the bat, the conversation could take a turn for the worst real fast. I might never get a chance to say what I came to say.

Just as he reached for his pipe, a sure sign he was about to launch into an unsolicited sermon filled with words of wisdom, I beat him to the punch.

"So, Dad. How is Sweets doing these days?"

He paused for a second and appeared to be shocked. He couldn't believe he heard Sweets' name coming from my mouth.

But, he passed it off as if I had broached an everyday subject. "It's funny you should ask, Chocolate. I talked to her just this morning. She's doing fine. She always asks about you, you know. She really misses you."

I didn't say a word.

"Why are you so quiet?" he asked.

The thought of Sweets having enough inside of her to still care about me left me breathless, but I had to say something.

"Oh. Well, I was just wondering about her and hoping that everything was going well for her, that's all."

"Sweets is doing fine. She's been going to school over there in Europe and has learned three different languages."

"That's great, Pops. I'm really proud of her. When we were kids she would mimic voices, so I'm not surprised learning languages has come easily to her."

My father was overcome with delight that I had said anything at all about Sweets. I could hear it in his voice.

"Oh, Chocolate. She has so many wonderful experiences to talk about."

He had written down her new address on a small piece of paper that morning when she called. When he saw I was interested in hearing about her, he reached inside his coat pocket and handed it to me.

"Here is her new address and phone number. I'm sure she will be glad to hear from you."

The late winter sunset was bringing a close to the day. It was just starting to get dark, and I didn't want my father staying out too late. In his late fifties his sight had started to fade. We hugged and said our good-byes.

On my way home I promised myself I would begin reading her letters I had saved all these years. It was now time for the spirit of procrastination to cease.

The drive home took only about fifteen minutes, but it took me even less time than that to fall asleep. I must have been exhausted because the next thing I knew it was morning.

Although it was true I needed to find myself, while doing so I might have lost my Sweets in the process. For years I had avoided this moment but it was time to invite her back into my life, and this time for good.

I walked towards my closest to get the boxes I had stored Sweets' letters in. Over time one shoebox had became three. The first letter I picked up was dated just two months prior. So, I began sorting through all of them, one by one, and placing them in chronological order according to postmark.

While my morning coffee was brewing I sat down at my desk, and placed the first stack of letters in front of me. Outside my bedroom window a gentle breeze caressed the large palm trees. I listened to the rustle of the palm fronds as I tried once again to visualize Sweets' face.

I took the letter opener and gently pried the first one open. I pulled the letter out to begin reading about Sweets' life.

Girl,

It hasn't been twenty-four hours and wouldn't you know it, I'm already missing you. We got delayed in the Miami airport so I took the time to write this first letter. I've never thought about life without you and I never dreamed that life would ever force me to. Please know that nothing or no one in this world could ever replace you. You are the friend that God sent me from heaven; you are the place that I hide when this mean world has removed all forms of shelter. I love you Chocolate. Please write back soon to the address on the envelope. My father says all our mail will be held until we arrive in Rome. I don't know how long I'll be staying in Brazil or Rome, but know that wherever I am, I'll make sure that you can find me. Raise your finger up to the sky and touch mine, now bring it down and point it at the one you love.

Love,
Sweets

By the time I finished that letter, my shirt was drenched. I felt so stupid, so frail and so unworthy of her love. Her absence might have taught me more than I wanted to know. I was the only guest invited to the petty party I had thrown. There were no balloons, no music and certainly no dances of celebration. All of my qualms about Sweets were self-induced.

I opened the second letter.

CHOCOLATE

Hi Chocolate,

My father and I are in Brazil. We are staying in a beautiful apartment, but all the buildings are so close together. Nobody has a yard! There are thousands of people everywhere. It seems much more crowded than California! The beaches are beautiful, but I haven't been able to spend much time there. Some people speak French, but most people speak Portuguese, and I have been able to pick up new bits of the language every day. The food doesn't taste like it does back home, but my father tells me I'll get used to it by the time we have to leave. Maybe he's right, but I'll never get used to not having you near. We're only staying here for a few weeks then we have to go to Italy.

Love,
Sweets

I read more of Sweets' letters one by one until I grew too tired to lift the pages. I was worn out by the confrontational truths that were woven inside each of her statements. I knew how to observe situations by placing myself in the third person in an effort to see things from an unbiased point of view. I had to force myself to do that now. By reading Sweets' letters, I was able to confiscate the facts instead of conjuring up my own. With each untainted word I was freed.

So many times the answers I was searching for were right in front of me. I refused to believe that peace was easier to find than obtaining riches. But I've learned that prosperity isn't measured by the acquisition of assets, but rather by the charity displayed in our willingness to give back. For years I felt exploited by my peers instead of respected, victimized by society instead of valued. I had confused my spirit of giving for being used, by failing to understand that no unconditional deed could ever be construed as such.

After reading a dozen or so more, I felt like the light inside my heart had come back on and it was shining brighter than ever before. The real truth was that it never went out.

Clouds of insecurity had hovered over my soul from time to time, but my love for Sweets was always there. I knew that the healing needed to start and I had to reinvent new hopes. But time never befriended anyone, and it was not about to make me an exception. There were some loose ends I needed to tie up; my only fear was that it might be too late.

Where I went from there depended solely upon me. Our future was now in my hands and I had to believe that my love for Sweets was better than anything All-State could offer. But I felt like time was running out.

My mind was running a mile a minute, and I was too excited to calm down. I was too ready to make things right to think about a tomorrow without my Sweets.

The order of the day was reconciliation and the gavel was about to come down. I was tired of endorsing deception and it was time to focus on what I knew was the truth. So what if I had been wrong? If time permitted, I was going to make amends.

In my boxes of letters I found almost two hundred reasons to believe. I was the reason they all went unanswered, and my new hope made it easy to begin reading them now. After fixing myself a fresh pot of coffee, I stayed in the kitchen with my boxes and began pouring over the letters one after another until I had read every last one of them. This was a pivotal point in my life and I wasn't about to squander the opportunity to correct a wrong.

I finally finished reading them all around eight o'clock, and immediately got the urge to go back and visit my father. I knew what had to be done and I was about to do it. I needed to tell him the great news.

I ran in one room and out the other like a mad woman in search of my car keys. As I turned circles in the kitchen, I finally settled down long enough to realize that they were in my pants pocket all along.

I ran back to my closet and pulled out a clean sweatshirt, put on a pair of gym-shoes, and was out the door as fast as I could go. I was too excited to even feel my feet moving, or to notice my route, and was on his doorstep in fifteen minutes.

At my father's house I quickly parked the car and ran towards the front door. I rang the doorbell twice. The house lights were on so I was almost in a panic when neither Nicole nor my father answered the door. I reached into my purse for the spare key.

I stopped short of barging in as I chuckled for a second, wondering if just maybe Pops had created a cinema of his own. Perhaps they were getting busy themselves... Naah. I opened the door.

"Is any body home? Nicole, Dad, are you here?"

Through all of my excitement I hadn't noticed that Nicole's car was missing, and no sooner had I placed my purse down on the kitchen counter did the two love-birds come strolling through the front door.

"What are you doing over here, child? I thought that you and Omar would be doing something tonight."

"Oh, so I can't come over unannounced any more?"

"Sure you can, Claudia. Any time. Your father's just playing around," said Nicole. "We just stepped out for a minute and ran down to rent a movie. Would you like to stay and watch it with us?"

"I wouldn't want to be a third-wheel. So no. Thank you, though. I won't be long, really. I just had something to discuss with my father. It won't take but a minute and I'll be out of your way."

Nicole smiled and said, "Don't be silly. I will give you two some time alone."

"Let's go into the study so we can talk," my father suggested.

When he sat in his favorite chair I walked over and gave him a kiss on his forehead.

"Guess what I did today?"

"No, you tell me. What did you do, Chocolate?"

"I read every letter that Sweets has ever written me," I announced.

The look in his eyes melted my heart. He had a smile on his face that could have lit up a whole city block. He got up and gave me one of the biggest hugs ever. The look in his eyes depicted the joy inside his heart.

I told him I felt that my prayers had been answered and the questions from afar had finally reached their destination. Though my response was several years late, my hopes were that our reunion would be on time.

"Sweets is going to be so excited to hear from you. When are you going to call her?" he asked.

I walked over to the other side of the room and began to twiddle my thumbs, the way I did when I was a child. I stared back at my father to gain emotional leverage.

"Dad, I'm ready to see Sweets now."

"Oh my God. I thought this day would never come. But I am so happy to hear you say those words. Why don't you just call her, though?"

"No, Daddy. I don't want to call her. I need to see her face to face. I have to apologize in person for being so selfish and mean all these years. Calling her wouldn't be right."

Before I could say another word, he reached inside his desk drawer and pulled out a round trip ticket to Paris.

"Well, if you're not going to call her, I guess you'll have to go and visit her, now won't you."

I have never loved my father more than I did at that very moment. His love for me was the driving force that kept my heart beating. It was not unlike the Olympic torch, for it has always burned forever bright. He had such a tender way of reducing my fears and minimizing my misfortunes. I couldn't have thanked him enough for what he had just done, but God knew that I would have to try.

"Daddy, thank you. I know you know how much this means to me. I'm so glad you are my father. I can honestly say that you are the best father in the world."

"Chocolate, go home and pack, and remember to save some of those nice words for Sweets. She and I have talked at least once a month for over six years now, and I've said all that I can in your defense."

"What does that mean, Dad?"

"That means, it's your time to speak on your own behalf, and that I'm tired on being the dispatcher of truth."

I let that sink in, and absorbed it with all sincerity.

"So when am I supposed to leave for Paris?" I asked.

"Baby, the ticket is open. I bought it several months ago, knowing it would be put to good use at the appropriate time. All you have to do is call the airlines and book your flight."

"You mean I can leave when ever I get ready?"

"Sure, just call and make your reservations."

"How should I connect with her, Daddy?"

"Well, there is a place she's mentioned to me in several letters. Perhaps you read about it too in some of her most recent correspondence. It's a small café where the French people do spoken word. It's in the bohemian, artsy area called *Montmartre* near the *Sacre-Coeur* church. I have the address right here. Let's see… Oh, yes. It's the *Café Verde*… here write this down... at 18, rue Saint-Rustique, underneath the hotel *L'Auberge de la Bonne Franquette*. There, how was that?" he asked.

He was quite proud of his French.

"But I think I said 'hotel hotel.'" He looked out from the top of his glasses and smiled.

"I think this is important too, Chocolate. All that is in the 18th *arrondissement*. All the neighborhoods are numbered like that in Paris. So this place is in the 18th neighborhood, I guess. Anyway, Sweets performs, *en Francais*, every Tuesday night. It might be a great place to surprise her."

"I think you might be right, Pops. That sounds perfect. *Absolutment!*"

In all my travels I had yet to visit Paris. Luckily my passport was in order, and a few days later, I boarded a United Airlines 747 out of San Francisco, nonstop to Paris.

The flight took almost ten hours and I was unable to get any sleep on the plane, even in first-class luxury. I didn't watch the in-flight movie, and I even avoided striking up the slightest conversation with any of the other passengers or flight attendants.

I looked out the windows a few times, once as the pilot pointed out the northern lights when we flew over Greenland.

I took advantage of the time to compose a poem about my friendship with Sweets. I wanted it to be effective; to display everything I felt inside. I wanted to include my deep love for her, my sincerest regret for turning my back, the loneliness I endured, and most of all what I must have put her through.

I kept to myself and wrote draft after draft until it was almost time to land. As the plane prepared for arrival I felt a glitch in my poem, a void in my appeal to my life long friend, but my brain was abuzz. The only other part of my plan was to get to the café early enough to persuade the owner to let me read.

It was Friday mid-morning, Paris time, when my plane arrived at the Charles De Gaulle Airport at the T-1 terminal, which accepted international flights from the U.S.A. I managed to make my way through the airport, reading and understanding enough bits of French to get to the baggage claim area without a problem. I collected my bags and hailed a taxi at gate 16. I had heard there were long waits at that taxi stand, but one arrived immediately. I gave instructions to the driver to take me straight to the *Café Verde* in *Montmartre*. It was a bit of a drive into the city, over 40 minutes, and I gazed at the countryside and the construction as we sped into Paris.

When we arrived, the cab driver pulled up right in front of the café. I paid him handsomely and asked him to wait for a moment. I went into the café and looked for someone who might be the owner.

The café was just as I imagined it to be: dark and close with low ceilings, no windows, colorful walls, and dozens of round cabaret tables. There was plenty of seating, yet even without a soul in the room; it felt crowed. There was actually a stage at one end, and a bar to the side opposite the entry. I was impressed by the true French character the café possessed, and blown away by its décor; impressionist era paintings and posters covered the walls. I knew that was fitting as Degas, Monet, Manet, Renoir and others had made their homes in Paris.

I walked over to the bar, picked up a menu and attempted to order my drink of choice. I got the bartender's attention and said, *"Vorrei il vino, s'il vous plait."*

I could find the bathrooms, and decipher the menu, but speaking French was another thing entirely. However, I was quite proud of myself until the bartender gave me a quizzical look.

"*Pardon, Mademoiselle,* but you seem to be speaking both Italian and French." He was kind enough to point out my faux pas ever so gently.

"*Je ne parle pas francais, monsieur. Je suis Anglais,* uh, *je suis Americain.* I'm an American that is." I crossed my fingers, and hoped that all my words were French that time.

"Ah, *une Anglais* American. *Vous etes tres jolie, Mademoiselle.* I do speak some English, if I may." He chuckled again.

"Oh, what a relief. In that case, I'll have a glass of chardonnay, if you have it."

"*Mais oui.* It is so nice to see such a beautiful woman come into our café. You look lovely today and it is my pleasure to serve you."

I lifted up my glass and responded to the gentleman by saying, "It is an honor to be served by such a handsome man. *Merci beaucoups, monsieur.*" He smiled widely at my little attempt at French.

"What brings you to Paris this time of the year?" he asked.

"I came here to reunite with *mon chere amie,* a long lost friend. I was told that she speaks here from time to time. She recites poetry here. You might know her, her name is Sweets."

"No, I do not know of a Sweets. I have never heard that name here before."

I thought I might be in the wrong place before it dawned on me to ask for her by her real name. "Perhaps you know her by the name, Pamela."

When I spoke her name, his eyes light up like the Eiffel Tower on New Year's Eve.

CHOCOLATE

"Pamela? Of course I know the lovely Pamela. She is so very *tres joile*, just as you are. You are a friend of our Pamela?"

"You know her?" I asked eagerly.

"Every one person knows Pamela. She is the most beautiful woman in all of Paris. Her smile is the only light we use to illuminate our humble café."

I smiled because I knew what he meant.

"Mademoiselle, how do you know Pamela?"

"I am her best friend," I said.

"What? *C'est vrais? Vite, vite. Avec moi.* Come with me."

He reached across the bar and grabbed my hand and led me to a room down the hallway. He turned to smile at me almost every step of the way. He knocked on a door and shortly it was answered. It was Sophie, the café's owner.

The bartender told her in French who I was, and suddenly I became famous. I was beautiful Pamela's beautiful friend from America. Although Sophie spoke very little English, she spoke well enough for me to comprehend what she was saying.

While smiling back at me she said, "*Eh, vous etes* Pamela's *amie?*"

"Yes, I am her friend, and I am also her cousin."

"*Ah, oui. Cousine, n'est ce pas?*" Sophie picked up on her own.

I could tell we were off and running.

Luc, the bartender, translated the rest of our conversation.

I turned to him and said, "Could you please ask Sophie if I may come later tonight as a surprise guest? I have something to read myself."

"I understand what you are saying and it would be my pleasure."

"I would like to go on late if that is possible. Is there a place I can hide out until then?"

"*Mais oui*. Just come around back and knock on the door three times, like this: *un, deux, trios*." He demonstrated the knock, and seemed delighted to be a co-conspirator for my secret rendezvous. "Just knock three times, Mademoiselle, and someone will let you in."

"What time do I need to be here?"

"The last poet will read about *dix-heures et demi*, around ten thirty, so can you be here by the ten o'clock?"

"Of course, Luc. I've waited a long time for this day. A few more hours won't kill me."

I went back out to the cab, and the driver took me to my hotel. I had chosen the elegant, yet more subdued L'Hotel de Sully. I gave the driver the address, 62, rue Saint-Antoine, and he knew it was in the 4th *arrondissement*. I checked in and was shown to my room.

I kept to myself once again, but wasn't even able to take a short nap. I stayed awake to re-read the poem I had written for Sweets. Before I knew it, it was nine o'clock and time to prepare myself for my long awaited rendezvous. My clothes were already laid out across the bed. I had taken my bath and relaxed as much as I possibly could.

In less than an hour, Sweets and I would come face to face. I was carrying more guilt, hurt and blame than would fit in my luggage. I anticipated the worst and was ready to confront my truths as I confronted my fears. I had lived with the repercussions of my shallow and selfish decisions, and was ready to accept more emotional punishment for my ignorant deeds if necessary.

Before heading down to the lobby to catch the cab, I clutched the room's doorknob, closed my eyes and knelt down to say a prayer.

CHOCOLATE

Father, I have betrayed my best friend...
>*and in doing so I have deceived myself.*
For years I have ignored my tears...
>*and by doing so I have displayed my fears.*
A part of me awaits a meeting that has no right to be...
>*brought on by a spirit of selfishness*
>*that has for too long lived inside of me.*
Humble my tongue and refill my cup of reconciliation...
Place my feet back on the path of patience,
>*and direct me past the shallow waters of self.*
Renew in me a change...
>*so insightful, that a blind man would be able*
>*to see my new found reality.*
When I begin to misinterpret the desires
>*of those I claim to love,*
>*make me understand*
>*that 'I' has never been greater than 'us.'*
I am sorry for all the pain
>*I have caused both myself and Sweets,*
>*and I beg you for forgiveness.*
Please don't abandon me...
>*tho I have often abandoned You.*
Have mercy on my fragile soul,
>*and mend that which has been broken.*
You said that if You shall be with me,
>*You were more than the world against me...*
So please re-unite that which once exemplified togetherness
>*and bring us together for ever more.*
Go with me, Oh lord,
>*as I walk through these un-charted waters.*
Unshackle my fears,
>*and dismantle the walls of blame.*

Rebuild new walls of emotional stability
with the sturdy bricks of harmony.
These things I ask in Your name...

Amen

After my prayer I felt a sense of relief from my moment of atonement.

When I pulled the door open, I proudly walked towards the greatest test of them all. My sense of calmness, that I never knew existed, guided me on my destination. I was relying on my faith; walking towards my destiny, which was long overdue.

I stood waiting for the down elevator, as tears of reassurance streamed in the same direction. I patted them dry as I reached the hotel lobby, and calmly walked outside as the doorman hailed my cab.

The first driver in the taxi stand was leaning against his sleek black Citroen talking to one of his fellow comrades, while a cigarette hung off his lower lip. He noticed the signal and immediately jumped into action. He pulled his cab up in front of me, and the doorman opened my door.

The driver was a nice looking older black gentleman with distinct features. He had a large nose and an even larger smile. He was bald down the center of his head and seemed happy to be alive. He wore an old brown sports coat, which had to have been a few years older than he was. But his body embraced it as if it were new. His shoes were scuffed and the heels ran over on both sides, yet he walked ever so straight and tall.

He was well over six-feet and 225 pounds, a giant among Frenchmen. He seemed to be driven to do his job well. He had a name I would never forget. John Henry.

"Mademoiselle, *Jean Henri* at your service… but just call me *Henri*," he said in easily understood English.

"I will be your driver for the evening if you like. Where are you headed just now, Mademoiselle?"

I eyed him suspiciously before I gave him the address. There was something familiar about *Jean Henri*.

"There is a café over on rue Saint-Rustique in *Montmartre*. The Café Verde. Have you ever heard of the place?"

I handed him a business card Luc had given me earlier that day.

Henri recognized the address and said, "Of course, I know the spot. Just hang on and I will have you there in no time."

We sped away from the curb at the hotel and started a hair-raising drive back to the café.

"Is this your first time in Paris, Mademoiselle?" *Henri* asked.

I nodded politely, but hung onto the door handle for dear life. He proceeded to give me a whirlwind sight-seeing tour when I nodded my head. We cut through obstacles and circled the *Place de la Bastille*, then raced ahead and proceeded down *Boulevard Beaumarchais*. We passed sidewalk cafés, crépe stands, and Metro subway stations.

I thought we might have to blast through a tunnel just the way the real John Henry, the Steel Driving Man, had done to lay down railroads in the 1870's. But I knew we weren't in West Virginia.

I was sure *Jean Henri* worked from six 'til five, but I hoped he wasn't trying to win a race against a machine. Finally, I could see what had to be *Sacre Coeur* in the distance.

I filled him in on my secret when I was able to catch my breath, and he dropped me off at the back of the café just before ten.

Before I exited the cab I recited a few lines from the John Henry legend, "A man ain't nothin' but a man. But before I let that steam drill drive me down, I'll die with this hammer in my hand."

Jean Henri winked slyly as if he knew what I was talking about. I got out of the cab hoping that he would not cut his life short by virtue of his own superhuman effort. I shook my head thinking, 'I had just been escorted across Paris by my own French Tall Tale, *Jean Henri* himself.'

I knocked on the back door of the café as instructed, and was ushered in by a bouncer of sorts. Sophie had apparently told him to be listening for me, because he never questioned my identity. I was escorted into Sophie's office where I could view the evening's entertainment on a monitor.

It wasn't long before I heard a familiar voice. It was Sweets. She was even more beautiful than I imagined. Her hair had grown and she was wearing a funky purple outfit, which enhanced her assets. Her face wore a radiant smile as she stood there speaking to the crowded room as though they were family. She was about to display the confidence she had spoke of acquiring years ago. After Sweets finished her reading, she walked down one side of the stage and immediately disappeared into the smoke-filled room.

As I came out of Sophie's office and made my way to the stage, I could hear chants of, "Pamela, Pamela." The crowd obviously had great appreciation and respect for hearing her wise, poetic words. Just seeing her face gave me the confidence I needed to walk the last few steps towards our moment of reconciliation.

All I could wish for was that it was her habit to stay for the last reader. Hopefully she would stay long enough to hear the poem I had written for her.

Sophie appeared before the crowd as I waited backstage.

CHOCOLATE

"Good evening," she said to her café patrons in French. "This next person comes from far away. She is here to relate a message to a person that is amongst us. Without further ado, I would like to present a friend to a friend."

When I first walked out on the floor, I felt the total rush of being in front of an audience, but all I could see was a sea of empty faces peering through the cigarette smoke. My smile was in need of assistance that I could only receive by giving. I couldn't see Sweets, but I had to believe that she was out there. As I stepped up to the microphone, I swallowed the last bit of pride I had, and began to speak. Even though I spoke English, the French audience was very gracious.

"*Bon soir, mes amis.* This poem is entitled, 'Friends.' I wrote it to a very dear friend of mine, whom I hope is present to hear these heart-felt words."

I began with a slight quaver in my voice, but gained confidence as the audience grew hushed.

"When you went away,
you took with you a spirit of calmness
and like a thief in the night,
you made it all seem so harmless.

"I had forgotten what was real,
so I prayed the words of a coward:
'God, God, please don't let me feel.'

"I closed my eyes and tried not to see,
but every time I opened them,
there were visions of you staring back at me.

"My thoughts of letting go
were stronger than my willingness to hang on,
but tonight those same realities
have me shaking down to the bone.

"My eyes were too afraid to see,
that I was nothing without humility.

"Yes, I know that it all was a lie.
How could I have ever lived on this earth
without there being a you...
and I."

By that time, a tall, magnificently built black woman emerged from the smoke-filled room, and had slowly made her way towards the foot of the stage. It was Sweets.

After all of her unanswered letters, not to mention ignoring her dozens of phone calls, there she was, standing in front of me with forgiveness in her eyes.

Sweets was so beautiful; alive and as vibrant as ever. So ready to go on. I cried as our souls reconnected. She cried too, as she smiled back at me, loving me as if I had never left her side.

I had my poem still to finish, so I swallowed and spoke humbly. Without taking my eyes off Sweets, I reached out to her with my words, and continued to recite the poem I had prepared.

"Hold my hand,
as I admit I am nothing without you.
Forgive me as I attempt to start anew.

"Your tears never fell in vain
and that is what I've come here to explain.

CHOCOLATE

"Run with me
as I move towards reconciliation
Sweets, let's move swiftly,
without hesitation.

"Make me no promises
and I will tell you no lies…
just please be that old spirit
that my soul will recognize.

"Though your smile taught me
never to forget…
it was the loss of my own
that made me remember.

"Missing you has taught me
that sharing makes us whole…
and through our giving,
our blessings will unfold.

"Thanks for the tears you've cried
while placing every mean thought aside
but more than anything else…unlike myself.
you've never hidden behind your pride.

"Sweets,
I love you and I'm sorry"

By the time I finished reciting my poem, there wasn't a dry eye in the café. There was no language barrier for compassion.

Sweets climbed up on the stage and said her first words to me in over six years.

She held both my hands and said, "Chocolate, I never stopped loving you. I never stopped believing in you. You are my girl. What we have is real and don't you ever forget it."

Our spirits prompted us both to raise our hands up in the air as if on cue, and before we knew it, our right index fingers touched as they had so many times before. And, like Peabo Bryson and Roberta Flack, we were *Back Together Again.*

I wouldn't trade anything in the world for what I experienced at that very instant. It was the moment I would treasure most in life. When we hugged for the very first time I felt time literally come to a stand still. The crowd gave us a standing ovation, but the greatest applause had already come when I first laid eyes on Sweets.

She had filled out in all the right places, and had probably learned more about life than I had. Just having seen her out there on stage gave me chills. She had no broken limbs, no cries of sorrow, even though she had made it through the world's cruelest tomorrows. That was far from being a shocking revelation, though. I knew she was going to make it, I just knew it.

"Let's go over to my place and catch up on everything," she said as the crowd thinned.

"That could take forever," I replied.

"That's okay. I don't plan on going anywhere until forever is over anyway, do you? Now, where are your things?" she asked.

"They're at my hotel over…"

"Hotel? I know you didn't think I'd let you stay at a hotel, now did you?"

"Well, I just thought that…"

"Thought what? That there was a chance I wouldn't forgive you? Please, Chocolate. I forgave you years ago. You are my sister, my cousin, my confidante, and, yeah, that's right, my best friend. And don't you ever forget it."

I could see she wasn't going to let me get a word in edgewise.

"It's going to take more than six years of unanswered letters to come between us. I didn't just meet you yesterday, I've known you all of my life. My love for you *isn't* conditional and it *is* omnipresent. The thought of never seeing you again has never crossed my mind. You don't know how many times I've wanted to get on a plane and visit you. Uncle Marvin told me you needed time to work some things out. Although there were times when I missed you more than others, I stayed away and allowed you the time you needed to get yourself together."

"But, Sweets, what about all the years I ignored you?" I asked.

She looked at me with compassion and said, "I took every second, every minute, every day that you weren't there, to take a good look at myself. I have attempted to make myself a better person in the meantime."

I could tell she had done a fantastic job.

"Now, what we need to do is just ride over to your hotel and check you out of there. We'll get your things and take them to my house. So how long are you staying anyway?"

"Well that depends…" I said.

"Now there you go again with those famous Uncle Marvin riddles. At least that hasn't changed. Just tell me how long you're going to be here, so that I can begin to make plans."

"Oh, I really don't know, Sweets. At least a week, but two at the most. I have to go back to work in a few weeks. My return ticket is open, so I can be a bit flexible."

"Girl, you are going to make me quit my job. I didn't really like it anyway."

"Well, I'm at the Hotel de Sully, do you know where that is?"

"Hmm, L'Hotel de Sully, eh? Not bad. Of course I know where it is. I live here."

"It's in the 4th..." I began.

"*Oui, oui*, 4th *arrondissement. Je* know."

Something had happened to Sweets and I couldn't take my eyes off of her. She was driving her own car, speaking French, and making it without me. I never thought for one second that my Sweets would grow up, but time had shown me different. Six years had gone by fast. She was so real, so cute, so... right there.

I clutched her free hand as if I might never let go. There she was, sitting next to me. We were together; we were emotionally home again. I had never felt so complete, so ready to win, yet so content with the moment. I was quite caught up staring at her, and could feel my composure waning. My emotions got the best of me and, though I was happy, I couldn't stop the tears from falling. I turned my head to look out the window, and felt my soul trembling. It didn't matter which way I turned, I couldn't hide what I was feeling inside.

By the time we reached the hotel, I had lost it completely. We left the car with the valet, and Sweets took my hand as we entered the lobby. I attempted to wipe away my tears, but by that time they were falling nonstop.

"What's wrong, Chocolate? What's wrong?" she asked gently. "Why are you crying?"

"I can't help it, Sweets. You're just so beautiful."

"Thank you, Chocolate. But I will never be as beautiful as you are. I've seen you in those magazines," she said trying to bolster my spirits.

My heart was still overcome with guilt, as I sat in the midst of shame with no one to blame but myself. It was finally time to readjust my thinking. I knew I had to let go, so I cried out to my best friend. Sweets reached over and hugged me and I began to absorb her forgiveness.

"Please, don't cry, Chocolate. It's over now," she whispered to me. "The time we were apart is not worth mentioning. What really matters is right now. The past is just that, the past. It is…what it is, and no matter how hard we try to, we can never undo what has been done. But girl, we have the power to redirect the course of our future."

She tilted my chin as if I were a child, and looked into my eyes. "I love you more than the circumstances, Chocolate. I have never loved you less for standing up for what you believed in."

There I was, gazing at my best friend in the whole wide world, trying to see past my remorse. While I listened to each comforting word, I was still reminded of the emotional treason I had committed. I wanted to respond to the wonderful things she had already said, but the selfish part of me desired to hear more.

She answered my silent plea.

"Chocolate, the only thing that kept me going was your strength. I had to honor your wishes by denouncing my own. I never stopped loving you, not for one day… not for one second. So, stop crying. You must stop crying, and let's enjoy ourselves, girl. 'Cause I know I am."

It felt funny being lectured by the same person I had tutored for the better part of our lives. And I was being humbled by her newly found wisdom. We rode the elevator up to my room, and talked some more while I collected the few things I had unpacked earlier that day.

"Hey, all that money you were going to spend on the hotel can be used on shopping! We're going to have a ball. Girl, the 'City of Light' is in trouble. We're going to turn Paris upside down. Sweets and Chocolate are back together again and you know what that means, don't you?"

I nodded and smiled knowingly.

"I've just finished all my finals and I'm free for summer."

"Dad told me you've been doing well in school and have even learned a few languages."

She held up her hand and spread her fingers. "I've studied five to be exact, but it's not like I'm counting or anything. And I really can only converse in three, French being one of them! College has been fun and I really enjoy studying new things. It's been such a great experience to attend school in Europe. With all our travels I'm a bit behind our dual timeline, but *j'etudie a la Sorbonne.* I've spent the last two years here at the university in Paris, the Sorbonne, and only have one more term. I'll finish next fall."

"What is your major?"

"It doesn't work quite like that here, but I've been thinking about a career in the social field, you know something where I can give back to the community."

"That's interesting, Sweets. I've been thinking along those lines for quite a while myself."

"Well before you leave, let's sit down and brainstorm to see what we can come up with." Her smile turned reserved. She looked very French at that moment.

"What's so amusing?" I asked.

"Oh, nothing really. It's just a thought. I get them all the time."

"Well, at least it's a good one, I mean it's got you smiling in an interesting fashion."

"Look, I'm not going to tell you about it right now, so stop trying to pick my brain. Grab your bags and let's get going."

We each took a bag and hurried back down to the lobby. She helped me check out with great efficiency, and by the time we were escorted out to the *porte cochere,* her car was ready for us.

As we drove to her place she said thoughtfully, "You know, Chocolate, it's true. I have learned a lot of things over the years, but one of the most important things I've learned is that I am nothing without my family. Since coming here, I've learned a lot about different cultures. Studying abroad has an amazing effect on a person."

She was silent for a while, and I took the opportunity to study the city. We left Notre Dame on the *Ile St. Louis* as it towered off to our left across the Seine. Shimmering lights picked up the silhouette of a *Bateaux Mouches* gliding by. I looked ahead to see the Eiffel Tower in the distance as we headed out of the city towards Versailles. I could sense that Paris had earned every right to be called one of the most romantic cities in the world.

She lived in the Parisian suburb of *Versailles* about fifteen miles out of the city. It was several minutes before we pulled into her long driveway.

"Girl, is this your house?"

"Yes, well my father's really," she said proudly.

"He bought this house years ago, and used it whenever he came to Paris on business. He has given it to me for as long as I wish to stay in Paris. Come on, let's go inside; I have something to show you."

As we stood at the door she said, "Chocolate, close your eyes."

She took me by the hand and led me down a short hallway.

"Watch your step here," she cautioned.

I took two steps down into her living room when she released my hand. I began to cheat a little and opened my eyes ever so slightly. I saw her walk over to a large drawing of two little girls that was painted on her wall.

At first I couldn't make out the images but as I opened my eyes wider, my heart began to flutter. I finally focused clearly on what I was seeing. It was the biggest mural I had ever seen. It was very colorful and quite moving. The mural was so vivid it was frightening. It looked like the artist had reached inside Sweets' head and pulled both of us out. It was a mural of Sweets and me, and if I didn't know any better I would think that the artist had been there with us on the morning in question.

We were lying on the bed, like we did the morning after she told me about her horrifying rape experience. We were lying close to each other with our legs intertwined. There was a brush that had fallen from the clutch of my right hand. We were asleep as the sun from my window crept in on us just touching our shoulders.

"Do you even remember that morning?" she asked.

"Yes, Sweets. Like it was yesterday."

"I remember you trying to get up without awaking me. You did not know that I had never fallen asleep. I just closed my eyes so that I could hide inside your comforting soul, while you brushed my pains away. You always knew when I was afraid and I always knew where to run."

She walked over to her bar and poured us a glass of French wine, white at room temperature.

She handed me my glass and said, "Go closer to the mural and you'll notice that my left eye is slightly open, just as both of yours were when I asked you to keep them closed when we entered this house."

"Oh, Sweets. You mean you knew I was going to tell my father what had happened?"

"Yes, I knew you'd tell Uncle Marvin everything, and I was ready for him to know. I knew that when he found out something would be done."

I smiled back at her and said, "So, you used me?"

"No, silly girl. I simply appealed to your weakness."

"And what weakness might that have been?"

"Helping people, Chocolate. That was you since forever started." She smiled warmly at me. "I knew you couldn't hold water, so I gave you a barrel of my truths for you to hold. I was tired of holding it inside, and who else could I tell? I was hoping that you would stay true to form, and what do you know? You took care of it for me."

"How are you dealing with it today?" I asked.

"There are times when I can still smell the bastard's sweat dripping on me, but then I'm sure all rape victims have that recollection from time to time."

"Have you had any counseling?"

"No. Perhaps I will soon," she said, reassuring us both. "I know what happened to me that night was wrong, I have acknowledged that, and today the right thing to do is move on. I can't let that one awful day ruin my whole life anymore."

I was so relieved she had dealt with her misery and pain. I was in awe of her honoring the memory of our closeness. And I was so relieved to hear she would consider some counseling to wrap it all up once and for all.

"That mural must have cost a pretty penny, Sweets."

She got up and walked back over to the wall. "Yes it did, but who presides over the price of memories and what memories are more priceless than ours? My father asked me that same question when I questioned this gift. He had it painted for me. For us."

I was astonished. Our faces were painted to perfection. Every physical and emotional detail was there, as if they were taken directly off of a photograph. Every wrinkle, down to the linen on the bed, even the crack along side the wall near my closet was now on her living room wall.

"How can you remember so much about that night?"

"Chocolate if you've never been raped, you can never conceive the things I'm able to remember, or the things I try to forget. When you're trying to forget, it's funny. You start holding on to the simplest things."

"Things like what?" I asked. "Tell me."

"I held on to the good times. I reflected back on the time when we almost burned down your mother's kitchen while trying to bake those cookies. Do you remember that?"

"Yes, girl. That episode was scary as hell. How could I ever forget that? We couldn't have been any more than seven years old, but *you* put the cookies in the oven."

"Yeah, but it was *you* who turned the oven up too high."

"I was so hungry, and I couldn't wait all day for those cookies to be ready. So I turned the oven up as high as it could go."

"*I* noticed the smoke first, and it was *you* who started running towards the door, screaming like the house was on fire."

"But, it was *you* who grabbed those little cups, filled them with water and tried to put out that fire."

Our story could have gone on and on, but Sweets cut it short to explain its usefulness.

"I replaced my fears with the vivid details of that day, and others like it. I was able to leave a great deal of pain behind by extracting what little I could from pleasant, optimistic memories."

"Sometimes we are able to realize a lesson after a painful experience. But what good could you possibly have gotten out of that horrible moment in your life?"

"Chocolate, I learned a great deal that has helped me grow and move on. I learned that this space between my legs could only be devalued if I allow it to be. I understand the consequences of disrespecting myself by defacing my self worth are tremendous. When a woman is raped, she is dishonored from the inside out. All of her rights are taken away, and no form of apology can ever dislodge the tremendous emptiness she feels at that very moment, or for years after.

"For the duration of the malicious act, a woman becomes a hopeless pawn in a game where the rules are known to the evil player alone. I understand the rules now, and I am the keeper of them. If I invite wrong into my house, I should be willing to accept its unclean spirit."

She pointed emphatically towards her front door and said, "Before a man walks through those doors, you best believe that there are validating circumstances surrounding his presence."

Her voice had risen with a commanding crescendo, and I could see she needed to regroup. I kept listening, still without comment.

"Chocolate," she said after a few deep breaths, "your original question was, 'what good did I get out of that moment?' I hope I am explaining it fully. I learned the power of what I possess between my legs, and girl, let me tell you, that I'm using it. The period of anticipation is the season of reparation. It is during that time when a woman is able to truly reap the benefits of the full lustfulness of a man's dogmatic mind."

Sweets noticed that my mouth had flown wide open as she was carrying on, and said, "Life is funny. The moment you think you've got it all figured out, it changes. I don't claim to understand life; my greatest claim to fame is that I understand who I am."

She knew I was impressed by her self-knowledge, and smiled in accordance.

"Hey, let's go and get your things out of the car before we forget, and it gets too late. Oh, and by the way, I've got one more thing to show you."

"What now?" I asked, eager to see.

"Don't worry, I'll show you when we get back inside."

I couldn't wait to see what else she had up her sleeve. I hurried out to the car and back inside, carrying my things as fast as I could.

Sweets had taken my small carry-on and my small suitcase. I tried to keep up with her as I pulled the rest of my luggage in, but she had disappeared by the time I made it into the foyer.

I called out, "Hey, Sweets! Where do I put my things?"

"It's the second door on your left," she directed from a far off place in the house.

The second door on the left was closed, which I thought was a bit suspicious. I set my shoulder bag and my medium suitcase down on the floor outside the door. I rested the large suitcase on its wheels, and reached for the doorknob. I turned it slowly, ready for one of Sweets' harmless pranks. She had always played tricks on me and I wasn't about to fall for one now.

When I opened the door, what I saw made me instantly weak and brought me to my knees. Sweets had brought my old room to Paris. I found myself standing in a replica of my childhood room. There were pictures of me and Sweets everywhere. I was stunned.

"I hope you like it," she said from behind me. She helped me as I lifted myself up off the floor.

"I made everything larger for you so that it would be more comfortable."

"It's great, Sweets. I mean, it's more than great, it's fantastic. I can hardly believe it. Really, I'm practically speechless."

"I had it done a couple of years ago," she said with modesty. "Every now and then, I come in and dust things off, but until tonight, no one has ever slept in this room."

"Girl, you better stop messing with me like this," I said. "My heart can't take another surprise."

She left again for just a moment and returned carrying two fresh glasses and a bottle of wine. While she was pouring our drinks I reached inside my purse and pulled out my brush.

"Hey, Sweets. Get over here and let me brush your hair," I said nonchalantly.

She turned around slowly and I could tell she had processed the relevance of what I had just said. Tears of joy began sliding slowly down her beautiful face.

"Is that the same brush?" She was incredulous.

"Yes, it's the same one," I replied, and sat down on the edge of the bed.

"Now set down here and let me brush your hair."

She walked over to me and handed me my glass of wine. She sat down between my legs. She twisted half way around and held her glass high. We kissed the rims together in a silent toast and smiled knowingly at one another. She turned her back to me and I could feel her smile tightening her cheeks with each stroke of the brush.

"Girl, you know what this does to me?"

"Yeah, but it was a long time coming," I said.

"Chocolate, I'm so glad you're here."

"Shhhhh. Be quiet and go to sleep now."

Made in the USA
Las Vegas, NV
12 May 2022

48809755R00213